T0327407

Trading Tools
and Tactics

Founded in 1807, John Wiley & Sons is the oldest independent publishing company in the United States. With offices in North America, Europe, Australia and Asia, Wiley is globally committed to developing and marketing print and electronic products and services for our customers' professional and personal knowledge and understanding.

The Wiley Trading series features books by traders who have survived the market's ever changing temperament and have prospered—some by reinventing systems, others by getting back to basics. Whether a novice trader, professional or somewhere in-between, these books will provide the advice and strategies needed to prosper today and well into the future.

For a list of available titles, please visit our Web site at www.WileyFinance.com.

Trading Tools and Tactics

Reading the Mind of the Market

GREG CAPRA

WILEY

John Wiley & Sons, Inc.

Published by John Wiley & Sons, Inc., Hoboken, New Jersey.
Published simultaneously in Canada.

For general information on our other products and services or for technical support, please contact our Customer Care Department within the United States at (800) 762-2974, outside the United States at (317) 572-3993 or fax (317) 572-4002.

Wiley also publishes its books in a variety of electronic formats. Some content that appears in print may not be available in electronic books. For more information about Wiley products, visit our web site at www.wiley.com.

Library of Congress Cataloging-in-Publication Data:

Capra, Greg.
   Trading tools and tactics : reading the mind of the market / Greg Capra.
      p. cm. – (Wiley trading series)
   Includes index.
   ISBN 978-0-470-54085-5 (hardback); ISBN 978-1-1180-9855-4 (ebk);
   ISBN 978-1-1180-9856-1 (ebk); ISBN 978-1-1180-9857-8 (ebk)
   1. Investment analysis.   2. Stocks –Prices –Charts, diagrams, etc.   3. Stock price forecasting.
4. Portfolio management.   I. Title.
   HG4529.C366 2011
   332.63′2042–dc22

                                                                              2011010990

Printed in the United States of America

10   9   8   7   6   5   4   3   2   1

To all the prior,
present,
and future
Pristine students.

Contents

The Journey Begins

UNDERSTANDING THE LANGUAGE OF CHARTS AND PRICE ACTION

Twenty-two years seems like a lifetime ago, but back then I did not know the difference between a stock and a bond. I had a successful business, which I had organized to pretty much run on its own with good employees to carry out the day-to-day work. I began to take an interest in the market as I looked for what to do with my business profits. This soon became an obsession to learn how the markets operated, which is not uncommon for those who are bitten by the market bug.

Learning or wanting knowledge about the markets can be like a drug you have to have. If you feel this way—and I hope that you do, because as a trader you must have a passion and hunger to learn, excel, and be good at anything you do—I believe that this book will answer more questions about technical trading than you could ever imagine. If you have been trading for a while with the typical tools, this book is likely to shake some strong beliefs that you now have about technical trading.

When I began my quest, things were much different from today. There was not much information available about the markets. Day trading, as we use the term today, did not exist for the masses yet and was a couple of years off still. Many things we take for granted today, like even an intraday chart, did not exist. You could not place a trade yourself. The trade had to be placed by a licensed person. The only method of learning at the time was by reading books, and there were not a lot of them. Some of the things in these books made sense, but they did not enable me to make money.

At one point, I took a home-study course on fundamental analysis. I felt that if I learned about a company's fundamentals, and found companies that were undervalued, with low PE ratios, it was a method that could not fail. I came to realize that whenever a company goes bust, it will go always through a process of looking like a bargain and having lower and lower PE ratios. These stocks were much higher in price in the past and the current price seemed to be "cheap." Strike one.

Somehow, which was just a gut feeling at the time, since I knew next to nothing, I realized fundamentals were not the way to the faster profits I was after. However, I knew enough to realize that my limited knowledge and desire to make faster profits were a dangerous combination. Put another way, I was dangerous to my own financial well-being. The allure of the market does that, so I was not different from many others. However, I was smart enough to realize the risk and was not going to go bust. For that reason, I put most of my savings into municipal and corporate bonds. My basic understanding of them was that holding quality bonds to maturity virtually guaranteed getting back all my money plus a profit. If you are not familiar with bond investments, while they are "relatively safe" if held to maturity, their value can swing up or down a lot before the bond's maturity date. So it is possible to lose money in these so-called safe investments if you have to sell prior to maturity. Luckily, my bonds appreciated nicely at the time, plus provided additional income.

My long-term bond investing and trading has always turned out well, which helped offset some losses in what turned out to be a bust in tax shelters I participated in. Honestly, I knew very little about these at the time, but saving on taxes with a potential for a return all sounded great. I lost virtually everything on them. Past performance is not a guarantee of future performance, or so it goes. It sounded too good to be true, but greed has a way of allowing us to rationalize a good sales pitch.

Greed helps drive the markets, and it is possible to make money in a hot tradable instrument. But without the knowledge of what you are investing in or having a trading plan for your short-term trades, it is a pure roll of the dice. Odds are that you have had or you will have similar experiences to mine at some time, if you are new to the markets. You may hit a winner from a friend's tip, or the tip may not work out. Either way, it is not your researched idea, so you are just gambling.

Information can and does come from sources other than you. However, as a professional investor or trader you will make sure that you have done the work so that the decision to act or not is yours. Everyone reading this book has had—or will have the experience if you are only just starting in the markets—of not having a stop-loss in place that turns into a freefall of prices. This disaster may raise the head of another known demon, that of averaging down in a loser to lower your cost, in an attempt get back to breakeven or better. This can result in financial suicide for those new to the market and even those who are experienced that trade without a thought-out money management plan for an advanced trading strategy.

If you are thinking that averaging down should never be done, it can be. But it should be planned out based on advance money management strategies combined with technical analysis of the instrument traded. There are many ways to lose money in the markets, but all "uncalculated losses" in the market come from not having a plan and the education to operate in the market or operating outside of that plan. But you will read much more on this later.

My mind-set began to change from the beaten down so-called bargains. It likely changed because what I was doing was not working, so my mind began to open up to other ideas I was reading. One of them was the concept of buying really strong stocks that were moving up already, rather than trying to catch bottoms that many times never formed (or when they did, prices often retraced back down quickly). Bottoming stocks typically retest those bottoms multiple times, since there are so many people that are tired of holding them. Each time prices rally, holders of the stock sell into the move. Bottoms just take time to form and a sustainable trend typically happens after multiple retests of the lows after one, and many times two, strong moves out of that base. As with all technical trade setups, there are future expectations as to how those setups are going to play out. Bargains or bottom patterns take time, sometimes a long time, so expecting quicker trading profits does not make sense. Sounds like common sense, but when you are trying to figure out how the market operates it is all a mystery. It was to me.

Okay, so why not take a stock that is already moving up and jump on board? Many of you probably know the outcome from this technique, especially if you have tried it. I found strong, on-the-move stocks. The day I bought them, however, they decided it was time to take a break. So they would begin falling. But not to worry, I would say. This is what happens when you buy strength. Falling from strength is not uncommon, but did I have a plan as to where they would likely fall to? Would that be a good place to buy more or would the fall have caused so much damage that the original reason for the trade no longer existed? And even before these questions, was a strong stock that was already up, up too much? It was too early in my development to have answers to such questions, but they are good ones for you to consider now. It will all come together as we delve into the coming chapters.

The only problem for me in buying strength was the late entry that is inherent with buying something once you know it is strong. The pullback then begins, and it always seems that when I went long, the pullback was above average. Then the stocks would continue to decline to the point where I would have to question whether they were strong stocks anymore. And right or wrong, I was in pain from being down so much money. I never really figured or accepted the possibility that the trade would fail. Out of pure desperation and fear of a greater loss, I would sell and move on. A week later I would check on the stock, and 100 percent of the time (I am making up that statistic, but if you have been there, you also believe it to be true), the stock had shot up by leaps and bounds—and I not only would have had my money back, but I would have been well in the black.

I also came to realize in this process that these really nice-moving stocks were not ones that the "experts" said to buy. Some did not even have PE ratios, because some did not even have earnings. By the time the experts recommended to buy these stocks, they were already up hundreds of percentage points. Strike two.

Through this process I began to learn a few things. First of all, if there is *any* correlation between the fundamentals of a company that are known to the public and the price of a stock, there is no way to predict it or profit from it. I began to realize that simply looking at what stocks were actually doing, rather than what people "said" they should be doing, was much more reliable. This was a huge moment for me and a step in the right direction. It led to what I now refer to as "the only truth" in the market (which you will read about throughout this book).

While it was a step in the right direction, I still had a long way to go. This led me into the technical world of stocks. Twenty years ago, when you became a technical trader, it was almost synonymous with saying a "technical-indicator" trader. The reason was simple. The faster method of trading was being instituted, and technical trading was fairly new to the masses.

Stock traders using technical analysis looked to the same programs and indicators that commodity traders were using. Computer-based charts and indicators were more commonplace when it came to commodities. This was not inexpensive at the time. For stock traders, there were chart books that could be bought and were mailed to you on a weekly basis. We've come a long way! Computers were showing their power (relatively speaking) and becoming more affordable, and data vendors were making daily price information available for download. This was the time of 286 speed computers and 2400-baud modems. It was not fast and compared to today, it was like the stone age of technical trading. It was new to everyone, and there was not a lot of information out there. The thrill of having a single silver bullet, one Holy Grail to predict price, was very appealing. This was especially true after being chewed and spit out by the market more than a couple of times.

The argument for technical indicators was also very well presented. The author always had charts of stock prices, and the indicator they were selling always moved up or down with the price nearly perfectly. It always seemed to be very accurate. Every big move up in price had a nice bottom set by the indicator. What a "no lose" situation. So I began trading with some of these much-touted technical indicators.

A funny thing happened. They did not really work. What do I mean by did not really work? Well, they would work sometimes. But anything works sometimes. If your system was to go long the market the day after your dog gets a bath, that would work sometimes also. But I would not want to trade by it. Also, these indicators often worked in hindsight, meaning, when the stock took off, yes, the indicator did also. But it did not lead as some suggested it did. And if it did seem to lead, sometimes it was wrong. And sometimes the indicator and the stock went up but then fell hard. There did not seem to be any way to distinguish real moves from false moves, and the best moves seemed to happen with price leading the way, with the indicator keeping me out until it seemed to be too late. Suggesting that indicators prices are same as saying the tail wags the dog. It was all an illusion.

I even took all of this to a new level. I not only tried *all* of the indicators available at the time, but I also tried various combinations of them. My thoughts were that if several point in the same direction at the same time, it must work. It did not. I then went to a level that few of you probably have; I wrote my own indicators. I figured that the concept was good; it was just that nobody had the right formula yet. With all of the research I had done, I already knew much of what did not work, so I should have been the perfect one to write the perfect indicator. You can guess the results of those many months of work.

Some of you are probably laughing at this point, and if so, it is only because you have been through this. It is at this point that the vast majority of people who set out to beat the market just quit. They quit out of frustration, losing too much money, or just lack of belief that it can be done.

Well, I was frustrated. I had lost some money. But I still believed it could be done. Something I always thought about was that the market is a zero sum game. For every dollar I (and all those like me) was losing, *someone* was making those dollars. This kept me motivated. Thinking back on it, the lack of information and the frustration I went through became my biggest allies. By sorting through so many things that did not work, I fell upon a hidden truth: the thing that did work. What worked was not a single indicator. It was not a single formula, and could not be explained in a single paragraph. What alone worked was understanding the language of charts and understanding price action. It was the knowledge that prices do move in certain repetitive ways. While these movements are not perfect, they are reliable enough to make money when understood properly.

While this seemed to me like a revelation at the time, today it just seems like common sense. It took a while to understand, but now it seems easy. The easy part comes from viewing or interpreting any chart in any time frame in the exact same way, without the subjectivity of indicators, trend lines, Elliot Waves, Fibonacci, Bollinger Bands, Gann, planetary alignment, and so on. This doesn't mean that every chart pattern is tradable (and we will discuss that in detail), but my analysis—and I hope soon yours—of any tradable instrument will be clear, based on a consistent, systematic method of analysis.

Currently, I am the President, CEO, and the majority holder of Pristine Capital Holdings. Since its inception in late 1994, Pristine.com has been dedicated to helping investors and traders find the truth in the market; to a way of reading price that keeps it simple and uses pure common sense. It is not always easy, but it is very learnable.

Years ago, I also formed a broker-dealer to help Pristine students get the best trading technology and service available. Back then (and even today), it was (and is) difficult to get the service active traders and investors needed. Many advancements and offerings at Pristine have been based on the question, what will help traders do the best in the market? Since then, many have found out about the great service, as well as very competitive rates, at Mastertrader.com. If you are a serious trader or investor you will want to contact them.

Like anything in this life, nothing is free, and the truly great things are worth working for. With that, I invite you to read and enjoy this book. At the end of the book, you will understand that there is only one truth in technical analysis. Enjoy.

HOW TO USE THIS BOOK

I suggest that you read this book through from cover to cover. In the beginning chapters I discuss, in a very detailed way, some of the essential concepts, such as candlesticks, support and resistance, and moving averages, and explain how the common use of many of these is incorrect.

We then move into some of the more detailed areas on the charts and again discuss the proper and improper use of tools like volume, retracements, and how to analyze every bar as it forms.

We next look at more advanced concepts. In a section called "market internals" we look at various ways to dissect the market. We examine the proper use of relative strength, and how to really understand the differences in trends. We then look at gap analysis and also take a look at how prices play out over multiple time frames, one of the most advanced topics there is for a trader.

Following, we delve into more specialized topics, such as how to make failures work for you, and we talk about the all-important concept of how to manage both the trade and the money. We then look at how to handle the trading day, and conclude with a wrap up repeating the most important truth you need to learn about the markets.

I am sure you will enjoy reading this book as much as I enjoyed writing it.

ABOUT THE CHARTS IN THIS BOOK

There are many charts throughout this book that illustrate the concepts being discussed. If you want to view the full color versions, you may do so at the companion website at www.wiley.com/go/capra. (password: trade123)

A NOTE ABOUT PRISTINE.COM

Our Trading Methods

As you may know, I am the founder of Pristine.com. We have been in the business of teaching our clients how to become professional traders and investors. We have been doing this since 1995. If you look around this industry, there are very few organizations that can claim that longevity. I am proud of what we have built at Pristine. Our clients range from regular people who want to manage and take control of their own IRAs, to people who want to become professional day traders.

You will notice throughout this book there are various references to the terminology we use at Pristine. It is how I talk, and the only way I know to look at the markets. I have tried to explain the terminology whenever I use it. There is usually an acronym associated with the terminology; if you begin to lose track of the acronyms, there is a list of most of them in Appendix A. As you will soon see, our trading methods do not rely on a myriad of fancy oscillators or proprietary systems. We read price patterns and have learned how to pull information from every bar that forms on a chart, and how those bars come together to form trends and turning points. If you have studied the market for any length of time, you know this is the only way to understand the market.

More Information for You

In this book, I sometimes refer to the courses or methods we use at Pristine. I did not want to bore you with continuous references to Pristine, so here in the Introduction I am writing to let you know that you can find further information about many of the methods discussed in this book by visiting Pristine.com. On this website you will find many useful pieces of information that are available for free, including many free webinars and free services. In addition, you will find a list of the offerings that we have. They range from our world-famous "Trading the Pristine Method Seminar" to a "Proprietary Trading Program," for those who want to trade firm capital please visit www.pristine.com.

Trading Tools and Tactics

CHAPTER 1

Subjective Doesn't Work in the Market

*Technical Analysis Is
the Objective Standard*

W*ebster's Dictionary* defines subjective as "characteristic of or belonging to reality as perceived rather than as independent of mind." When we want an opinion from a critic on how good a movie is, we are expecting a subjective review. When we read a restaurant write up, we also get a subjective review. We may see the movie or eat the meal, and have a different experience than the critic did. We will tend to follow the critics who agree with our subjective notions.

This is fine for movies and dinner and many other things in life. But the market is not a matter of opinion. There are several ways in which "subjective" enters the marketplace. Subjectivity can enter when traders try to rely on the latest guru in the marketplace, when they try to use fundamental analysis in their decision making process, and when they use technical indicators on their charts. While there are some others, these are the three biggest culprits. I am going to explain how you can fall into each of these traps, and how you can avoid them.

THE GURU SYNDROME

The first common way in which people let subjectivity enter their trading comes to people before they decide to do it on their own. There is a tremendous tendency for people to want to follow a guru, or anyone who speaks with authority. Often these people are followed without any track record, simply because they say things that "make sense" or agree with our views in some way. Unfortunately, what appears to be common sense rarely works in the market place.

If you take a look at the famous gurus over the years that made a name for themselves, most of those names are gone. There may be new names today, but they will be gone tomorrow. People make names for themselves by standing up and taking a firm

1

stand on the market. For example in the 1990s, you may remember (if you were following the market then) several big names who decided to take a very bullish stance once the market began moving up. As time went on they got fame for their "prediction" and continued to pound the table to be long. When the market turned in 2001, it also turned on them. They dropped off the map or were even heckled for their views. Very few gurus maintained a name for themselves when the market turned. Just like many did with their stocks, these gurus rode fame as the market rallied, and crashed with the market.

Did some predict the crash? Sure. The problem here is that many predicted the crash up to eight years earlier. Again, little fame is justified for such predictions. In every market you will find bulls and bears. Some are right, some are wrong. Those that are consistently right are harder to find. Those that are consistently right are often looked at as foolish for periods of time where they go against popular opinion, even though it is the right thing to do at the time. They have found their own method or style, and know how to use it properly. New people to the market usually find in short order that the "experts" on TV are not making them any money.

After a while, many learn it may be best to find a way to develop a system, method, or style of interpreting the market, or individual stocks, in order to find their own plays. For traders or investors of the market who decide to do the work themselves, there are still two ways in which subjectivity is introduced to their studies. The first way is by relying on fundamental rather than technical analysis. While this debate has continued since the beginning of time, my view is unquestionably that there is no debate: technical analysis is what works in the marketplace.

However, even when traders take the technical route subjective issues can still creep in through the use of technical indicators. Following is a discussion of both of these issues that new self-directed traders may face.

THE PITFALLS OF FUNDAMENTAL ANALYSIS

Going back to the first time anyone charted the price of something that was sold in an open market, the debate between fundamental and technical analysis has existed. Fundamentalists claim that technicians are trying to look at the past and predict the future. Technicians claim that fundamentalists are trying to find the value of a company, which is impossible to do, and that is not relevant even if you determine what it is.

Fundamentalists look at the accounting numbers of the company. They look at things like price to earnings ratios (PE ratios), book value, and other accounting type numbers. They also look at things like the ability of current management, new products coming out, and recent acquisitions. They then take all this information, and come up with an exact price that the company should be worth. From that, they calculate the price per share, and if the number is higher than the current stock price, they consider it undervalued, and a buy.

On one hand, it sounds like looking at hard numbers may be very objective. But there are several problems with this. First, how do you know to trust the numbers you are looking at? Back when Enron was trading over one hundred dollars a share, it was considered a great fundamental value. The problem was, of course, that the numbers that were being looked at were all lies. They were made up by accountants and CEOs. Was that an isolated incident? Not in the least. WorldCom and many other companies have gone out of business or had huge price swings as the underlying accounting numbers were found to be a "tad bit off."

Even if you are less skeptical, talk to an accountant of any business. There are huge ranges in acceptable accounting measures that are allowed. Some are just allowed, while some are in constant debate as to what is correct. So the officers of a company can have huge swings in their profit and loss statements, based on the decisions made on how to account for certain big numbers. Fundamentalists often look to a change in profits by even a penny as being a big deal, when the accounting choice may have changed the outcome by a dollar. It becomes quite silly at some point. So, using the fundamental numbers of a company is a very subjective way of valuing a company when you come right down to it.

Beyond that, there is a more basic problem with fundament analysis that makes it even more subjective. It assumes that someone knows the value of a company based on last year's or last quarter's numbers. But that picture is immediately clouded when an analyst says, "That was last year, you should see what they are likely to do this year." So now they start talking about increasing the value of their "objective" analysis by a guess as to what may happen in the future. This is why hundreds of companies in the 1990s (and this still continues today) had soaring stock prices, with no earnings. Fundamentally, without earnings, there are really no numbers to work with to justify any price, let alone a higher value than the current price. Yet the promise of future earnings had stocks rise from one dollar to literally hundreds of dollars, based simply on the promise of great earnings someday. Does that sound like how you want to make your trading and investing decisions?

There is one more problem that puts an end to the conversation. It simply does not work. Many companies that show undervalued prices, and have low PE ratios are often undervalued for a reason. There is a tendency for the cheap to just get cheaper. They are rarely good buys. Likewise, companies, or their stocks, that seem overvalued, rarely come down when analysts say they should. They are overvalued for a reason. If you have ever tried investing using fundamental numbers, you have likely discovered these issues for yourself. Fundamental analysis is actually totally subjective, hiding under only a veil of objectivity.

Most Wall Street analysts use fundamental analysis, though the number of technical analysts has increased dramatically. The opinions of Wall Street analysts on a particular stock or the overall market really have not been much help at all to investors and traders over the years. Take a look at Figure 1.1. Back in 2000 as the price of the stock was reaching all-time highs, everybody loved shares of Yahoo. Merrill Lynch had it as one of their best ideas. As the price declined they reiterated their buy recommendation believing

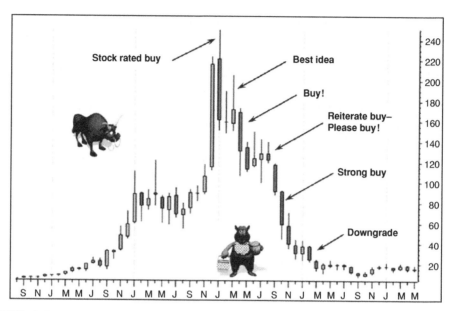

FIGURE 1.1 Actual Analyst Calls Getting Yahoo! 100 Percent Backward
Chart courtesy of Mastertrader.com.

it was such a great company the price of the stock had to rebound. The price continued to decline throughout the year as the Wall Street analysts continued to suggest investors snap up the shares. Finally when the stock had declined by about 90 percent, Merrill Lynch downgraded the stock and stopped urging investors to buy!

Technical analysis, on the other hand, looks to one thing: what the company, or price of the stock, is *actually selling at*. Technical analysis assumes that the price a stock is selling at is the perfect price based on the fact that all known quantities, whether in the past, or anticipated in the future, are built into the price. Tens, hundreds, thousands of investors and traders take positions on both sides of the stock price, and it trades at the price that they have determined based on supply and demand. It *is* the price. There can be no argument. When you think of it that way, any other method is useless.

Now, to determine the future price, technical analysis relies on patterns. Seeing prices that occur consistently in such a way it shows that there is ongoing demand for, or supply of, a stock. Learning these patterns is exactly what learning technical analysis is all about. Are their drawbacks? Of course, or else this debate would not exist. However, all drawbacks are a function of not understanding how to use technical analysis. For example, technical analysis finds patterns that are predictable, but it does not mean that every pattern you see will be a predictable pattern. Another example is the concept of multiple time frames. Smaller patterns exist inside bigger patterns, and if you do not know how they should interact, it can appear random. These concepts will be discussed more, later in this book. Most important for this chapter, regarding subjectivity, is the misuse of technical indicators. Many traders rely on technical indicators, but unfortunately these indicators take the objective chart and turn it subjective.

TECHNICAL INDICATORS: ADDING SUBJECTIVITY TO THE CHART

The term "technical indicator" refers to all the things on a chart other than price, which are derivatives of price. You may know some of them: Moving Average Convergence Divergence (MACD), Relative Strength Index (RSI), Stochastics, Gann Lines, Elliott Waves—the list goes on and on. There are charting programs that literally have over 200 of them. This alone should tell you the value of any one indicator. Even moving averages are technical indicators. While moving averages can have a useful purpose, they too are often used subjectively to a trader's detriment.

Technical indicators are subjective in nature for a couple of reasons. They all rely on past prices. Also, while they claim to add objectivity, they all have so many settings that it comes down to everyone's individual opinion of how to read them.

It Is All in the Past

As I just mentioned, all technical indicators rely on past prices and apply a mathematical formula, which is supposed to help predict the future move. The past prices are already on the chart in front of you. This is the objective part of the chart. Price is what matters. Once you create a derivative of that price, it is open to interpretation as to what it means.

Some who use indicators say that they remove the noise from the price movement. However, it's that noise that can provide some of the most valuable information to us. We'll get to this later on.

There is some subjectivity in reading a price pattern. Trading will always have some subjectivity. If it did not, the future of all prices would be known to all and there would not be a market. Our job as traders is to keep things as simple and objective as possible, to find the patterns we know. Indicators add just another layer of mystery, and rely on someone else's setting to tell us what is happening.

It Is Still a Matter of Opinion

Indicators rely almost entirely on opinion or how each individual reads the tea leaves of the various indicators. There have been literally hundreds of different oscillators and indicators developed over the years and when most of them have the option to change the settings it makes the choices endless. The simple truth is that they alone do not tell you anything about what is going on in a stock or in the markets. Investors and analysts over the years have developed countless methods to take the measure of the market.

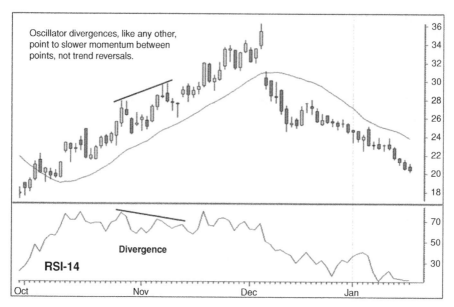

FIGURE 1.2   An RSI Divergence Is Often Meaningless
Chart courtesy of Mastertrader.com.

In reality, you do not need to measure or guess the market. The answer is in the price and it will tell you what it is going to do if you know how to listen to it.

Subjective analysis is based on what you think is happening. In contrast objective analysis is based on what is happening. Prices are directly observable in the real world and tell us what we need to know. Making decisions on subjective measurements leads to what we at Pristine (recall that I am president of Pristine.com, and may occasionally reference what we do there; please see the preface for more comments about my trading company, Pristine) call "mirage trading." It almost always leads to failure. A stock can hit its moving average and go down just as often as it might go up. A stock can remain oversold for months at a time. Perhaps you have already made some of these observations.

Take a look at Figure 1.2. You can see a clear divergence in the 14-day RSI, a very popular oscillator. A divergence such as this would tell the trader that since the oscillator is going down, the stock price should follow according to traditional technical analysis. As you can see that simply does not happen. All an oscillator can measure is slower momentum between price points. This does not necessarily mean that prices will change direction any time soon. Momentum can increase and decrease and the trend remain the same for a long time.

As we can see in Figure 1.3, using absolute levels for many of the indicators does not work either. In this example the RSI never reaches the levels that would indicate the stock was oversold and should be purchased. The price just kept going up for months. This leads to traders trying different settings until the indicator reaches the buy and sell levels where prices turned in the past assuming that this will predict the turns in the

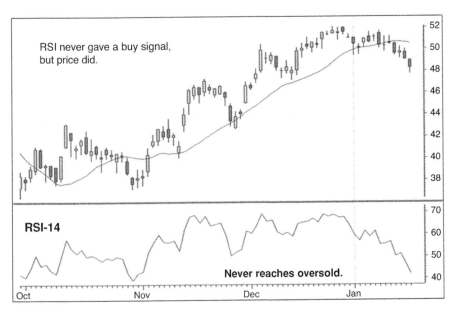

RSI never gave a buy signal, but price did.

RSI-14

Never reaches oversold.

FIGURE 1.3 Most of This Move Was Missed by the RSI Indicator
Chart courtesy of Mastertrader.com.

future. As the market environment changes or a different stock is used the indicator doesn't line up any more. This typically leads to a long cycle of constant changes in settings and indicators to find the perfect indicator.

Unless there is a very strong trend in place, using oscillators leads traders to buy tops and sell bottoms in stocks. The tools you learn in this book will show you to focus on the price itself. It does not matter if you are a day trader using five-minute charts or a long-term investor looking at weekly ones, all the information you need is in the price bars themselves. Why use anything else? The price is the truth.

You may notice that these conversations can flip back and forth between a stock and the market. That is intentional. The market is just a sum of several stocks. What is taught in this book works across all price patterns on anything that is bought and sold in an open market, with sufficient volume. Stocks, futures, commodities—the market itself—they are all the same.

Another problem with some of the technical systems that traders use is that they may lead the trader to believe with 100 percent conviction that the trader knows what will happen next. These are the ultimate in providing those new to the technical analysis with a false sense of security. Everyone wants to feel secure—to know what will happen next. This is human nature, but this is a major obstacle to succeeding as a technical trader or investor. Methods like Gann Angles, Cycle analysis, and Fibonacci retracements profess to offer precise measurements and predictors of stock movements. This creates a belief for traders that they know what is going to happen and can lead traders to make serious mistakes. If your conviction causes you to over-bet on a particular trade the results can be disastrous. Operating with a false sense of belief can also cause you to stay with a losing trade far too long, rather than exit with a small loss when the market told you your bet was wrong.

APPROACHING THE MARKETS OBJECTIVELY

To succeed at trading and investing you need to develop confidence, patience and discipline. I have found over the years that the key to developing these traits includes, ironically, operating in a state of not knowing what will happen next. This is just the opposite of what the majority of technical analysis techniques are based on. You have to eliminate subjective analysis based on indicators from your day-to-day activities in the market. To do this we need to learn a systematic objective approach to the markets.

At Pristine, we teach traders to recognize two key factors when approaching the markets:

1. A stock is always in one of four stages: we name those stages simply stage one, two, three, and four. All stocks, markets, anything, are always in one of these four stages. This is what I consider to be the first basic truth of trading and investing. Understanding this will always keep you on the right side of a move, and also let you know when it is best to leave a stock alone as it becomes less predictable. This is a basic concept to our method that I will be referring to throughout this book.

2. The stages always come in the same order. Once we know what stage a stock is in, there are very specific strategies used to play the stock, and this process keeps us objective in our trading.

The Four Stages of the Markets

For every stage, there is a correct way to play the stock. There is a direction, and there are certain strategies that can be played that will maximize the movement due to the stage we are in. Once you know what stage you are in, you know *how* to trade the stock, and you will know what *strategy* to use on the stock, which will tell you *when* to enter the position. Simple, objective, clear. Trading against the stage a stock is in accounts for 80 percent of losses.

Is it always easy to tell what stage a stock is in? No, of course not. In hindsight it is. In real time it is sometimes easy, and sometimes more challenging. Subjectivity can never be totally eliminated in technical analysis; you must accept this. But it must be controlled, minimized, and understood.

Here is an important point to remember: *When it is not easy to tell what stage a stock as in, you, as a trader, have the right to pass that particular trade. Wait for a better stock, or a better time.*

Re-read this paragraph; it is one of the keys to trading in my view.

Winning traders and investors are those who have learned to identify which cycle a stock or market has entered and buys or sells accordingly. You want to buy at the beginning of stage two and sell it before it enters stage three. Again, this is true regardless of whether you are day trading or investing for the long term. Losing traders and investors are those who react emotionally or rely on subjective indicators. Inevitably these individuals will buy late in stage two as the excitement peaks and sell near the end of the fear stage when all hope of an imminent recovery is gone.

Stage One: A Time of Ambivalence   In stage one, the stock is in what I call a state of ambivalence. Nobody really cares much about the stock, and the stock trades back in forth in a range. There is usually very low volume, as there is little interest in the stock. The range is usually very small, as again, no one cares about this stock. Stage one always follows a period of selling, and often this selling can be enough to totally turn off the bulls from trying to buy any more. They are wounded, hurt, out of money, and no longer interested in the stock. Other bulls may be watching, and may soon want to buy, but at the moment, no one is interested as this stock is weak, and no one knows how far it may fall. There are many failed breakout and breakdown attempts, as neither bulls nor bears can find follow-though anymore, as there is just not enough interest. Breakouts always fail, as all the traders that held the stock long on the way down, sell into rallies trying to recoup their money.

Stage Two: The Uptrend   After enough time goes by, many of these sellers exit or give up, and are no longer selling on rallies. All of a sudden, instead of a rally getting slapped down, it holds. Bulls look around and notice there are very few bears left. This attracts the attention of other bulls, and a snowball effect develops. When selling does come, it is just profit taking from the new bulls, and the stock doesn't go as low as it was before. More bulls come in and the next rally goes to new highs when compared to the prior rally. If this process continues, the early bulls are rewarded as the stock continues to set higher highs on rallies, and higher lows on pullbacks. This turns into an actual uptrend and attracts more buyers. This is now stage two, the time of buying: bulls, uptrends, and the emotion is greed. In the beginning this is what drives the price higher, and the beginning of stage two is the sweet spot that traders should strive to hit. You can see this in Figure 1.4.

Stage Three: Uncertainty Sets In   Even after stage two has been in place a while, it can continue higher. Never bet that a trend is going to end unless you have good evidence. One of the odds we have in the market is relying on the power of the trend. At some point, new intelligent buying now becomes irrational exuberance. However, sometimes after a reasonable move, traders take profits, and new bulls are not as easy to find. The stock or market cannot find enough buyers on breakouts and they fail. Yet, when things seem weak, potential buyers who missed the move view dips and breakdowns as buy opportunities, and breakdowns do not work. The stock or market goes sideways, in a very sloppy manner in a wide range. The bulls and bears have to battle it out until a victor

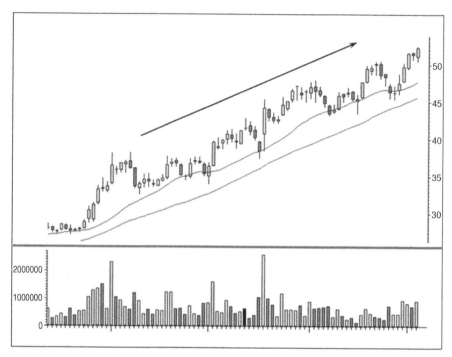

FIGURE 1.4 The Power of a Stage Two
Chart courtesy of Mastertrader.com.

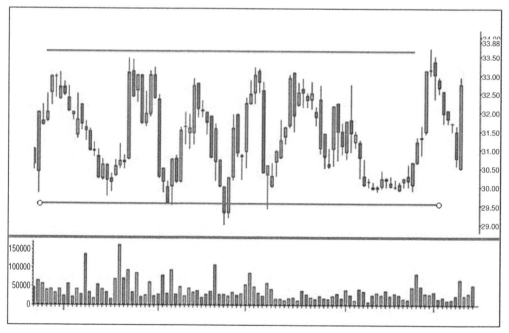

FIGURE 1.5 The Uncertainty of Stage Three Produces a Wide Sideways Pattern
Chart courtesy of Mastertrader.com.

is found. This is a period of indecision, where prices go sideways, and where unknowing traders try to play breakouts and breakdowns and they lose money, never knowing why.

Stage 4: The Downtrend   The pattern may settle down and simply go higher, which would continue the original stage two. This is known as a pause in stage two, and can be distinguished. We will discuss these two types of bases in more detail later. But sometimes the balance of power changes and, all of a sudden, one of those breakdowns does not find buyers and the price drops. The bulls who have been relying on that base to hold now realize they are in losing positions, and they begin to exit. Again, the snowball starts rolling and selling begets more selling. The rallies stop short of prior rallies, and the declines go lower than the last decline. Selling, fear, good news is bad news, are all the signs of stage four (see Figure 1.6).

As fear accelerates, selling increases and begets more selling. This drives prices to the point that even those who swore they would not sell cannot stand the pain and they sell, vowing never to buy another stock again. At some point all sellers, that are ever going to sell, have sold. The stock has run out of sellers and it stops falling. There are no buyers, as the pain has kept old bulls away, and the falling stock has kept new buyers away. So the stock drifts sideways, with no one caring. We are back to ambivalence; we are back to stage one.

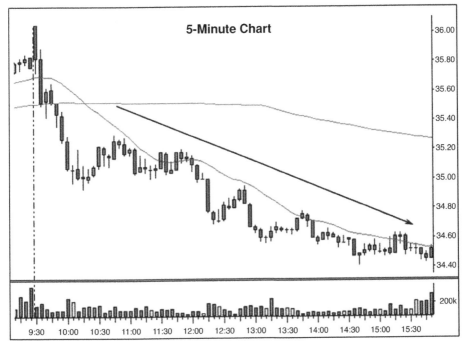

FIGURE 1.6 Stage Four: The Bears Take Control
Chart courtesy of Mastertrader.com.

This will play out across all time frames. You will see it on intraday charts every day. You will see it on daily and weekly charts.

Observing Trends: Up, Down, or Sideways

The second truth is that throughout these stages, a stock or market can really do one of three things. Go up, go down, or go sideways. When a stock goes sideways, it can trend sideways in a reliable pattern, or it can be sideways in a wild erratic pattern.

Stocks go up in up trends (stage two), where the price movement forms higher peaks at the highs and higher dips at the lows. Stocks go down in down trends (stage four), where the price movement forms lower peaks at the highs and lower dips at the lows. A sideways price pattern will have a series of roughly equal high peaks and low dips and requires a slightly different approach to trading. Knowing which condition exists is a key to consistently making money in the markets. Once we know which stage and trend a stock or market is in at a point in time, we can begin using what prices are telling us to find: high probability price movements.

One of our biggest tools to help spot where we are and how to read what the prices are telling us, are what I call the Pristine Buy Setup and Pristine Sell Setup. As you can see in Figure 1.7, I use candlestick charts to read the price of a stock or index. For analyzing

FIGURE 1.7 A Bullish Changing of the Guard Bar Tells Us the Stage Two Uptrend May Be Ready to Resume
Chart courtesy of Mastertrader.com.

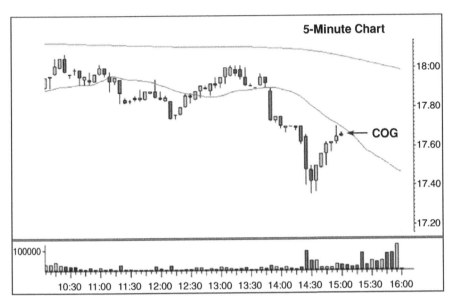

FIGURE 1.8 A Bearish Changing of the Guard Bar Completes This Sell Setup
Chart courtesy of Mastertrader.com.

all normal price action on most charts, I do not consider a chart useful unless it uses candlesticks. I will explain why in greater detail in Chapter 2.

For now let's take a look at what this chart is telling us. The big picture of this stock is a bullish stage two, moving up with higher highs and higher lows. The recent pattern shows the stock has been moving down for several bars in a row, but has not violated the stage two pattern. Once we get a reversal of this price action, as long as we have identified that the stock is still in an uptrend, or in the early part of stage two, it is time to buy. We also call this reversal bar the "changing of the guard" (COG).

In Figure 1.8 we can see that a Pristine Sell Setup (PSS) is simply the reverse of this. The big picture of this stock is a bearish stage four, moving down with lower highs and lower lows. The recent pattern shows the stock is moving up for several bars but has not violated stage four. If we looked at the movement as a line it would be pretty much a straight line up. When the price action reverses it is time to sell or short the stock.

These setups can be used in any time frame. They can be used to establish short-term swing trades or to time long-term stock purchases. It is an easily recognizable pattern that uses a specific series of candlestick charts. Generally speaking once we get reversals we find out very quickly if we were right or wrong and can react to what the market tells us most of the time. Generally this set up occurs when there has been a countermove due solely to profit taking, and the buying or selling activity of the underlying trend is going to reassert itself. Because we already know that we do not know exactly what is going to happen we can let the price tell us what to do once we place the trade.

There are several beautiful things about this Pristine Buy or Sell Setup you may have noticed. First, we are playing in the direction of the primary trend. Second, we are not

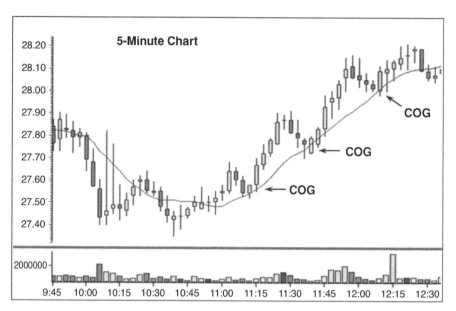

FIGURE 1.9 The Uptrend Is Punctuated with Bullish Changing of the Guard Bars
Chart courtesy of Mastertrader.com.

chasing high prices, we are getting in right at the maximum pullback. Which leads to the next beautiful thing, we have a larger move to whatever price target may be out there. We also have a place to limit our losses very quickly, because if we are right, that entry bar should be the resumption of the trend. If it does not hold, we will be out quickly.

Take a look at Figure 1.9. The stock opens up and begins an uptrend around 10:30 A.M. Then, at 11:15 A.M., we get a changing of the guard buy setup. After momentum stalls and the stock fades out, we pull back setting up another buy signal and move still higher into the close. The patterns are very precise and easy to recognize.

Once we eliminate emotional thinking and subjective analysis we can begin to read what the market is saying. The price is the truth and it is all we need to determine what trading or investing action to take next. We do not need to rely on indicators and tools that are derivatives of price when we can use the price itself. There are no fundamental or technical measurements that will allow you to develop absolute certainty about what is going to happen next. Using the tools you will learn in this book you can tip the odds in your favor but you have to be willing to trade based on probability, not absolute certainty. This allows you to react properly to what does happen and to profit.

IN SUMMARY

The price patterns that form every day and every week are true objective indications of what is actually happening to prices. When stocks are being bought or sold they usually develop very specific patterns that can be learned and identified. Relying on or even considering any of the subjective notions we discussed is only a mirage as they do not involve the truth.

We are going to build on this notion. I have introduced you to the concept of the four stages of price action. We now get more specific and look at the basic units that make up these trends, starting with the individual candlesticks that make the charts we follow.

CHAPTER 2

Candlestick Analysis

*Using the Language of Candles to
Profit from Market Moves*

When I first began my study of technical analysis, candlestick charts were rarely heard of or used. The few books you could find on technical analysis all had bar charts that displayed the basic patterns like rising wedges, flags, head and shoulders, tops and bottoms, and others that can be found in hundreds of books today. The first charting software program I used didn't even have candlestick charts, can you imagine? That's unheard of today. In time, I found a more advanced program that was able to scan stocks within my database for specific criteria, which was a huge advancement at the time, and it had candlesticks. However, the data provider did not provide the opening price at the time. What was available was only the high, low, and the closing price, which leaves you with a candle that has incomplete information.

Years ago, if you wanted to have your own charts you had to buy data from a vendor and download it into your computer over a 2400-baud modem each day and then copy that data with DOS commands to a file within the charting program. Of course, this was after downloading the several years of historical data you wanted, which took all night. Yes, all night! This process of downloading that day's data and then scanning several hundred stocks on what was a fast computer at the time, an ATT 286, would take about an hour. Today that happens in seconds.

The charting of stocks was coming out of the Stone Age, so to speak, and what I was using was as high tech as you could get at the time. Most traders or investors that were interested in viewing price charts would buy chart books that would have hundreds of daily charts. But, of course, those charts would always be a week or more old and were bar charts. I don't believe that such services exist today since virtually a chart of any stock is available on the Internet for free. This should give you a greater appreciation for the technology available today.

Once I found a data provider that had opening prices, I began the process of downloading data on hundreds of stocks again. Having the advantage of candlestick patterns began to take new meaning. The messages were clearer and could be seen faster. In my opinion, this is the real advantage of using candles rather than bar charts. The pictures of what you are looking for are easier and faster to spot than using a bar chart. That being said, don't get caught up in the candlestick hype of today. The use of candlesticks will not ensure that you will make money in the markets. There is no magic to them. They are just one of the tools that we will put together to form our method. However, I will show you a simpler, more enlightening way to use candles with the mindset of a trader.

Candlestick analysis will be the foundation of our approach to reading the mind of the market. We use candlesticks at Pristine because they give us an insight into the thoughts of traders and the expectations of others at the moment for future prices. Each candlestick speaks to us about how traders have acted, how they are acting, and what they are expecting for the future. For us, it allows us to form insights into likely stock or market direction.

A SINGLE CANDLE

Let's start with the basics of candles. You may know some of this information, but many traders do not appreciate all there is in even the most basic information. Candlesticks give us all the information there is about the time frame that the candle represents. Remember, a candle may represent any amount of time from one minute or lower, to a week or year. As I said, this information can be seen in bar charts, but it is not easily recognizable and does not help form patterns we can see at ease.

The candle consists of four pieces of information. This information includes the opening price for that period, the closing price, the high of that time period, and the low. You can see this in the black-and-white representation in Figure 2.1. Remember, if you want to view the full charts in color you can view them at www.wiley.com/go/capra.

The open and the close are important pieces of information and determine the starting point if the bar was a "bullish bar" or a "bearish bar." If the close was a higher price than the open, the space between the close and the open is filled green. (The color is

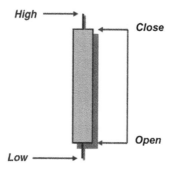

FIGURE 2.1   A Candle Gives Us Four Basic Pieces of Information
Chart courtesy of Mastertrader.com.

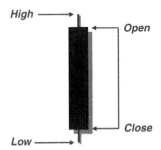

FIGURE 2.2 The Candle Turns Red When Prices Close Lower Than They Open
Chart courtesy of Mastertrader.com.

of your choosing, but green is the most common color of a candle that closes above the opening price.) It is considered a bullish, or green bar (gray represents bullish green bars in this book), because the bulls were able to close prices above the opening price. The bulls won the battle for that period of time.

The high of the period can be seen by the top of the wick or tail. The low of the period can be seen by the bottom of the wick or tail. I will call them tails; however, you also may see them called wicks. Don't get stuck on terms. A wick or tail is just what is above or below the space between the open and close. The top tail is the difference between the close in this case, and the high of the period. The bottom of the tail is the difference between the open in this case, and the low of the period.

Likewise, if the open was a higher price than the close, the space between the close and the open is filled red (black represents bearish red bars in this book). See Figure 2.2.

It is considered a bearish, or red bar, because the bears were able to close prices below the opening price. The bears won the battle for that period of time. The high of the period can be seen by the top of the top tail, and the low by the bottom of the bottom tail.

I want you to think of the opening price of a candle as the start of discovering the supply and demand relationship between sellers and buyers. The high price is where the market or stock began to run into resistance that kept prices from moving higher. Supply began to outpace demand and prices dropped. The low is the point where buyers stepped in and kept prices from falling further. The body or difference between the open and close of the bar tells us who won the supply and demand battle for that time period.

While that is your basic candle, the configurations that can develop between the open, close, high, and low can tell us a lot about prices. Just from looking at one bar!

Figure 2.3 shows a variety of single candles. They all have varying opens, closes, highs, and lows. The patterns above are some of the patterns you will come to recognize from single candlesticks. Look at the first bar. This is called a bullish-wide-range bar. It opens very near the low, closes very near the high, and has very small tails. It is unusually wide as well. This is one of the most bullish bars, and often times even this one bar can tell us a lot. We know bulls totally controlled the period. We see later that this bar is very significant, as it can tell us that a new move is beginning, or an old move is ending.

Bulls Win

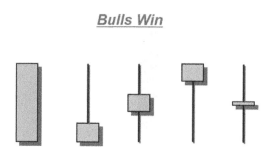

FIGURE 2.3   Five Different "Bulls Win" Candles
Chart courtesy of Mastertrader.com.

Look at the fourth bar. This is the bottoming tail bar. This bar is also a very bullish bar. It alone tells us a lot, and is arguably more bullish than the first bar. A battle was fought here, and the bulls ended up victorious. A lot of emphasis is placed on who was in control at the close of the bar. You will also learn that this bar can mean a lot when combined with other bars.

Now check the third bar, in the middle. This is the next most bullish bar. The bulls were in control part of the time (the bottoming tail), and the bears were in control part of the time (the topping tail). In the end, the bulls had a slight edge as the bar closed green.

The fifth bar, the last bar, is a neutral bar. It has both a topping and bottoming tail, and closed very near the open. This bar is called a doji. While this single bar is neutral, it can tell us something when combined with other bars.

Finally, the second bar. It is green (remember that green shows up as gray in this book, and you can see the color pictures for all of this book at www.wiley.com/go/capra), but it also has a big topping tail. If you follow the progression, you may have already guessed that this bar is slightly bearish. Yes, it did close above the open price, but remember, we care a lot about who ended up in control. That bar at one time was a bullish-wide-range bar like the first bar. Then the bears brought it all the way down to near the low. While they did not bring it under the open, the momentum is down.

Likewise, here are the same patterns on the bearish side in Figure 2.4.

Bears Win

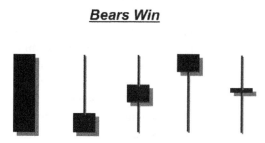

FIGURE 2.4   Five Different "Bears Win" Candles
Chart courtesy of Mastertrader.com.

All the comments from the "bulls win" picture apply to the "bears win" picture, in reverse. The first bar is very bearish, as a bearish wide range bar. It may only be beat by the second bar, which is the bearish topping tail bar. The third bar is moderately bearish, and the fifth bar is the doji, and is equal to the prior doji. The fourth bar is arguably more bullish than bearish even though it is red, because the bulls were in control to change it from a bearish wide range bar to a topping tail.

Each candle tells us something about the supply and demand relationship within the particular time frame being studied. It doesn't matter if you are a day trader using five-minute candle charts, or a long-term investor studying weekly charts, the same principles will apply. They are universal. Candlesticks that form definable patterns give us an insight into the likely direction of prices. Once you have learned to recognize these patterns you will be fluent in what I call Candle Language. In a short time, you will see how the candles are telling you a story and I want you to view that story as if you are in it. Once you understand candles, technical analysis itself will take on new meaning. The patterns or stories will become repetitive and you will intuitively realize the next chapter. If the next candle pattern follows through you will see the end of the story, as it was in the past, and profit from it.

MULTIPLE CANDLE FORMATIONS

While one candle tells us something, two candles tell us more, and groups of candles can tell us even more. There are many strategies or concepts that are spawned from a single candle. There are many that are spawned from two candles. Many also come from groups of candles that form patterns that we have come to recognize. Simply said, we are looking for pictures that reoccur from our studies of price patterns of the past that we understand. You don't have to understand all price patterns to make money. Actually, there are many times that patterns signal confusion among traders and it is a message for us to sit on the sidelines and wait for more information.

It does not matter if it is a basic changing of the guard or some of the other patterns with fancy names like Bearish Engulfing pattern, Evening Star, Dark Cloud Cover, or other esoteric patterns. The patterns are simply tools that help us determine what others are thinking and doing as well as the future directions of prices. Taking this approach to candlestick analysis will help you lift your understanding and trading to a whole new level.

When we talk about candlestick charts we often hear exotic terms to describe each pattern. They can be as exotic sounding as the charts that were developed in Japan many years ago. Patterns have names like Hangman, Thrusting Line, Hammer, Shooting Star, and Doji Star. There are at least 50 different descriptive phrases used to identify various candlestick patterns. At Pristine, we like to simplify things.

The name of a candle or the pattern does not matter to us as traders, so don't waste our time remembering names. Doing so will not make us money. Names do help communicate larger pieces of information with a word or two and are useful in that way. But when it comes to candlesticks, the number of names for a candle or multiple candles is unnecessary. What is important is what the candle is telling you in the moment in relation to the prior candles, trend, support, and resistance.

Changing of the Guard

Let's talk about some multiple bar patterns. The first we will talk about is a changing of the guard. This occurs when we have three or more candles of the same color, and then the changing of the guard (COG) is the opposite color. See Figure 2.5. For example, a bullish COG would occur when we have a red bar, red bar, red bar, followed by a green bar. There could be more than three red bars. The green bar would be the COG. The reverse would be true for a bearish COG. This pattern shows a likely reversal (from the three or more bars, to the COG), at least in the short-term pattern.

Now, while that pattern is a COG, not all COG, patterns are the same. What we want to look at is how far the COG bar penetrates and closes into the prior bar. There are dozens of different names for different changing of the guard patterns, but they are all telling us the same thing. We don't need a lot names for them, just an understanding of how far the COG penetrates. They really can be broken down into three categories, depending on the potency of the reversal. Let's take a look at each of these three types, shown in Figure 2.6.

Note the differences in the three setups. In the first example of each set, the COG penetrates the prior bar by less than half of the candle's body length. In the second, the penetration is half or more of the length. The third and most powerful reversal candle is more than 100 percent of the body of the prior candle.

The level of penetration into the prior bar is the valuable information we are looking for. Recall that we are using candlesticks to measure the supply and demand relationship that exists in the market. The further a bullish setup penetrates and closes into the prior candle the more we know. If it is just barely touching or slightly into that prior

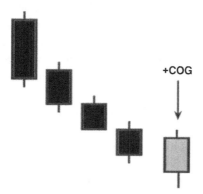

FIGURE 2.5 A Bullish COG Must Follow at Least Three Red Candles
Chart courtesy of Mastertrader.com.

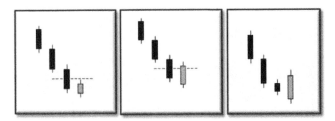

FIGURE 2.6 Three COGs with Different Penetration
Chart courtesy of Mastertrader.com.

bar, supply may be decreasing but we do not have enough information to determine that there is enough demand to push prices higher. If it climbs halfway into the prior bar we can see that most of the supply is being met by demand. A higher open (gap up) of the next bar would give us confirmation that demand had regained control of prices. When a candle exceeds the prior bar by 100 percent, demand has exceeded supply and prices are going higher. All of these candle formations have names you know, but this last one is the most common. Even at Pristine this formation may generate several names, such as a Bear Trap, a Bull 180 Reversal, and a Bullish Engulfing Bar. Again, call it what you like, just so you know the effect that this visual pattern has. It's simple and common sense.

Obviously with a bearish COG setup the opposite is true. The further prices fall into or below the prior bar, the more potent the sell signal. With the bearish setups we want to see that demand is waning and supply is coming back into the market and will take prices lower. If you refer back to the first illustration in this chapter, with the five bullish and five bearish candles, any one of those could be a COG bar. Any bullish candle shown there could be a COG bar if it followed three or more red bars. Note the more potent COG bars will be the bullish wide range bar shown first, or the bottom tail bar shown fourth.

Narrow Range Bar

Likewise there are many different names of bars that fall into the class of what I refer to as narrow range bars. A narrow range bar (NRB), where the range between high and low is smaller than prior bars, is telling us that momentum is slowing. We saw the NRB in Figure 2.3 and 2.4. Again, a single narrow range bar by itself does not mean much, but following at least three prior bars in the same direction we now can read more about the pattern; a slowing of momentum. We often separate a narrow body bar (NB) where there is a small difference between the open and close. In Figure 2.7 you can see the difference visually.

The NBs include a popular candle known as a doji, where there are top and bottom tails, but the body is not there (having the same open and close) or is very narrow. The NB in Figure 2.7 is a doji.

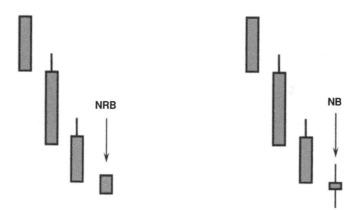

FIGURE 2.7 A Narrow Range Bar and a Narrow Body Bar
Chart courtesy of Mastertrader.com.

As we look for potential reversal, one of the things to look for is NRBs/NBs. As you can see in Figure 2.8, this is simply a series of bars where the range of each is narrowing compared to prior bars. Again, these single bars are most effective after a series of bars in the same direction.

There are several different variations of this but the message is always the same. The momentum of the price trend is slowing. Obviously this is true whether the trend is up or down at any given point in time. It is not an actionable pattern. A NRB simply tells us that momentum is slowing and a reversal is more likely. We have to let the next bar form to tell us what is going to happen. While the odds of a reversal are now higher, the next bar could well signal a continuation. We must wait for the candle to form and presents us with the market's message.

So why is this useful? Well, as we will see later, if this candle formation is happening in an area of the chart we care about for other reasons, the slowing of momentum may mean even more. This is something we will talk more about later in this book.

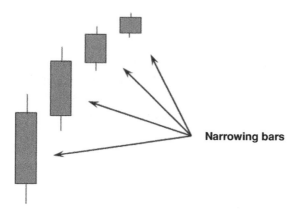

FIGURE 2.8 Bullish Bars Losing Momentum
Chart courtesy of Mastertrader.com.

Wide Range Bar

A wide range bar, or WRB, is a bar that you have already seen as a single bar. Figures 2.3 and 2.4 show the first bar as being very bullish or very bearish. They are almost all green or red, so they have very small tails. They are also larger than the average bars. The best WRBs should be at least 50 percent greater than the average of the series of bars you are looking at.

As we discussed, the WRB has meaning by itself. It is a very bullish or bearish bar. But when combined with other bars, it can show us one of the most powerful patterns in candlesticks. There are two things a WRB can tell us, depending where they occur in the price pattern. A WRB after an extended period of low volatility and a consolidation of prices usually leads to a continuation of prices in the direction of the WRB bar. Figure 2.9 shows an example of a WRB coming after a period of indecision.

When this occurs, we note that this is a bar that is likely starting a new move. A period of inactivity, indecision, or sideways churning (stage one or three, from our earlier discussion) can turn into a new uptrend or downtrend when the move explodes out of the old area with a WRB. View this bar as buyers (demand) overwhelming sellers (supply). Buyers have crushed sellers in this battle and they are committed to continue doing it. In extreme cases, an extended move down could be reversed by a bullish WRB. Here the bullish WRB would be acting as a COG (changing of the guard) bar as well.

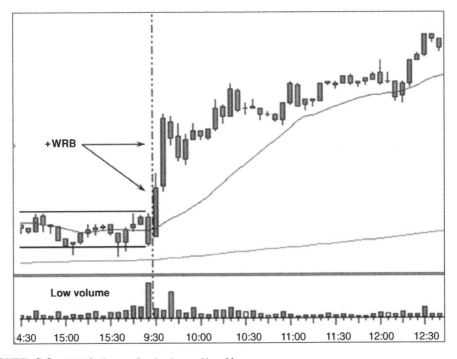

FIGURE 2.9 A Wide Range Bar Ignites a New Move
Chart courtesy of Mastertrader.com.

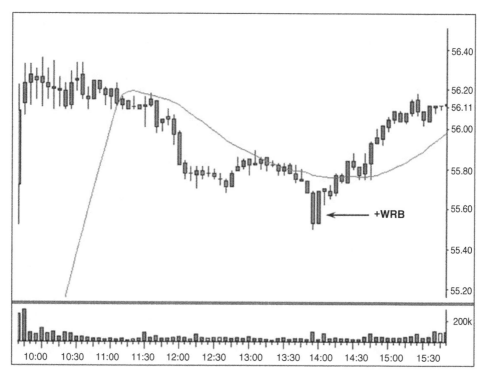

FIGURE 2.10 A +WRB Forms a Potent +COG as Well
Chart courtesy of Mastertrader.com.

It would be a very potent COG, and can start to change the trend from a downtrend to an uptrend. An example is shown in Figure 2.10. Naturally, the same is true for a bearish WRB after a bullish move. When this combination of bars happens, we refer to this as a WRB that is igniting a new move.

The other time a WRB has a message for us is when it occurs after several bars that are moving in the same direction. When there are a series of bullish green bars, and then a bullish WRB forms, that tends to end the move to the upside. As prices are moving higher it's becoming more and more obvious to traders that prices are really going up. I say really going up because traders always have doubts whether prices will continue to move up, even the traders that already own the stock. The traders that don't own it are hoping for a stall in the move and pullback to buy. As prices continue to move up to the amazement of all, those that own the stock now have little doubt that it can go higher and supply-sellers become fewer. The tension for those that were not able to get on board becomes unbearable. They cannot take being left behind any longer and have to get on board this rocket knowing that it's going higher! They send their buy orders into whatever supply there is, exhausting the remaining bulls and a WRB forms on that time frame. Patterns are pictures that are a reflection of emotion and expectations on a continuous basis. Have you ever sold the bottom of a move or the top of one? If you

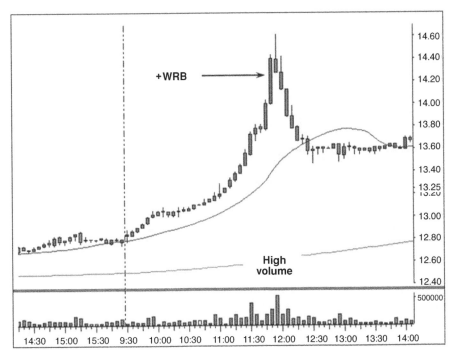

FIGURE 2.11 A Wide Range Bar Ends the Current Move
Chart courtesy of Mastertrader.com.

have a journal of your trades, and you should, odds are you'll find those entries were in a
WRB. Figure 2.11 shows a WRB ending a move.

Be careful: ending an uptrend does not always mean beginning a downtrend. Remember, there is a third trend that exists, called sideways. Whether a bullish WRB ending a
move up turns into a sideways pattern or a downtrend will depend on the surrounding
pattern and other time frames, something we will get into more in future chapters.

Bars That Form Tails

Now let's take a look at bars that form tails after a move in one direction. These are
my favorite candles and I'll show you a pattern later with a tail that I call a money bar.
We have already seen topping and bottoming tails in Figures 2.3 and 2.4. A topping tail
bar (TT) is a bar where prices close below the midpoint of the entire bar. This tells us
that supply is now starting to overwhelm demand within that time period. After an initial
move up during that time frame, sellers stepped in and pushed prices below the midpoint
of the range. There has been a change and a distribution has occurred.

Like the other bars in this section, this individual bar has meaning, but much more
meaning is conveyed when the bar happens in a pattern of other bars. Just like the COG
discussed above, the pattern we want to see is three or more bars in one direction, then a

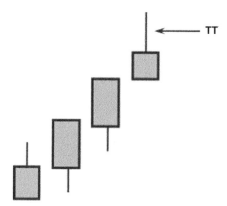

FIGURE 2.12 A Topping Tail Follows at Least Three Green Bars
Chart courtesy of Mastertrader.com.

tail pointing the other way. For example, green bar, green bar, green bar, then a topping tail. This is a signal that the recent trend may be about to reverse course. See Figure 2.12.

A bottoming tail bar (BT), as seen in Figure 2.13, is exactly the opposite. The price closes above the midpoint of the bar. If this is happening after three or more red bars, this tells us that prices started to move lower and continued the trend, but buyers stepped up in the face of falling prices. A bottoming tail bar tells us that demand is starting to absorb the supply and price could be about to move higher.

An important point to remember with tail bars of either type is that the most potent signals are those where the range of the bar is greater than previous bars. The wider the range of a topping or bottoming tail bar, the more dramatic the change in momentum that has occurred. Remember a wide range bar after a multiple bar move signals that the move is likely to end. A wide range tail bar was a WRB and tells us that the supply

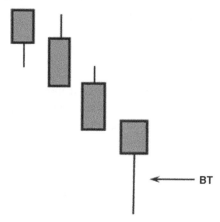

FIGURE 2.13 A Bottoming Tail Follows at Least Three Red Bars
Chart courtesy of Mastertrader.com.

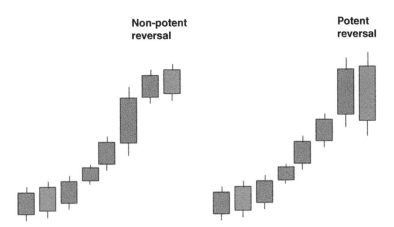

FIGURE 2.14 When a COG Becomes a WRB It Is More Likely to Reverse Prices
Chart courtesy of Mastertrader.com.

and demand relationship has changed and a reversal in trend is likely to occur. A narrow range tail bar could just simply be a brief rest in the trend and is not a tradable signal.

Additional Comments

This concept of the wider move is true for all the patterns we have looked at. In general, when we are looking for buy and sell signals, keep in mind that the larger a reversal bar is in relation to the prior bars, the more potent the signal is. This is true for the COG, the WRB, or the BT. (By definition, this concept does not apply to the NRB.) We want to see concrete evidence that the supply and demand relationship has changed within whatever time frame we are studying. For a COG, I want to see the bar penetrate the prior bar by at least 50 percent or more before I am confident a change is about to occur, and the wider that prior bar is, the better. For a BT, I want to see the tail be at least 50 percent of the bar, and the bigger the overall bar, the better. For a WRB, I want to see the bar at least twice the size of the average bar. When this happens, the odds are also very good that the WRB that becomes a COG will reverse the pattern. Examples of these are in Figure 2.14.

FAILURE IS NOT ALWAYS BAD

One of the first great things about the proper use of technical analysis is to understand that things do not always play out as we read them. Understanding that anything can happen, and to focus on what is happening, rather than on what you think is going to happen, keeps you in the moment and focused on reading the pattern properly. There is an expectation created by a pattern for those who understand it and are viewing it. Is that expectation being fulfilled or is a pattern showing signs of failing? Some patterns

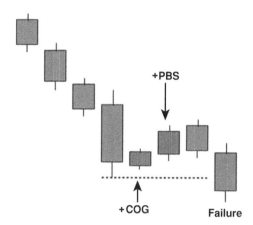

FIGURE 2.15 A Pattern That Failed
Chart courtesy of Mastertrader.com.

fail, because of the nature of stocks and markets. We are always looking for odds, not guarantees. There are no guarantees in the market. I wait for high-odds patterns and manage them as they unfold.

Some patterns fail because we know they are low-odds patterns. This begs the question if anything really failed, but the point is that many traders have views that they continue to follow, even though they are very often wrong. Using subjective indicators (as discussed in Chapter 1), and looking to certain common patterns, without a deeper understanding of the big picture, causes many traders to keep looking to losing patterns. Price patterns must be put into the context of the other concepts or those patterns could be a fast track to lost money. At Pristine, we teach traders to look for the failures (which may not even be failures to us), and take advantage of those instances. When we get into failed patterns you start to learn how to take advantage of them.

In Figure 2.15 we see a Pristine Buy Setup (PBS) that occurred after a bullish COG bar. Two bars later the pattern failed. We say it failed, because this pattern called for an entry when it traded over the COG bar, but then it traded lower below the point where the play would be stopped. Was this a good play that just stopped because some plays fail, or was this a play that was destined to fail because it was a low-odds setup? In this case we cannot tell from just looking at the few bars above. We know that it was not a potent COG, which may have been part of the problem, but we are not seeing the whole picture.

What is an example of seeing the whole picture? Trends are one of the most reliable things we have in technical analysis. Let's say in the above example, the big trend was down. While there may have been a buy setup forming in some fashion, I know that the odds are slim of it working. As a matter of fact, I could be expecting the pattern to fail, and actually taking an entry on that failure. This is a great example of a pattern I know and use. It is known as using the failure of a pattern on a smaller time frame to confirm the trend of a bigger time frame. In addition, I may have already been short when that PBS formed. Of course this would be of some concern to me since the pattern would signal that buyers have stepped up for the moment and could take prices higher. However, the failure of the setup would confirm my bias and how I objectively monitor the trade.

It is critical that you allow each bar to complete its time frame. Do not assume that a candle will close in a manner or pattern that it seems to be before the candle is complete. This can change quickly. For example, in a daily candle, just because a bar is bullish through most of the day does not mean it will be bullish at the close of the day. There were times years ago where I would enter a swing trade (several day hold) at one o'clock because the daily candle was forming as I expected. However, at the close of trade at four o'clock the candle didn't look anything like it did at one o'clock. Can you manage a trade that you should not have taken in the first place? Of course not and that is my point. The same statement applies to any time frame from minutes to weeks. The candle is not complete until the time period has ended and the bar is closed. We want to hear what the market is telling us, not what we want or hope it will tell us.

IN SUMMARY

All of these concepts have different names using traditional candlestick analysis. But if you learn to ignore those names, and concentrate on what the candle patterns are telling you, you begin to learn the language of the market, rather than learning a collection of isolated pattern names. What is the message? Is supply (sellers) or demand (buyers) in control? Is volatility expanding (candle range increasing) or contracting? Is the expansion of range (WRB) starting or ending a move? How likely is it that the supply-demand relationship has changed (potent reversal or wide-tail bar) and momentum is going to swing in the other direction? All of this information is found in the basic candle patterns we discussed in this chapter.

Several times when talking about a candle or candle pattern I've said "in that time frame." I mention this because changing time frames will change the candle and candle pattern. This can be a point of confusion and needs further discussion that we will get to.

Now that we have learned how single and multiple candles can tell us much about prices, we now want to focus on how prices react when the candles run into prior candles. This is the concept of support and resistance, which we tackle next.

CHAPTER 3

Support and Resistance

Price Is King

Mark this chapter right now. It is one that you will want to revisit many times in the future. The concept covered here on support and resistance levels is one of the keys to understanding price movements. Once you understand these ideas, you will understand why prices move rapidly from one pattern but do not form a similar-looking pattern.

PRICE PATTERNS

Patterns tell us what has happened in the past and what might happen in the future. The idea behind pattern recognition is that patterns reflect the analysis and thoughts of the other investors and traders. People often act emotionally, especially when it comes to their money. These thoughts and emotions form patterns and since emotions and human nature are universal, similar patterns form in all tradable instruments. It does not matter if you trade stocks, commodities, currencies, or bonds, the patterns are universal to all of them. Once we recognize one, we then have to put that picture in the context of the bigger picture or structure of support and resistance. When we see that pattern or picture again, odds are that result will be similar.

As I touched on in Chapter 1, we must remove all forms of subjective analysis from our charts and our thought process. Reference points of support and resistance analysis must be based on what is real, not on analysis tools that we can fit to our liking. As always, in any type of technical analysis of markets and stocks, price is the truth and the only thing that matters.

Many traders use analysis tools, such as moving averages, Fibonacci lines, Fans, Circles, Gann Lines and the relatively simple trend line to find support and resistance levels in the market place. I used some of these for years, since that is what others did,

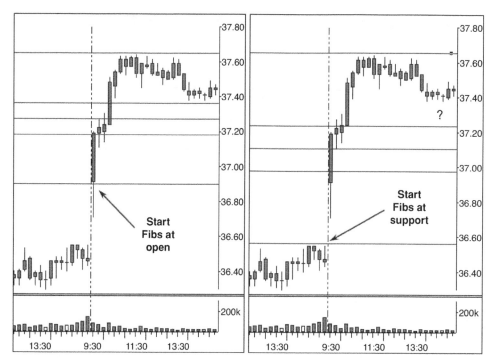

FIGURE 3.1 The Subjectivity of Fibonacci Lines
Chart courtesy of Mastertrader.com.

and thought that this is how one found support and resistance. However, I found them to be completely subjective in nature. I questioned whether I used the right moving average or if I drew the trend line between the correct points. There were often multiple trend line possibilities based on where they were drawn from.

This was also the case with Fibonacci lines or levels. Then I thought of a more interesting question that added to the uncertainty of using these tools. If trend lines or Fibonacci levels were drawn from different points, would that change the location of where support or resistance was? For example, if the lines were drawn from closing prices rather than the highs or lows, it would place the lines in a different place. Another concept related to drawing Fibonacci levels is when they are drawn from multiple high and low points. Look at Figure 3.1. This may result in some of those Fibonacci lines (Fib) overlapping each other. In theory, this is supposed to be a stronger or more reliable reference point of support or resistance. Sometimes it worked, but many times it did not.

There is no consistency in this type of technical analysis and it does not stop when using moving averages either. The type of moving average used will change the location of the so-called support or resistance as well. Using simple versus exponential, 20-period versus 50-period versus 200-period, on a half dozen different time frames, gives quite a variety of support levels. You see this example in Figure 3.2.

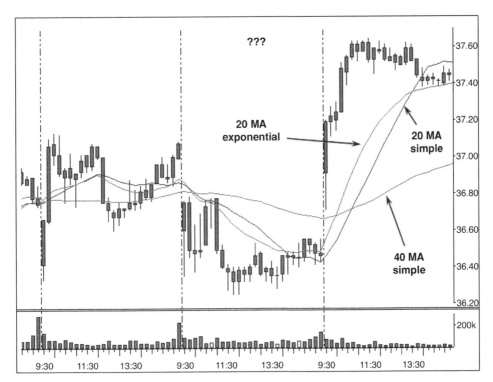

FIGURE 3.2 Which Is the Correct Moving Average?
Chart courtesy of Mastertrader.com.

Using these subjective tools leads users from one level of uncertainty to another. When prices hit these points, they may or may not react to the level based on these tools. When they do, it is usually a self-fulfilling prophecy. Realize that a lot of technical analysis is just that, a self-fulfilling prophecy. If enough people believe in a level, even if it is not based on actual price points, it may temporarily affect prices. Other times, there is not enough buying or selling to change direction around these tools, particularly in a strong price trend. The concept of self-fulfilling prophecy works best when prices are truly on or near a real support level, and then the subjective indicator kicks in. It becomes the catalyst to initiate the real move. The key for us as traders and investors is to read what the market is telling us and what does happen as current prices reach actual support and resistance levels based on price.

The only thing that matters in reading price movement is the actual price. When prices congregate or reverse, this forms support and resistance levels. These levels are some of the most important things we will look at in technical analysis. That is because these areas are actual prices where traders made entries and exits and they will be affected in one way or another when prices return to those areas.

By the end of this book, my hope is to convince you that analysis tools like those mentioned above are not needed. If you move away from using them in the way that most do—which is to think that they are needed to locate support and resistance—understanding price movement will be a lot clearer and less mysterious to you. Even at this point you may be asking yourself, why would anyone use such tools to find or see support and resistance when they only have to look at the chart to see it? In general, people believe that the markets are complicated, so the analysis needs to be complicated through the use of esoteric or proprietary analysis techniques. You'll see how exchanging complexity for common sense will create "light bulb moments" in your trading.

I interchange the words "support and resistance" with the words "demand and supply" at times. Demand and supply provide a more meaningful and accurate explanation of what we are looking at on a chart, as supply and demand are what form resistance and support levels. Support is a reference point where demand will increase (buyers step up) and a downward move may reverse as demand overcomes supply. Resistance is a reference point where supply will increase (sellers step up) and a move higher may reverse as supply overcomes demand. We know without any doubt that buyers and sellers will show up at prior areas of price support and resistance, at least for the moment. The unknown is how many, but we'll get to that. These areas represent places where real money changed hands and are not subjective. As I have said before and will many more times in this book, only truth in technical analysis is based on price.

Actual support and resistance levels are found only in the price. Prior lows are real support levels, and prior highs can also become real support levels once traded above. Prior highs are real resistance levels, and prior lows can also become real resistance levels once traded below. That may sound confusing, and we will talk about that in a moment. It is actually the difference between major (MS) and minor support (mS) (see Figure 3.3). Actual support and resistance can also be a series of price bars that form a base in prices. A gap that fills is a real level as well. I'm talking about the structure or patterns that price bars take, which form the reference points called support and resistance.

All the other tools that are used, whether they are trend lines, price envelopes, Fibonacci levels, or moving averages are subjective in nature and often provide you with misleading information about an area being support or resistance. Their use suggests that there is some mystery to the market's movement that requires their use. This type of thinking is what keeps so many in search of that elusive Holy Grail or ultimate indicator. This is nothing more than a need for ultimate certainty that will never be had in the markets. Accept that now, or move on to another endeavor, my friends. The markets are not for those that need ultimate certainty. We must have rules that guide us to the odds of what may happen, not to what will happen. Let's continue to build on those rules.

RECOGNIZING REFERENCE POINTS

To build a systematic step-by-step process of viewing support and resistance, our first reference point is the prior bar of whatever time period we are examining. The prior bar's low is the first reference point of demand and the high is our first reference point

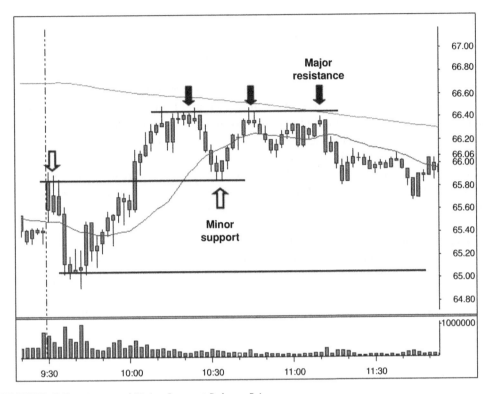

FIGURE 3.3 Minor and Major Support Rely on Price
Chart courtesy of Mastertrader.com.

of supply. Let's take a little closer look at that concept. Look at the two sets of bars in Figure 3.4.

The prior bar's low and high will always offer some support and resistance, even as a self-fulfilling prophecy; how much may depend on the actual pattern. Notice in Figure 3.4 that in between either pair of bars nothing happens. Let's assume these are

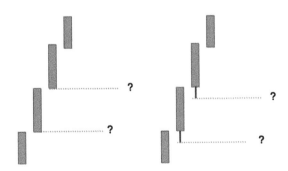

FIGURE 3.4 How Much Support Is in a Candle?
Chart courtesy of Mastertrader.com.

intraday bars, let's say five-minute bars. The one bar closes, the clock strikes twelve, and the next tick forms a new bar. Are there any real buyers or sellers in this area? No. If this were a four-minute bar this area would not exist. It exists only because we decided arbitrarily to start a new bar.

Now, as a side note, this is one of the rare times that a daily chart may be different. There is more support and resistance in the top and bottom of a daily candle, only because the market is closed in between the formation of the candles. This is not true on any lower time frame. This closure causes gaps and void areas that make for some support and resistance at daily highs and lows.

However, what about those intraday candles? Is support and resistance at the prior bar's high or low always just a self-fulfilling prophecy? No. Look at the pair of candles to the right in Figure 3.4. See the difference? Those bottom tails on the right-hand set of bars make the difference. The bars were not at the low when the clock ticked twelve. Prices fell, and then rallied, leaving a bottoming tail. The closing price of the prior bar is not very relevant, but the bottom tail bar is. It does not care when the new bar started. That bottoming tail shows that a battle was fought and there was a victor. When that area is visited again, there is a much greater chance of finding support at the low of the prior bar. Note also that the reversal that caused the tail will show up on all smaller time frames as a reversal of some kind.

Our second reference points are going to be pivots. We use the term "pivot" to describe the inflection point formed when a series of bars form a V or an inverted V. Figure 3.5 shows examples of this.

For now, let's not worry too much about how strong a pivot is. Let's just say that when a bar is the low point in the series, as soon as there are two bars with higher lows to the left, and two bars with a higher low to the right, and the bar on the right has closed, we have a low pivot. The reverse is true for a high pivot. We need two bars with lower highs on the left, and two bars that have closed with lower highs on the right. As you might guess, the more bars on each side with descending or ascending bars, the stronger

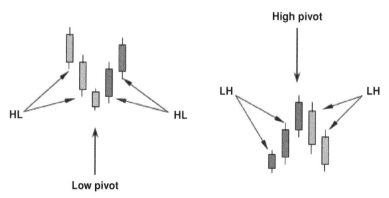

FIGURE 3.5 Basic High and Low Pivots
Chart courtesy of Mastertrader.com.

the pivot becomes. Also, the steeper or more pronounced the V is, the stronger the pivot. Also, just so you are aware, a weaker form of a pivot can form with only one bar on the right, if that one bar has a higher low and a higher high. The same is true in reverse for a weaker form of a high pivot.

Understanding pivots becomes a very important part of technical analysis and the Pristine Method. Pivots are what tell us when a trend exists, what kind of trend, and how strong it is. They tell us when trends are weakening, broken, or have changed. They also can be used to manage positions to set, raise, or lower stops. They can be used to set targets.

Unlike all the subjective things, pivots contain the battles between actual buyers and sellers. They are the pure example of price in action, the ultimate truth. No one is lying about prices that reversed in an area. It is what happened. Prices came from the exchange, are displayed on your chart in the time frame chosen, and cannot be manipulated. No one is lying or guessing if the bulls lost control, it is in the chart. This is just like watching a war zone and seeing the front move up or back: battles are fought, there are victors, and there are losers.

Note that there is a relationship between different time frames. A pivot on a smaller time frame will show up as a tail on a larger time frame. There is an example of this in Figure 3.6.

Our third reference point of supply and demand is a cluster of bars. In an uptrend, most bars will have higher prices than the prior bar. When the opens, closes, highs, and lows start to go sideways, or jump up and down, it will form a cluster, or consolidation, of bars. Regardless of what happens next, this cluster will form a reference point of supply and demand in the future.

Sometimes that cluster of bars may reverse prices and show up as a pivot on a larger time frame. You can see this example in Figure 3.7. If prices cluster but then continue in the same direction as before the cluster, this point will become a form of minor support or resistance when tested again. You can see this in Figure 3.8. If prices begin to move up after a cluster pattern that would be our point of reference for demand rather than a

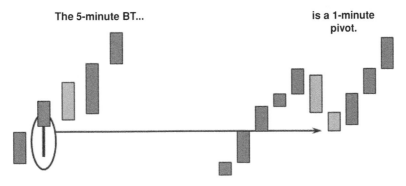

FIGURE 3.6 A Tail May Contain a Pivot in the Smaller Time Frame
Chart courtesy of Mastertrader.com.

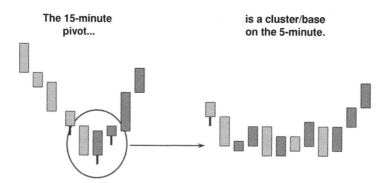

FIGURE 3.7 A Pivot May Contain a Cluster in the Smaller Time Frame
Chart courtesy of Mastertrader.com.

pivot low. These cluster patterns often form in the midst of strongly trending markets. This can also be used as a form of trend analysis. When clusters form in an uptrend, and the prices continue above the cluster, it shows the trend is still strong.

THE TWO FORMS OF SUPPORT AND RESISTANCE: MAJOR AND MINOR

Let's look at some examples of what actual price support and resistance looks like. I view support and resistance in two forms: major and minor. The difference between them is that a violation of minor support (mS) does not change a trend. A violation of major support (MS), on the other hand, will change the trend. To remove any subjectivity to this we have to clearly define this concept. In technical analysis, there will always be some areas that are black and white, but some areas will be grey. Support and resistance is something that we can make black and white.

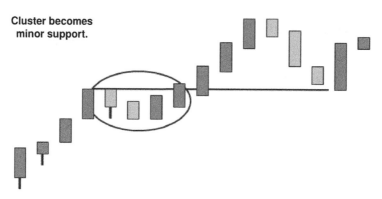

FIGURE 3.8 The Cluster Later Becomes Minor Support
Chart courtesy of Mastertrader.com.

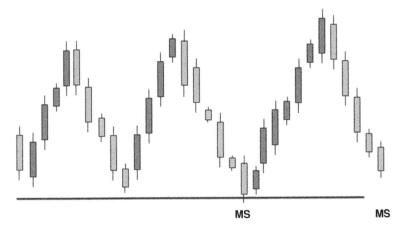

FIGURE 3.9 Revisiting Two or More Prior Lows Is the Most Common Form of Major Support Chart courtesy of Mastertrader.com.

Everything we are discussing applies equally in both uptrends and downtrends. For simplicity, I am going to talk about this concept in uptrends for now. In an uptrend, we generally describe major support as a prior reference point that has the memory effect of holding the current price pattern by reversing a countermove. All major support has one thing in common: if it is violated the uptrend is over, by definition.

The most common form of major support is a series of prior lows that have held the same area on prior tests. You may see this form as a consolidation or base. It may be a tight, consistent base, or a loose wild one that fell to the same level a couple of times prior and held. Figure 3.9 shows this example. We generally want to see the price hold twice before, and then this becomes a major support area. Otherwise, any bounce in a downtrend would be considered major support and it is not.

Next, we will often see price make a very significant rally from an area. If the rally was so extraordinary that it stands out on the chart, this area will have memory affect and can be treated as major support. This rally can occur in a downtrend and, if so, it must be significant enough to break the downtrend in a meaningful way. See Figure 3.10 for an example.

Any time a downtrend becomes climactic, a significant bounce from that low could also be considered an area to treat as a major support, even if the bounce does not break the downtrend. This is a very similar concept to the last one. You can see that example in Figure 3.11.

What we are doing is identifying patterns that form possible areas of major support. This is significant, because what we are saying is that these patterns tell us that buyers stepped up aggressively from these areas. Demand overcame supply and buyers will likely have enough demand there again. When prices get there a bounce will happen. We want enough of a bounce to play the area as a trade if we get an entry that makes sense.

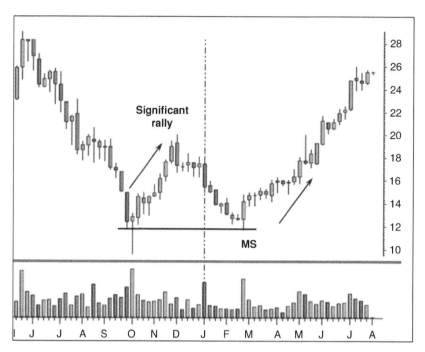

FIGURE 3.10 The Origination of a Prior Significant Rally Can Be a Form of Major Support
Chart courtesy of Mastertrader.com.

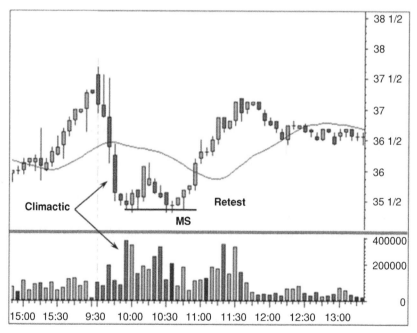

FIGURE 3.11 Climactic Reversals Can Also Be Major Support on the Retest
Chart courtesy of Mastertrader.com.

FIGURE 3.12 The Prior Pivot in an Uptrend Is Also a Form of Major Support
Chart courtesy of Mastertrader.com.

Finally, and maybe most common, major support can be defined as the pivot that preceded a higher high in an uptrend. We label this as major support because, if violated, the trend is no longer up. See Figure 3.12.

However, this kind of major support is a little different. It is major support because it is the area of last resort. If it fails, the trend is no longer up. However, when the pattern has been in a strong uptrend, and prices move to major support levels, it is negative for the underlying trend since the strongest of trends do not retrace to these levels. Remember, an uptrend requires higher pivot highs and higher pivot lows. When we return all the way to the prior low, it may be major support, but the quality of the trend is now in question. With the strength of that trend now in question we need to watch very carefully to learn what the stock or market has to tell us about future price direction.

Remember, we have been discussing major support in an uptrend for simplicity, but everything we have discussed holds true for major resistance (MR) in a downtrend (see Figure 3.13). Major resistance in this last example is the prior pivot high that preceded the last lower pivot low. Again, it is called major because if it has been violated the trend is no longer down.

The concept of major support (and resistance) is rather easy. In the case of major support, the support area is key because it has a memory affect. Buyers were rewarded, so they anticipate being rewarded again for buying at the same place. Notice though, that

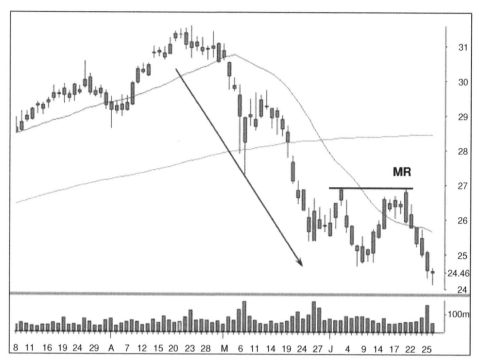

FIGURE 3.13 The Prior Pivot in a Downtrend Is a Form of Major Resistance
Chart courtesy of Mastertrader.com.

only in the case of multiple prior areas of support can we say that major support is a reliable event to continue a trend. In that case, the trend would be a sideways trend. Major support in an uptrend is playable, but by definition, the uptrend has been challenged by prices falling to major support. Major support that is a retest of a dramatic rally or a climactic area is perhaps starting a new uptrend, but the price was falling to set up the first low. In other words, the way prices rallied or fell suggests that the prior downtrend may be over.

On the other hand, minor support is exactly the support that is adhered to in strong trends. Minor support is defined as the support that is formed when an area that was resistance is broken above, and then prices pull back to the area that was resistance. An example of minor support is shown in Figure 3.14.

The area of resistance that is broken can be a difficult or larger resistance area, or it is most commonly the prior high in an uptrend. This area of resistance is known as the prior pivot resistance, and is expected to be overcome. Why? Because uptrends are expected to make higher pivot highs. Once overcome, the pullback that sits on the old high is known as minor support. See Figure 3.15 for an example of how minor support reacts in a typical uptrend.

Remember, the same would apply for minor resistance (mR). Once a prior low is broken in a downtrend, the rally back to that prior low will find minor resistance, which will

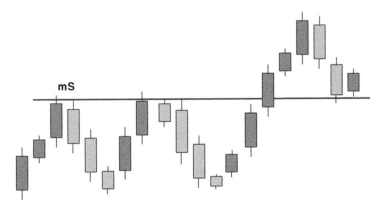

FIGURE 3.14 Minor Support
Chart courtesy of Mastertrader.com.

help to continue the downtrend. Just to give fair time to the downtrend/bearish picture, Figure 3.16 is an example of minor resistance in a downtrend.

Now for something that may seem confusing. The greater the resistance that was broken, once broken, the greater the support will be as minor support. For example, as we will learn in a few minutes, certain tops form very strong resistance areas. They are

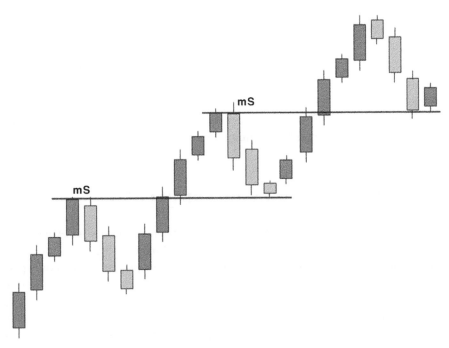

FIGURE 3.15 Uptrends Rely On Minor Support
Chart courtesy of Mastertrader.com.

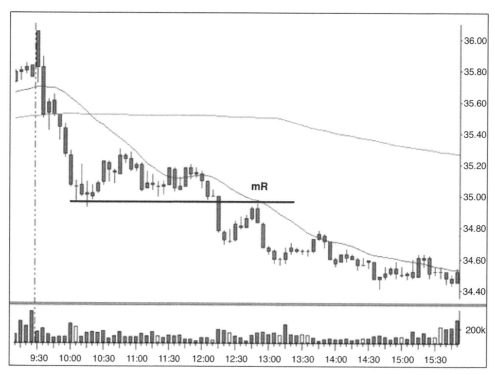

FIGURE 3.16 Minor Resistance in a Downtrend
Chart courtesy of Mastertrader.com.

expected to hold prices below the base and usually do. However, if a price breaks that resistance area, the stock or market is telling us something. The pullback that comes back to the area of original resistance will find a very strong area of support. This area is what we call minor support. Figure 3.17 is an example of price that was below a strong resistance area, broke above, and found minor support to continue the new rally.

HOW SUPPORT AND RESISTANCE AREAS FORM

Once support is broken, it becomes resistance, and when resistance is broken, it becomes support that may act to keep prices from falling further. This is the idea behind minor support and resistance and is a widely followed concept. Like many concepts related to technical analysis that are widely followed, this concept can and often does become self-fulfilling, which is why we use it. But it can also be misleading if not understood. To stay objective and focused on what is most relevant as support and resistance we want to use reference points that are directly to the left of current prices, not what is beyond it. As you can see, this concept of minor support is one that focuses on prices that are not directly to the left.

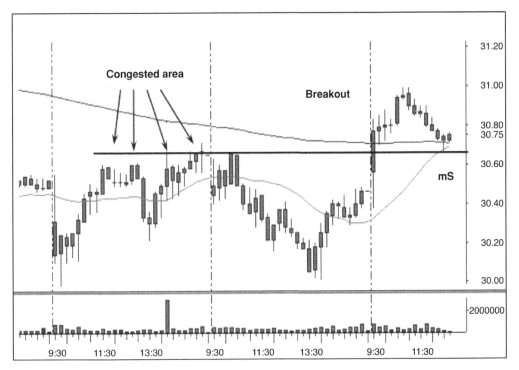

FIGURE 3.17 The Bigger the Resistance, Once Broke, the Better the Support
Chart courtesy of Mastertrader.com.

To understand the concept of how resistance becomes support, we simply have to follow the actions of traders at the prior reference points. As prices are coming to the resistance area (prior high) traders begin to sell into that area. At times, prices can be seen stalling as overlapping bars or narrow candle bodies at the prior high as supply increases before demand overcomes it and pushes it higher. This clearly displays a reference place that buyers will use to enter. Other times, when demand is very strong, prices will appear to push through the prior high without stalling, or as if the prior high was not there. I say appear because the majority of the time there is a stall, but it can only be seen by taking an x-ray into a lower time frame.

The concept of using minor support as a reference across prices that are beyond what is directly to the left provides us where buyers are likely to be. What I've explained gives you a black-and-white understanding of why this subjective concept does work.

I'm often asked; how far to the left is it necessary to look? You look to the left until you see some form of congestion or a prior turning point. Anything beyond that is too far in the past and will have been used as a reference point already. An example of this is seen in Figure 3.18.

We need to understand why prices move between demand and supply levels. This is the basic foundation of technical analysis and price movement. As prices come back to a prior level where demand came into the market, traders will be bidding at that prior

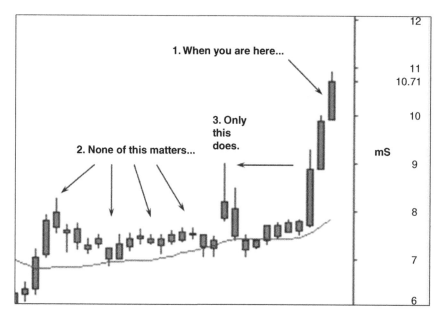

FIGURE 3.18 Only the Price Bars Immediately to the Left Matter
Chart courtesy of Mastertrader.com.

support level that created this price point. Bidding is a passive way to buy. As prices decline to a prior reference point of support traders will bid in anticipation of a turning point. If those bids (demand) overcome the supply from active sellers that are been selling at the bid and have been pushing prices lower, a reversal will form. Once the turn occurs, traders that are waiting for the turn or confirmation of the support level in the form of a reversal bar will become active buyers (meaning that they will buy at the offered price). In addition, those that were hoping to get filled as bidders now have to decide when to become active buyers by buying at the offer or by raising their bids. This action is what drives prices higher to the next reference point of resistance. As prices approach prior resistance levels where supply took over in the past, traders will be offering to sell (passive sellers) at that price level. If their offers overcome the demand that is pushing prices higher, prices will stall and turn. If demand is stronger than supply, a new higher level will be made. This is the ebb and flow between buyer and sellers that is occurring in different time frames on a constant basis.

We need to look for patterns that tell us if prices are reversing or are continuing in the direction that they had been moving. Prices are either going to move between prior reference points that formed support and resistance levels or there will be a change in the supply and demand relationship as they near the target area. My goal is to teach you to assess and use this information about price direction as the patterns emerge. When there are price voids prices are likely to move rapidly in the direction of the trend. A price void simply means there are little or no reference points of support or resistance to impeded price movements. Remember, technical analysis is largely a self-fulfilling prophecy where traders and investors are all looking at the same reference points to buy and sell. When they have nothing to use as a reference point, the odds are high that prices will move rapidly to the next reference point or trend to that point. When there are multiple reference points in the market place close together, price action is far more likely to be choppy, moving between the price points where supply and demand enters the market.

When prices move sideways within a void, it is going to create new areas of support and resistance. When a breakout or breakdown occurs from these new supply and demand points we have a trade with good odds if the next reference point is far enough away.

As you recall, our first reference of supply and demand can be the highs and lows of bars, though some of these will be very minimal areas. The next references for supply and demand are pivots, which can create very substantial areas of support and resistance depending on the strength of the pivot. We then talked about how these points all come together in a way that either forms minor or major support and resistance areas. Let's look deeper at some of the types of patterns that form minor and major support and resistance.

A more significant type of resistance comes from what we call a rounding pattern. In an uptrend, for example, there will be one to several bars that carry into a new high then move back down and sideways. Eventually prices fall below the starting point of the pattern. Once it breaks below the levels where the rounding top began to form and there is a price void below, it is likely prices will fall down to the prior reference points. An example of this is seen in Figure 3.19.

In a sense, a rounding top is the next form beyond a V top. In other words, when a rally runs into a prior bar's high, there is some resistance. When we have a clean pivot, like a clean inverted V, there is more resistance. However, when that prior high is a rounded top, there is even more resistance.

To understand why a rounding top is more bearish than a pivot high we have to understand the psychology or thought process that created it. As prices are moving up, buyers are confident and in control. Once prices reach a level, even if there is no resistance to the left, buyers become less aggressive and would rather wait for a pullback to enter. However, the strongest of uptrends will not pullback. They will move sideways for a few bars, which create a point where prices move higher from again. The initial sideways movement signals that while buyers are less aggressive, sellers are not aggressive either. As time passes, it becomes obvious that prices are not pulling back, and a decision to enter at current prices or on a breakout has to be made by those interested. Once prices do breakout, it happens for one reason. Buyers become aggressive again and overcome the supply that was holding prices within a base. But this time, prices come back into the base, and those that bought during the basing process are in pain and sell their positions. The pullback causes some buying, but not enough to get back to the top of the base. This process is repeated, with prices slowly moving away from the high that was created.

The reason why this is a more significant area of resistance when compared to a regular V pivot is that when prices form a regular pivot high and pullback, it signals

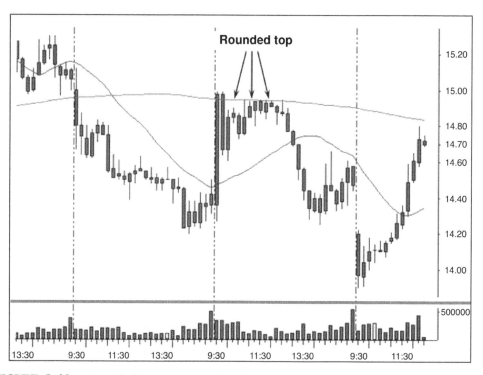

FIGURE 3.19 A Rounded Top Is an Example of a Strong Resistance Area
Chart courtesy of Mastertrader.com.

that sellers were aggressive and buyers had little interest on that pullback. This leaves a relatively small area of overhead supply where long traders are caught. If prices are in an uptrend, buyers should enter aggressively on a pullback and absorb what supply there is. If this is the case, a pivot low will form quickly and signal what is happening. Buyers should easily be able to push prices above the V high, and a strong uptrend will form with a series of higher pivot lows and higher pivot highs. In a rounded top, there are several instances of buyers trying to go long, all unsuccessfully. Many of those will be holding long positions hoping prices will go higher. As they go lower, they will experience enough pain (losses) that they will welcome the opportunity to sell close to their poor entry. This generates a constant flow of selling that new buyers have to overcome.

This pattern may take the form of a square top as well. The concept is similar, but there will be a breakout attempt late in the pattern that forms a corner on the top right. This can bring on extra selling created by the shock of the failed breakout, as buyers think the breakout is real this time, but it also fails. You can see this pattern in Figure 3.20.

Sometimes prices are moving up, and they just stall, going sideways. This can form a series of bars that have similar opens and closes. We call this a cluster. As you can see in Figure 3.21, there is a cluster of opens and closes that indicates a pause in the

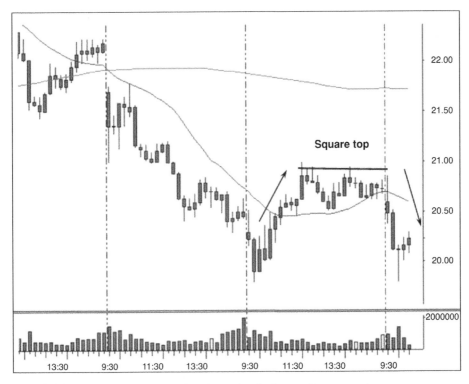

FIGURE 3.20 A Square Top Is Another Example of a Strong Resistance Area
Chart courtesy of Mastertrader.com.

uptrend. This cluster is a short-term source of supply. When this area is overcome and prices move past the clustering area, demand is back in control.

Clusters are different from rounded or square tops because they do not have repeated failures of breakouts. Usually, one bar will put in a top tail, and then a couple bars will stay under that top tail. If it is a new breakout, the move is confirmed as prices move above the cluster and hold.

Let's look at how to spot the supply and demand areas in the market and just how strong each point may be. When we look at Figure 3.22 we can see that prices have moved down rapidly creating a price void. Once the reversal is in place, there is nothing to stop prices from moving higher until profit taking sets in. Then demand slows and supply comes into the market place forming a V-Top. This tells us that traders are taking their gains and exiting the position.

Once price pulls back to the area of the top of the wide range bar where prices consolidated a bit, buyers step in and push prices higher. This causes a V-Bottom to form and prices rise back into some resistance of the prior V-Top. At this point, prices do not retreat but rather consolidate sideways for several bars. Traders and investors are not dumping their positions, and they are content to hold. Once demand re-enters, the market prices overcome the resistance area and move higher.

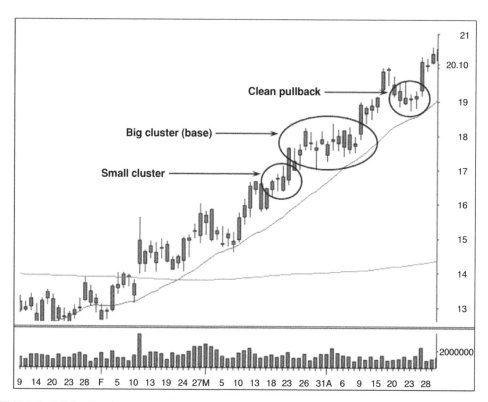

FIGURE 3.21 Clusters Can Be Short-Term Sources of Supply
Chart courtesy of Mastertrader.com.

We can see in Figure 3.23 that near the top of the move a breakout occurred that failed to move higher. Think about what caused this bar to form. More demand (buyers) than supply (sellers). Prices closed at the high of the bar and this indicates that prices should go higher. They do form a new high but then fail in the very next bar as prices gap down and form a bearish candle. This is how rounding tops are formed. Price shows several bars reaching new highs and then failing. The market tries to consolidate but cannot and prices fall lower.

This is a far more significant form of resistance. As prices pull back, they form the first Pristine Buy Setup (PBS). Here is where we put our knowledge of support and resistance to work to make money. If a Pristine Buy Setup forms, it is likely to fail. Many traders will not realize this. They see a pattern fail, and just think it failed. With the knowledge you are learning, you will learn why some setups are more likely to fail. The first PBS after a rounded top is always a lower odds setup. There will be sellers on the first move up, as I explained earlier.

It will be the second PBS that has a good chance of overcoming overhead supply and carrying prices above the more powerful rounding top. The reason for this is the further correction will move price farther away from the rounding top and during that correction more of those that were caught at the high will exit. You see, over time, the

FIGURE 3.22 Once a Difficult Resistance Area Is Overcome a Void Can Make Prices Rise Rapidly
Chart courtesy of Mastertrader.com.

prior reference point of support or resistance become less significant as such. The supply is being absorbed with every attempt to attack it.

We have to add some common sense to the technical analysis. For example, in the bear market that occurred after the year 2000, prices fell for several years and to date current prices are below some of those levels in the NASDAQ market. Some day prices will retrace back to those levels. Are we to think that what occurred that many years ago is really a relevant reference point of resistance? I say no. It will only affect those who have bought and held since then, so that affect will be minor. The more time that passes, the less likely people are still affected. However, those that view and teach technical analysis from a purely academic point of view, rather than a common sense trader's point of view, will view the past with the same importance as the present. The more traders that have positions within the recent past, which is reflected in the patterns, the more relevant that reference point. What is most important is what is currently happening.

The key is to know where to anticipate where buyers and sellers will enter the market place. We see to the far right of Figure 3.23 that prices have formed a low in the form of bottoming tail bars. These bottom tail bars are breakdown bars that did not carry through to the downside. As demand enters the market place, prices rallied.

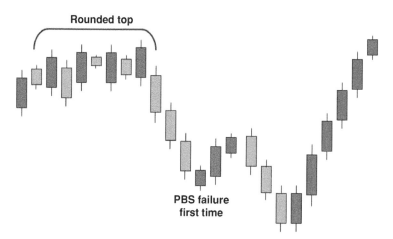

FIGURE 3.23 Rounded Tops May Cause the Next PBS to Fail
Chart courtesy of Mastertrader.com.

When prices pull back into the area of the bottoming tail bars, we can now anticipate buyers coming into the market. If buyers stepped up and took control at that level once we expect that they are going to do it again. This fresh demand, if strong enough, will push prices back toward the prior highs. As prices near those levels, we will see supply starting to come back into the stock. Traders who bought at or near those prior highs have losses. They thought prices would go higher and they were wrong. The stock pulled back and they are anxious to get out if prices rally to near breakeven.

Prices now begin to consolidate, forming a new pattern. Demand is absorbing supply and the market is moving sideways. What I look for, as this pattern forms, is evidence that supply is not strong enough to push prices back to the major support levels. I like to see several bottoming tail bars in the consolidation where prices are unable to push through to the downside. Bottoming tail bars tell me that buyers are stepping up on the dips as supply increases, and stronger demand overwhelms that supply and is reflected in the pattern. Bottom tail bars are minor corrections in themselves and we want to take note of them when they form. They tell us that larger buyers are putting money to work and there is nothing subjective about that.

When the prices move above the consolidation area, demand has overwhelmed supply. We see in the chart that a bottom tail bar has formed. Before that bar closed, it was a strong bearish candle at one point before the tail formed. Buyers emerged however, and there was no follow through to the downside. The narrow range bar that follows, closing at the top of the bar, is our signal that demand is in control and prices are going higher.

In the same fashion, we will look for sellers to emerge in the areas of prior highs. When we begin to see topping tail bars in the congestion pattern we know that demand is insufficient to overcome the supply that is coming into the stock. When the prices move below the congestion area, there is excess supply and we can assume prices are going lower. See Figure 3.24.

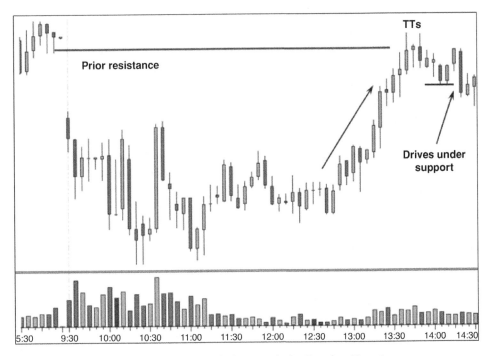

FIGURE 3.24 Prior Highs Stall Prices and Then Break the Trend to Move Lower
Chart courtesy of Mastertrader.com.

When we deal with the issue of supply and demand patterns in the marketplace, there are a few important things to keep in mind. We always want to ask our self how potent the support and resistance actually is in a particular stock or market. Is the support or resistance a one to three bar V pattern or have we formed a more potent rounding top or bottom, consisting of multiple bars in whatever time frame we are considering? How far apart are the support and resistance levels? Is there enough potential profit to make the trade worth considering? In other words, is there a void to trade within? Choppy markets form support and resistance levels that are so close there is no real profit opportunity.

Now that we have gone through some patterns, here's a quick reminder about something I discussed in Chapter 1 that might be clearer now: Notice that everything we have looked at has involved price formation. Actual prices, actual buyers, actual sellers, and how they reacted. A lot of investors and traders like to use trend lines to determine support, resistance, and the trends in prices. As we have discussed these are very subjective analytical tools. If you do use them, always look to the left so you can see what the prices are aligned with.

If enough people use a technical tool like a trend line and believe in it, they will react on those beliefs. For example, a trend line drawn on a daily chart of the S&P 500 would have greater odds of a reaction to it than a stock because many more will be drawing trend lines on a market than a stock. Sometimes that reaction will bring enough buyers to be the catalyst for the real move, if prices are aligned to form a true area of price support.

If they are not, you are merely connecting the dots and projecting a line from them with the thought that this line is going to be support or resistance. It is really a ridiculous idea when you give it some thought. Can drawing the lines from different points change the location of where support and resistance will be? As I said it's a ridiculous concept. When it does not work, those beliefs are shaken and a loss in confidence emerges. We need some consistency in our analysis or understanding of why we are doing something. In this case, buying or selling at a certain point. Drawing lines between points on a chart will not provide that consistency over time. Of course, if you draw enough lines, as many that use them do, your lines will catch a turn eventually. If you want to understand why prices turn when they do, look to the left to see where the price reference points are. It's really that simple.

IN SUMMARY

Indentifying support and resistance levels is one of the most important parts of trading. We do not need subjective tools like trend lines, moving averages, or retracement levels to calculate where these levels are in the markets. We only have to look to the left to see where they are. No proprietary indicators or levels needed. It is simple; price itself will tell us where the reference points are to focus on. The supply or demand forming the current bars or candles at those reference points will tell us who is in control and if that relationship is likely to change.

Now we start to look at other technical tools that, when used with support and resistance, can give us even better odds of determining how well these areas might hold. Next we focus on moving averages.

CHAPTER 4

Moving Averages the Right Way

Visual Aids to Price Action

Before I introduce the concept of moving averages, let's look at where we are at this point. I have already discussed that price is the true king to all technical analysis. We also discussed the fact that various technical indicators that many traders like to use are subjective and are in fact not very useful. In addition, there are really only three things that I like to see on any chart, and only three things that I put on my charts:

- Price: My charts are dominated with a large picture of the price pattern. We discussed that in Chapter 3.
- Volume: I keep volume at the bottom of my charts, which we discuss in Chapter 5.
- Moving Averages: In addition, overlaying the price pattern I have two or sometimes three moving averages on my charts, which we discuss in this chapter.

Technically, moving averages are a technical indicator (no pun intended). Therefore, a moving average is an exception to my "no technical indicator" policy. However, when you see how we use moving averages, you will discover why they are an exception and are only used as a visual aid to price action, not an indicator of it. Simply, I use them as a tool to speed up the analysis that I could do without them though, as you'll see, not for the same reason most traders do.

A VALUABLE TECHNICAL MEASUREMENT

Moving averages (MA) are one of the most widely used and discussed technical measures in existence. Just listen to the financial news channels or open a newspaper any day and there is a discussion of how the market or a particular stock is above or below a moving average (see Figure 4.1).

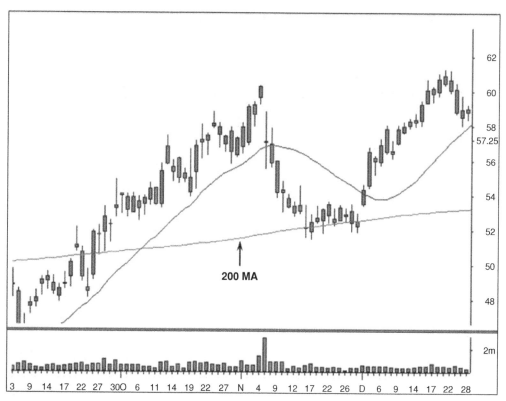

FIGURE 4.1 Daily Chart Sitting on the 200 MA
Chart courtesy of Mastertrader.com.

The truth is that moving averages can be one of the most valuable technical measurements when used correctly. However, the traditional methods of evaluating moving averages are far too subjective. More importantly, the purpose for which most traders use moving averages is flawed. Most traders will use a moving average as support or resistance. As we discussed in Chapter 3, this type of support and resistance is very subjective. This is why traders get frustrated with only the basic and often flawed understanding of technical analysis.

Using Moving Averages Properly

Whenever moving averages are talked about, one of the first things out of a novice trader's mouth will usually be "moving average crossover." Once again, this is not only a subjective indicator of price direction, but it is almost always a useless one. Waiting for moving average crossovers is a flawed concept. Depending upon which moving averages you use, they may give very early and false signals, or the signal may be so late that it is good only for confirmation, as seen in Figure 4.2. Traders then attempt to adjust the two

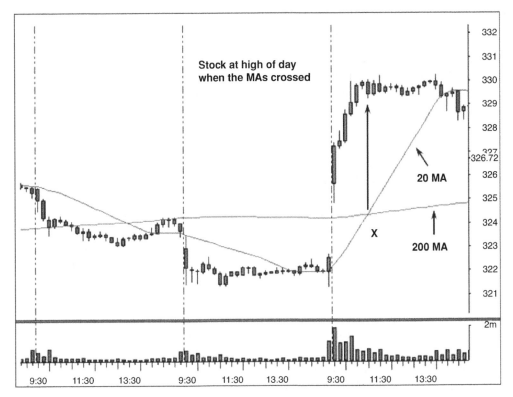

FIGURE 4.2 Moving Average Crossovers Often Come Very Late in the Pattern
Chart courtesy of Mastertrader.com.

moving averages to match the current price pattern. This is one of the biggest downfalls in technical analysis. Trying to adjust the parameters of any technical indicator based on the past, even an MA, to fulfill your view on what is happening only works for the current price pattern. The next price pattern, whether it is a stock or futures contract, will have to be adjusted again, thereby rendering your scheme of that technical indicator adjustment virtually worthless. This concept of reverse engineering works for stable things like discovering how computer software works, but not for the dynamic flow of price movement.

Here is a rule that you can take to the bank. Moving averages should never be used as a buy signal. It is not a buy signal just because the price touches a moving average or crosses it. Nor is it one because the moving averages cross. Moving averages never give accurate entry signals all by themselves. So why do moving averages have the distinction of being one of only two items that belong on our price charts besides price itself? The answer is because moving averages are a superior guide to assisting in trend analysis. The approach to using this tool as we do is one that gives you a clear direction as to what the market is *likely* to do in a given time frame. Let's review.

Which Moving Average Should We Use?

Let's begin our discussion with which moving averages are appropriate. The first question that comes to mind when we begin our research of moving averages is, which time frame should we be looking at, and which MA should we use? Traders may have a variety of moving averages on their page and some of those may include the 8, 10, 20, 40, 50, 100, and 200. The answer may shock you, but perhaps it will get the point across. The answer is that it does not matter.

If you ever try to use moving averages for actual support for entries, you probably have already discovered that there is no magic number or magic spot that always works. Since we are using moving averages only as a guide to determine trend analysis, the exact moving average is not relevant. We are looking for certain consistent relationships between the actual price and the MA, and sometimes between two different moving averages. If you can see and get to feel (feel comes after long study of price movement) the flow of a particular trend by looking at the price compared to the 7-period MA, as compared to the 31-period MA, that is just fine. With that being said, since we do have to pick one or two moving averages to use, I like to pick the ones that most traders will be using, rather than what most are not. Why? Because when an MA does work as an actual support level, it is due to a subjective method based on a self-fulfilling prophecy. If that prophecy is going have an effect, I want to see what other traders are looking at. In a sense, we, the traders looking at the same MA, will work together as a group to fulfill our belief that the MA will be the point where prices will reverse.

To reinforce my point that moving averages are not actually support or resistance and subjective as such, just think of all the choices we have. The most commonly used moving averages will be the most reliable as a reference point, so don't fall into the trap of thinking it's better to use what other traders aren't looking at. When it comes to technical analysis tools, you do want to use what the majority are looking at.

Based on this, the number one superior moving average to have at every chart, and that I do have on every chart that I look at, is the 20-period MA. It is the perfect MA to analyze most trends. It reacts properly and quickly. Most long-lasting trends, by mathematical computation, usually end up retracing to an area very close to the average of the last 20 periods. This means that statistically, when in a nice trend, prices that retrace to the 20-period MA have a statistically enhanced chance of moving from that area. If enough traders are looking to this as a self-fulfilling prophecy as well, and most are, it may help make the move. Beautiful trends, such as the one in Figure 4.3, will have prices responding to the 20-period MA consistently.

As I will demonstrate shortly, it is also helpful to have another trending moving average running close to the first one. For this I like to use the 40-period moving average. Over the years, many traders have used a 50-period moving average and, as I just indicated, that is perfectly fine. I will use the 40, but there is nothing wrong with the 50 if you like it. The 40-period moving average has very little or no self-fulfilling prophecy effect. However, it works well to keep the 20-period moving average in check—so to speak—because it will track the 20 closely and provide us with a visual aid to spot

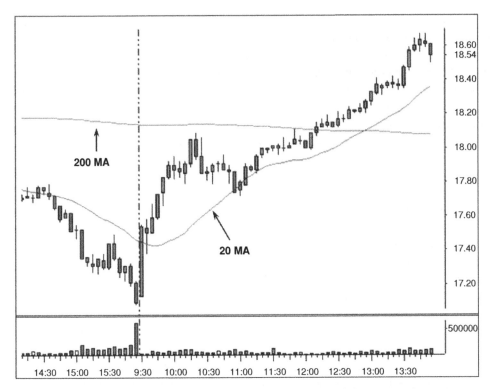

FIGURE 4.3 Nice Uptrends Have Prices Responding in the Area of the 20-Period MA
Chart courtesy of Mastertrader.com.

extended patterns quickly. We will look at how this works next. In addition, the 40-period moving average is equal to the 8-period moving average in the weekly time frame. So, when the 20-period moving average is trending higher and the 40-period moving average is parallel to the 20 and trending higher, it tells us that the daily and weekly time frames are aligned. This picture will place the odds in our favor for swing trades.

The third moving average that belongs on my daily charts is the 200-period moving average. This moving average is based almost entirely on a self-fulfilling prophecy, but it is one that is recognized throughout the trading community. You probably do not have to listen to CNBC long before you hear the 200-period moving average being cited. The 200-period moving average is not a trend setting moving average like the 20- and 40-period MAs. Prices tend to live either above or below the 200-period moving average. In addition, as prices start to accelerate away from the 20-period moving average, there becomes a greater likelihood of return to the means. Again, we will look at some examples of this in more detail in just a minute.

What about the other moving averages? The 100 or any other moving average that you may want to look at falls into the same category as any other technical indicator we have discussed up to this point. The three moving averages I mentioned, or any similar one you'd like to use, will do the job that needs to be done. Adding extra moving averages is simply adding more "spaghetti" to your charts. There is one exception that would allow you to substitute one moving average in exchange for another if you prefer. The 20- and 40-period moving averages work great in tandem on larger time frames. However, on fast-moving issues, and on smaller time frames, such as anything below a 15-minute chart, you may want to substitute the 8- or 10-period MA for the 40. This allows the moving averages to more accurately follow the price for fast-moving issues. This is optional, and if you choose to do this, it should replace the 40-period MA so that you are never looking at more than three moving averages at any one time. Remember the smaller moving averages such as the 20 and 40 will be trendsetting moving averages. The 200 will always be a line in the sand.

Another question always asked and easily answered is what type of moving average to use. I use simple moving averages. Some people prefer to use exponential or weighted moving averages. These are not more accurate at defining a trend or support and resistance. Those that believe they are fall into the indicator trap of believing that one will better define price direction than another. This belief typically results in the never-ending search for the Holy Grail that will insure all profitable trades. Forget it. There is no right or wrong length and do not fall prey to those trying to sell you an optimized moving average. You will always be optimizing again for the next stock or change in the market environment.

Again, since we only use moving averages to help speed the analysis of a trend, the exact length of the moving average used, or the type, doesn't matter. You just need to get used to the look and feel of the relationship. Since all the other types of moving averages tend to add another layer of analysis, keep the simple moving average—it's a clean representation of price.

The 20-Period Moving Average

Let's talk about the 20-period moving average. I use a 20-period MA in every time frame. That means daily charts, weekly charts, and all the intraday time frames right down to a one-minute chart. A trade in the direction of the 20-period MA has the highest degree of success. If the 20-period MA is moving up, the stock is likely to go higher when the proper trade set up occurs. Likewise, if the 20-period MA is down, then I want to look for a sell setup. When prices are above the 20-period MA, I want to buy dips. If the price is below the 20-period MA I want to be looking for opportunities to sell rallies.

If you are taking notes, there is one trading axiom that you should right now highlight with your yellow marker. And that is: You should always trade in the direction of the 20-period moving average. I have found that doing this, and this one thing alone, can eliminate up to 80 percent of the average trader's losing trades. Whether it is an uneducated trader, or an educated trader who thinks he knows better, it is still the case that 80 percent of losing trades come from fighting the trend. While much more analysis can go into what makes a trend, for right now it would benefit all traders to simply

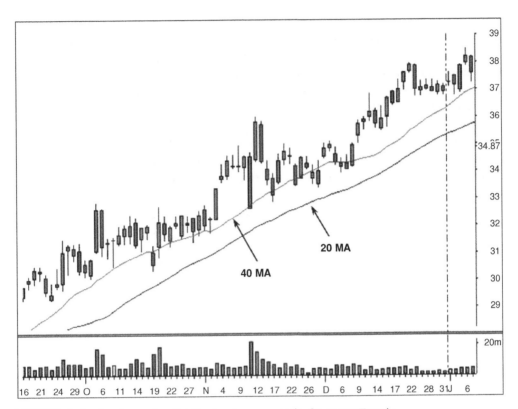

FIGURE 4.4 Consistent Parallel Moving Averages Make for Better Trends
Chart courtesy of Mastertrader.com.

acknowledge that when you trade against the direction of the 20-period moving average, you are likely in for a losing trade.

CONVERGENCE CAN HELP

In addition to the direction of moving averages, I watch for convergence between two different averages. This is the reason for keeping the 40-period moving average on the chart right alongside the 20-period moving average. When prices are staying in close proximity to the 20-period MA, and the 20-period MA is paralleling the 40-period MA without accelerating, that is usually the basis for outstanding trend. You can see this example in Figure 4.4. Prices may occasionally accelerate away from the 20-period MA, only to return to the 20-period MA and maintain the pattern.

However, when prices accelerate away from the 20-period MA, and the 20-period MA accelerates away from the 40-period MA, that pullback will likely no longer be buyable. This is one of the great uses of comparing the two moving averages. We look for a "railroad track" type of relationship between the two moving averages. As long as this exists, the trend is likely to remain valid. When the gap between the two moving averages becomes large and continues to increase in size, the pattern is accelerating to a point that will no longer maintain a healthy move after the next pullback. The same logic may be applied to the relationship between the 20-period MA and the 8-period MA on smaller time frames and faster moving issues. This concept is simple, but powerful.

Now let's take a look at the third moving average and how we can use it to help understand trends better. The 200-period moving average will stay much flatter and not follow price as closely as the other moving averages we use. This is just a simple mathematical result of having a longer time period moving average. It will react slowly since it is averaging 200 periods. Once a new closing price has formed in the time frame used, the closing price that occurred 200 periods ago will be dropped and the current one added and averaged in. This means that the change in slope and direction of the 200-period moving average will change slowly. For that reason prices tend to live either above or below the 200-period MA. You can see this in Figure 4.5.

Naturally, as you may have guessed, it is most bullish for prices to be above the 200-period moving average. That is rule number one. If we are playing a stock bullishly above the rising 20-period moving average, we would prefer the price pattern to be

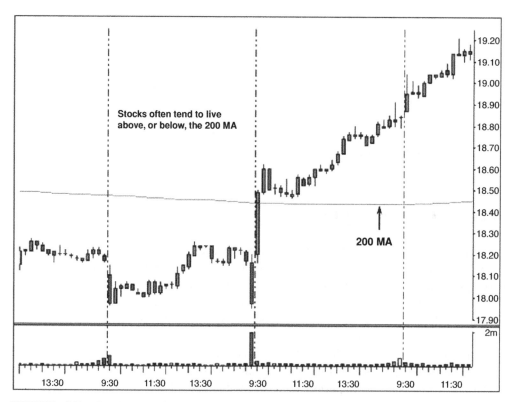

FIGURE 4.5 The 200-Period Moving Average Is More of a Rock
Chart courtesy of Mastertrader.com.

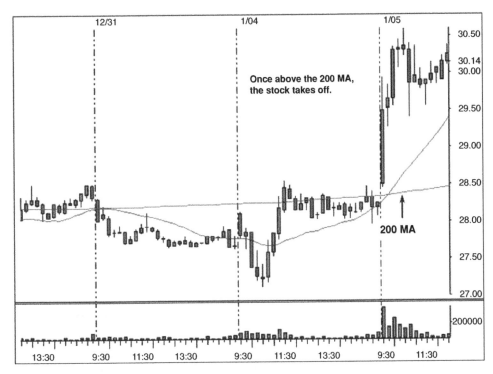

FIGURE 4.6 A New Trend Beginning Above the 200-Period MA
Chart courtesy of Mastertrader.com.

occurring above a flat or slightly rising 200-period moving average. Likewise, if we are bearish on the stock, we want to be shorting the stock while it is below a declining 20-period moving average, while that price pattern is living beneath a flat or slightly declining 200-period moving average. This is the real sweet spot for trending-type trades, as you can see in Figure 4.6.

However, there is more that we can learn from the relationship between price, the small moving averages, and the 200-period moving average. Remember when I was discussing the likelihood of a trend ending because price begins to accelerate away from the moving average, or if the 20-period MA and 40-period MA begin to split apart? There are times that it may be difficult to tell when the trend is truly ending and when prices are simply enjoying an exuberant run or decline. The other piece of information you can use is how extended the entire pattern becomes from the 200-period moving average. In other words, while it is beneficial to begin long trades as prices stay above the 20-period MA and that pattern exists above the 200, at some point an extended pattern way above the 200-period moving average begins to lose its luster on pullbacks. Likewise, at some point, sharp declines in price that accelerate the 20-period moving average away from the 40-period moving average—that happen while the 20-period moving average is way below and accelerating away from the 200-period moving average—may lead to sharp

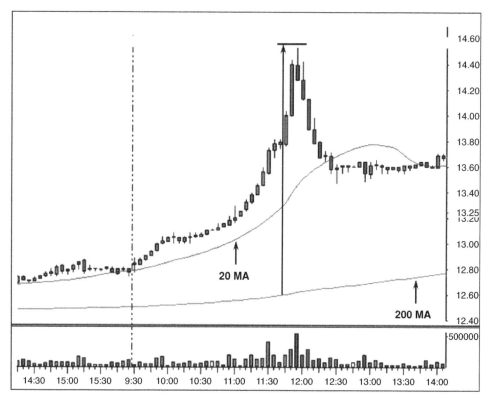

FIGURE 4.7 Prices Are Accelerating Far Away from the 200-Period MA
Chart courtesy of Mastertrader.com.

reversals. These reversals can be either temporary or permanent in nature depending upon the overall larger price pattern. This type of reversal is shown in Figure 4.7.

The faster prices move in one direction without stalling, the further they will get from the moving averages and the further the moving averages will move from each other. This is a simple, objective way of observing price momentum increasing and the odds of a pullback or retracement occurring.

Everything we have discussed so far involves how to use moving averages to find the best trends. Another use for moving averages is to find focal areas in which prices may reverse a short-term countertrend move in favor of the presumption of the primary trend in the direction of the moving average. In other words, another way to look at moving average analysis is when prices decline to an MA that has an upward slope. This is an alert that there may be a rally in the direction of the underlying trend. It is not an action point but a message that I need to be watching for the candles to form a buy setup. The same is true of a stock whose price rallies into a down sloping 20-period MA. This is particularly true when prices drift along the level of the average for several bars. Prices are likely to move back in the direction of the trend when this happens. You may know these as breakdown or breakout plays. An example is shown in Figure 4.8.

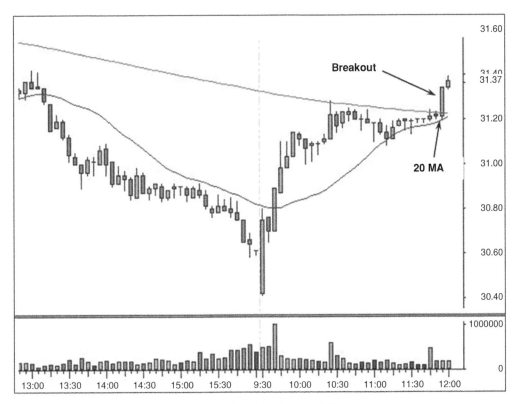

FIGURE 4.8 A Breakout Is Occurring Right at the Rising 20 MA
Chart courtesy of Mastertrader.com.

MOVING AVERAGES AS FOCAL AREAS

Remember the discussion of candle formations in Chapter 2? We talked about bullish COGs and PBSs, as individual bars formed. The priceless concept that I want you to understand right now is that we want those bullish candlestick formations to be happening in the area where price retracements against the bigger trend meet the moving average. In other words, a properly formed PBS that is occurring on a price retracement downward into a rising 20-period moving average is the type of trade that is going to put the odds in your favor. This is illustrated in Figure 4.9.

When prices move toward the MA we want to look for what I call attention points. If we have a stock whose price is consolidating along the MA line and we get a bar that closes on its high, this is a sign that the trend is about to resume and prices are likely to go higher. The reason for this is simple and based on the time frame viewed. For example, if you are using a 5-minute chart and buying (demand) increases, that buying does not stop because you want a new bar to start. It should continue and the new bar should start

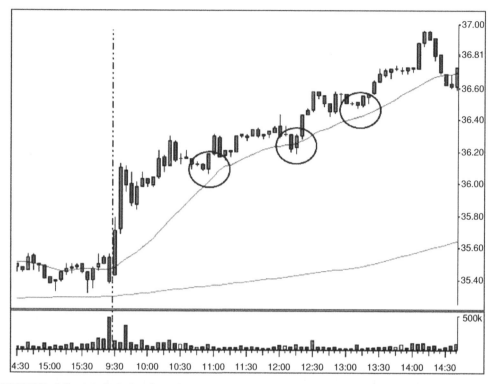

FIGURE 4.9 A Bullish Candlestick Formation Happening in an Uptrend at the Rising 20 MA
Chart courtesy of Mastertrader.com.

where the prior closed. If however the price bar closes at or near the low, we need to be aware there may be a change in the supply and demand relationship.

We know that many other traders use moving average breaks so we need to be watching for important changes. Sometimes there are enough traders selling the break to move prices lower. This can be another self-fulfilling prophecy, but one to be aware of. Confirm the break by looking to the left when this happens and see if price violated a key support point and not just the subjective MA line. When this happens, we know that the supply and demand equation has changed and we need to change our bias for the stock. This is illustrated in Figure 4.10 where you can clearly see the prices break not just the MA line, but also a prior support area.

Used properly, moving averages can give us a lot of information quickly. By examining the relationship between price and simple moving averages, we can determine if a particular stock is overbought or oversold at a given point in time. We can find potential points of support and resistance in the price of a stock. They can also serve as an indication of how strong or weak a particular trend is for a market or stock. Because we know so many traders are watching the moving averages, we know that as prices approach these levels, a reversal may be likely and we can look for tradable candle patterns to form. This is why I say that moving averages are one of the most useful tools we have.

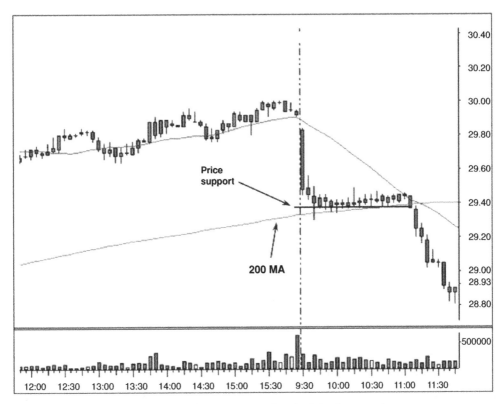

FIGURE 4.10 Prices Break Not Only the MA but Also the Prior Support Area
Chart courtesy of Mastertrader.com.

STAYING OBJECTIVE

Once you begin to understand this relationship between the moving averages, you can begin to eliminate the need and desire to have other technical indicators on your charts. Many of the technical indicators, such as MACD, are simply comparing the relationship of two moving averages and plotting the difference. Nothing can compare that better than to have the actual moving averages in question on your chart and to be watching their behavior. This relationship will give you a much cleaner picture of what being overbought and oversold really means, as opposed to looking at yet another indicator that is supposed to tell you when something is overbought or oversold. Don't clutter your charts with redundant information. Less is more when it comes to technical analysis. The more you have to interpret, the more difficult it becomes to make a decision.

Let me remind you again that we want to avoid subjective analysis. When we say a stock is oversold it sets up a thought process or belief that the stock has to move higher. That simply is not true. If we rely on subjective indicators we fall into a conventional trap that can lead to losses or missed opportunities. A stock or market that is oversold

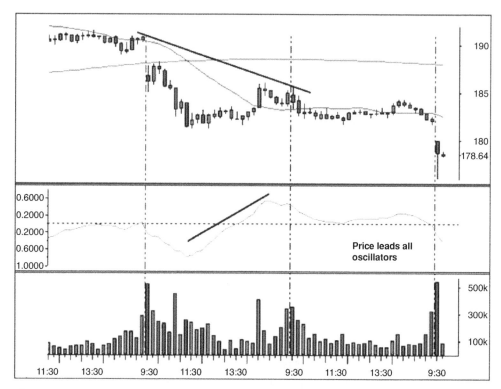

FIGURE 4.11 An MACD Indicator Is Giving Us No Useful Additional Information
Chart courtesy of Mastertrader.com.

can become even more so. It happens in every bear market. If we act on purely subjective information, we are likely to lose money. Prior use of moving averages can tell
us is that there is a higher probability of a reversal and we need to be on the lookout
for reversal patterns. We do not want to buy a stock and have it do nothing, or even
worse, plunge to even deeper oversold levels. By using moving averages and price support and resistance levels we gain an enormous edge over traders who rely on traditional
oscillators. As seen in Figure 4.11, popular technical indicators may look flashy, but give
no additional information and can be misleading. Adding colorful indicators can make
you a "chart artist" and look impressive to your friends, but they aren't going to make
you money.

Moving averages can also tell us something about the momentum of a move in the
market. When we see prices falling far below the 20-period MA we know it is a fairly
strong down move in the stock. However, as the MA catches up with prices and new
moves fall a shorter distance from the MA, we know that momentum is slowing. If you
get a changing of the guard pattern after a new low and the price is closer to the MA
line than previous moves, we know there is what is called a momentum divergence in
the price. A change in the supply and demand relationship is taking place. Buyers have
absorbed the recent supply and are ready to take price higher. You can see an example

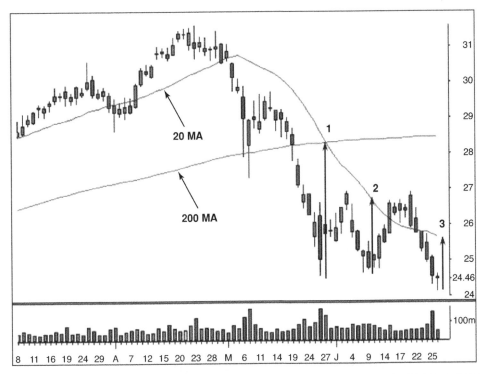

FIGURE 4.12 Momentum Is Slowing When Looking at Prices Compared to the 200-Period MA
Chart courtesy of Mastertrader.com.

of this in Figure 4.12. You can see that as the stock breaks support, it quickly moves away from the 20-period MA line, leaving a wide distance between price and the moving average (arrow 1). As the supply is absorbed, new selling does not push the price as far from the moving averge (arrow 2) and eventually we expect demand to reverse the downtrend on the next move up (arrow 3).

Divergences can be a tricky concept. Many traders use various price oscillators to find divergence and use them as a signal to trade. This is dangerous. Divergences merely tell us that momentum is slowing, not that it has changed. A divergence is defined by price making a new low or a new high and when the oscillator does not make a new low or new high.

What oscillators do in various ways is compare the current prices to some period in time from the past to determine momentum divergences. You can do this with a simple moving average by comparing the distance between the moving average and price on the last move and the current one. If you want to check this, put a 20-period moving average on your chart and a RSI oscillator or any other momentum oscillator set to 20. Check the divergences shown by the oscillator and look at the distance between price and the moving average. This is a lot simpler. As I said earlier, moving averages simply help speed the analysis. We can see these momentum divergences even without the moving

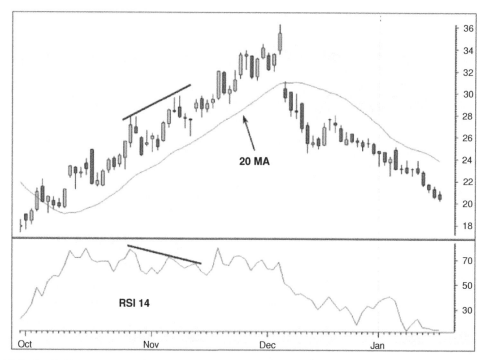

FIGURE 4.13 Price Chart Showing a Meaningless RSI Divergence
Chart courtesy of Mastertrader.com.

averages by looking at the number and/or size of bars in a prior move compared to the recent one.

Look at Figure 4.13 and you see what can happen with a traditional oscillator. As prices move higher initially, the price bars are longer and the oscillator moves higher. As prices continue to move higher, the momentum does slow and the bars are smaller. This causes a divergence in the oscillator. But look at what is happening. Even though momentum has slowed, it has not changed the direction of prices. The price bars are all higher, even if at a slower pace. There is still demand and no price bar retreats below the prior bar. It is only when the 20-period MA catches up to prices later in the up move, and a bearish changing of the guard occurs, that you can really determine that momentum has reversed. Relying on the oscillator would have been a losing trade.

When using moving averages remember to make sure they are in alignment with support and resistance levels. Meaning, there is a prior high, low, or congestion to the left of it. We know that traders pay attention to moving averages as a reference point so they can often be a self-fulfilling prophecy. However, if the averages are not in line with prior price levels, this is far less likely to happen. We want to see the price penetrate not just the MA line but prior periods of support or resistance before trading. If the MA break is not in an area where prices formed significant patterns in prior time periods, it is far less relevant. Always look to the left and see what prices are telling you. Price

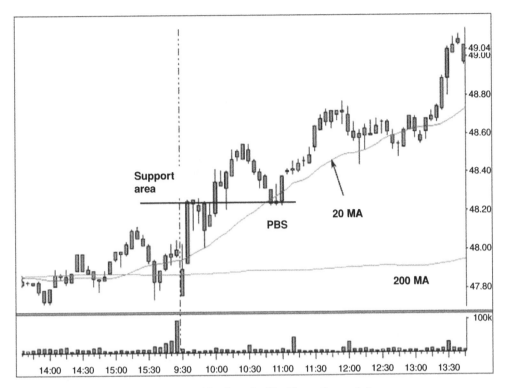

FIGURE 4.14 The Moving Average Matches the Significant Support Area
Chart courtesy of Mastertrader.com.

and patterns are far more important than just the MA line itself. Figure 4.14 is a good example of this.

We can see in Figure 4.15 how this works. The prices have broken above the 20-period MA and are consolidating back toward the line. When we look to the left we see that there is an area of prior resistance that has formed. We can also quickly see that the 20-period MA is far away from the 200-period MA. This tells us that there has likely been a steep decline at some point and there is probably a price void above the initial resistance levels. When we get a changing of the guard at the area of the 20-period MA we know it is significant. Our risk is just below the buy pattern and once the price clears that initial area of resistance it should quickly move higher.

Think about what is happening here. Prices have fallen below the 20-period MA and supply is in control. Bottom fishing traders push prices higher only to see them fall back to new lows. When the price breaks above the 20-period MA initially, subjective traders push prices back into the area of resistance. Buyers who bought at that prior high quickly sell out their positions, eliminating a source of supply. When demand comes back in at the 20-period line, as seen by the changing of the guard, there are no sellers left. Prices can quickly move back toward the 200-period MA as there is demand that is clearly in control and buyers will rapidly move the stock higher.

FIGURE 4.15 The Moving Average Acts as Resistance Only Temporarily When There Is No Price Resistance
Chart courtesy of Mastertrader.com.

A FEW GOOD RULES WHILE USING MOVING AVERAGES

We can use moving averages to set up different rules in different time periods. These will put the odds in your favor. When day trading, we want to consider long trades when prices are above the 20-period MA on a 60-minute bar chart. From an intraday focus we are trading in the direction of the long-term trend. We will then look for buy signals as long as prices are above the 20-period MA on a 5-minute bar chart. For short trades we want to look for prices to be below the 20-period MA on the 60-minute chart, and again look for the signal itself in the 5-minute chart as long as prices are below the 20-period MA. I don't need a buy or sell price pattern on the 60-minute time frames, only prices trending above or below the 20-period MA.

Once you have this relationship, trade strategies or entries may come down to any time frame you choose to play, even the 1-minute chart. An example of a good intraday bullish bias hourly chart is shown in Figure 4.16, where the hourly chart bias is upward and all pullbacks are buyable with proper setups including the smaller time frames.

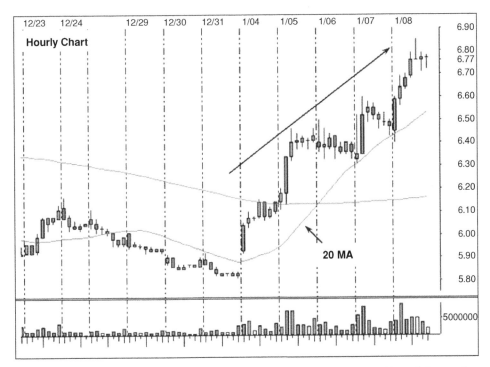

FIGURE 4.16 The Hourly Chart Bias Is Upward and All Pullbacks Are Buyable with Proper Setups
Chart courtesy of Mastertrader.com.

For countertrend trades, if prices are far below the 20-period MA on the 60-minute MA, or what we call a Climactic Buy Setup (CBS), but have moved above the 20-period MA of the 5-minute chart, take buy setups in that time frame. The reverse of that is true when looking for countertrend short trades. If the price is far above the 20-period MA on the 60-minute chart, but has fallen below the 20-period MA on the shorter 5-minute time frame, supply is taking over and we need to be looking for bearish patterns to form. Keeping these two time frames in check will always keep you on the right side of the trade when day trading.

On longer-term charts you can consider a similar relationship between the weekly MA and the daily set up. In other words, when the weekly 20-period moving average is heading up we will find the greatest likelihood of successful daily buy setups when they encounter their rising moving average.

OTHER POINTS TO CONSIDER

There are a few more concepts to discuss regarding moving averages. At this point you may be asking, if they are good for determining uptrends and downtrends, how useful are they in sloppy markets or for sideways trends? The answer here is a very simple one.

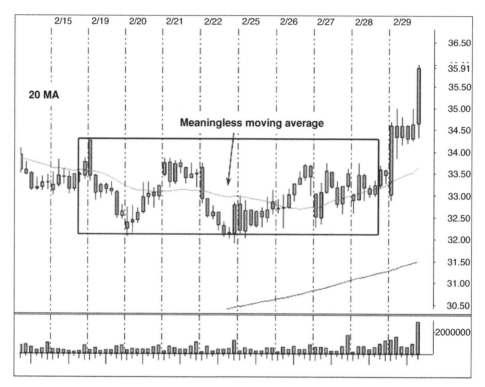

FIGURE 4.17 Moving Averages Become Worthless in Sideways Sloppy Patterns
Chart courtesy of Mastertrader.com.

Basically, in sideways or sloppy markets, moving averages have no valid use. The beauty of the moving average only comes into play when prices are moving in one direction. When averaging a series of inclines it becomes useful information. When averaging a series of sideways patterns it gives us no more information than what any sideways price can tell us. If prices are sloppy or sideways, we expect that pattern to continue until it breaks. See Figure 4.17.

In other words, if the moving averages are no longer parallel, and the price is no longer adhering to a rising or declining moving average, the moving averages have done their job to tell you that that trend is likely ending. A moving average crossover may also be confirmation that this is the case. If there is an immediate reversal in trend, let's say from an uptrend to a downtrend, following the moving average crossover, the moving averages may fall directly into place in the downtrend with that parallel look, with prices adhering to the newly declining moving averages. If this is the case, you simply have changed from following a perfectly diagrammed uptrend using the moving averages, to a perfectly diagrammed downtrend using the averages. However, this particular situation happens very rarely. Most of the time when an uptrend breaks, prices go sideways in a rambling and sloppy manner. The moving average often becomes intermixed with the price, and the two moving averages, the 20-period MA and the 40-period MA, begin to intermix with the price in an indiscriminate way. When this happens, it is important to understand the moving average may no longer have any value whatsoever. Prices touching the moving average do not even have a self-fulfilling prophecy effect. To the extent it does, it is so minimal that it will be overridden by the next price move that occurs.

In addition, moving averages can be phenomenal timing indicators to help understand when an extended price pattern may be ready to resume its upward move. We have talked about retracements and prices that come into an area of a rising moving average (and the reverse for declining issues). However, sometimes prices move up very sharply and refuse to pull back in terms of price. As we discussed earlier, prices may consolidate over time. After a very sharp move up, the question often becomes how long prices need to consolidate sideways before they are ready to resume their upward movement? The answer is very simple. When encountering the moving average again, no matter how strong the move, the resting time required to meet the rising 20-period MA usually indicates that the stock is rested enough to move upward. This can be seen in Figure 4.18. Naturally, a Pristine trader does not simply buy the contact point. However, we understand the stock is now rested enough that if the proper setup forms, we will look for prices to move higher once again.

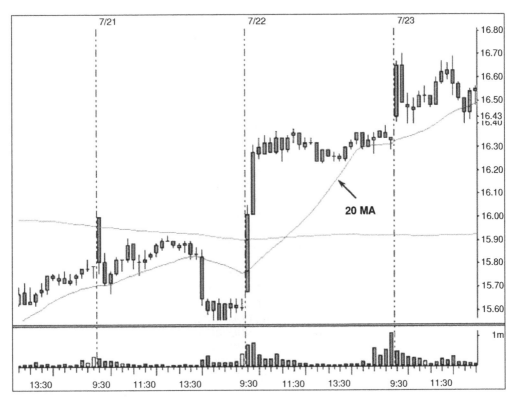

FIGURE 4.18 A Strong Move Up Has Consolidated Enough When It Meets the Rising 20-Period MA
Chart courtesy of Mastertrader.com.

MOVING AVERAGES TO FIND PLAYS

Just a quick note on another great way to use moving averages. If you were to scan for stocks that were above the 20-period MA at the current bar, and were above the 20-period MA 30 bars prior, and were above the 20-period MA 30 bars prior to that, you would have a list of stocks that would have some of the best uptrends. Naturally, you would want to review that list visually, but it would be a short list to review and would have some of the most powerful patterns.

Figure 4.19 is a stock minder out of a RealTick trading platform and shows us another idea. RealTick is the preferred trading platform of MasterTrader.com. This minder has the symbol listed in three columns, and it is either green (represented as black here) or

Symbol	Symbol	Description	Symbol
$DJI	$DJI	Dow Jones Industrial Avg	$DJI
AA	AA	ALCOA INC	AA
AXP	AXP	AMERICAN EXPRESS CO	AXP
BA	BA	BOEING CO	BA
BAC	BAC	BANK OF AMERICA CORPORATION	BAC
CAT	CAT	CATERPILLAR INC DEL	CAT
CSCO	CSCO	CISCO SYS INC	CSCO
CVX	CVX	CHEVRON CORP NEW	CVX
DD	DD	DU PONT E I DE NEMOURS & CO	DD
DIS	DIS	DISNEY WALT CO COM DISNEY	DIS
GE	GE	GENERAL ELECTRIC CO	GE
HD	HD	HOME DEPOT INC	HD
HPQ	HPQ	HEWLETT PACKARD CO	HPQ
IBM	IBM	INTERNATIONAL BUSINESS MACHS	IBM
INTC	INTC	INTEL CORP	INTC
JNJ	JNJ	JOHNSON & JOHNSON	JNJ
JPM	JPM	JPMORGAN CHASE & CO	JPM
KFT	KFT	KRAFT FOODS INC CL A	KFT
KO	KO	COCA COLA CO	KO
MCD	MCD	MCDONALDS CORP	MCD
MMM	MMM	3M CO	MMM
MRK	MRK	MERCK & CO INC NEW	MRK
MSFT	MSFT	MICROSOFT CORP	MSFT
PFE	PFE	PFIZER INC	PFE
PG	PG	PROCTER & GAMBLE CO	PG
T	T	AT & T INC	T
TRV	TRV	TRAVELERS COMPANIES INC	TRV
UTX	UTX	UNITED TECHNOLOGIES CORP	UTX
VZ	VZ	VERIZON COMMUNICATIONS INC	VZ
WMT	WMT	WAL MART STORES INC	WMT
XOM	XOM	EXXON MOBIL CORP	XOM

FIGURE 4.19 This RealTick Minder Can Make Short Work of Finding Strong or Weak Stocks
Chart courtesy of Mastertrader.com.

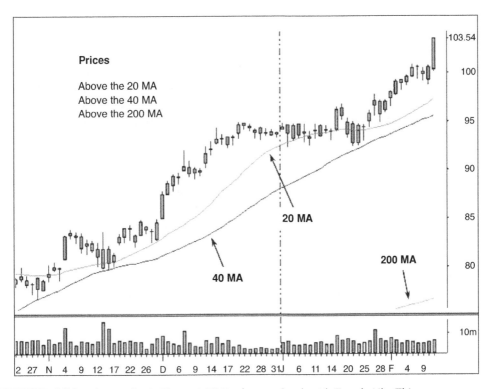

FIGURE 4.20 The Minder in Figure 4.19 Produces a Stock with Trends Like This
Chart courtesy of Mastertrader.com.

red (represented as gray). Being green in the first column means that the stock closed on the daily chart above the 20-period MA. When it is green in the second column, it means it closed above the 40-period MA, and the third column means that the 20-period MA closed above the 40-period MA, all on the daily chart. You can sort by any column, giving you the ability to find the strongest of the strongest stocks (and the weakest of the weakest stocks).

Using a method like this can save time and also produce some of the best results. One of the stocks that was green in all three columns, meaning it was above the 20-period MA, above the 40-period MA, and the 20-period MA was above the 40-period MA on the day this was done, is shown in Figure 4.20.

Finding truly strong trends is the first step in finding really great plays, and the moving averages can help do that.

IN SUMMARY

The proper use of moving averages will not only enhance trading results as much or more than any other technical item, but can also speed up the process tremendously. When in a bullish environment, searching for stocks that simply have a smooth rising 20-period MA that is paralleling a smooth rising 40-period MA will produce the best trading results. If traders were to take the total universe of stocks that they follow, and use this criteria to establish the trending stocks and discard all the rest, they would have the best of the best stocks to play on pullbacks. In addition, those traders that use scanners will find that you will achieve incredible scan results by simply finding stocks that have prices above the 20-period MA and the 20-period MA above the 40-period MA during the current time period, as well as two to three prior periods. The reverse is also true to find the best downtrending stocks.

Moving averages are the ultimate tools for helping to determine the proper trends we want to play. They also can be useful in determining approximate areas of retracement that will enhance the entry techniques we discussed earlier. While part of their use may be self-fulfilling prophecy, Pristine traders know how to use that to their advantage while not developing a premature bias based on subjective indicators.

We have talked a lot about support and resistance, and moving averages. These all have to do with *where* the price action may occur. Next, we talk about something that can really emphasize the "where": That something is known as volume.

CHAPTER 5

Volume Is Money

Commitment to Prices

A nother indicator that is overused, and sometimes incorrectly, is volume. Much noise is heard everyday about volume and how the tea leaves can be read. Volume is part of our analytical process but it is just a tool. I think of volume as a secondary indicator. Our primary indicator of when to take a trade is always the price. The analysis of volume is in the past but is never a part of the in-the-moment decision process, with one possible exception. At the time of the trade, you are part of the volume that is influencing price.

In its basic form, volume indicates a commitment, or lack thereof, to current prices. It can be useful as a confirming indicator to candlestick patterns. But I cannot emphasize enough that it is price action and its patterns that are the reason for any trade, never volume alone. Just because volume is rising or falling does not give us any objective information by itself. It is the candlesticks that reveal the supply and demand relationship. Volume just tells the magnitude of that relationship. See Figure 5.1.

Volume is perhaps one of the most talked about indicators in trading. Volume earns a unique distinction with me. On one hand, it is one of the three important things that I keep on my charts. Remember, I only keep three things on my charts: price, moving averages, and volume. On the other hand, volume's message is perhaps the most overrated and misunderstood by traders.

THE FALLACIES OF VOLUME

It would be best to begin talking about some of the fallacies and misconceptions regarding volume. We cannot understand the proper uses of volume until we understand what trading volume really means.

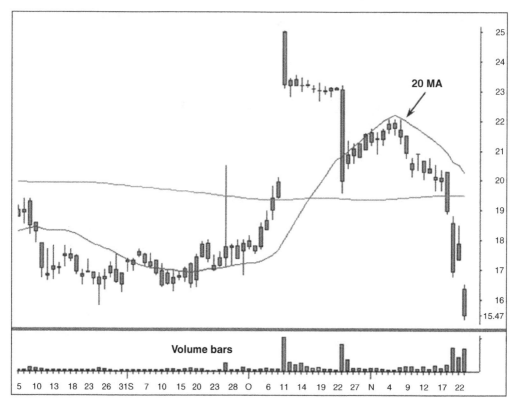

FIGURE 5.1 Volume Is One of Three Things You Should Have on Your Chart
Chart courtesy of Mastertrader.com.

The first misconception may simply be a matter of semantics but it is important to make the distinction. When asked why a particular stock rallied, a typical answer from an educated trader might be to say, "There were more buyers than sellers during that time period." While we perhaps know what the trader means when he says this, that statement is actually not true. There are not more sellers than buyers in any time period for any stock regardless of whether it rallied or declined. At the end of the period, at the end of the day, there are always just as many buyers as sellers. For every buyer there is a seller. For every seller there is a buyer.

What the trader perhaps means to say is that there are more potential buyers than potential sellers during that time period. When potential buyers outnumber potential sellers, there is an increase in demand. However, we also have to keep in mind that volume is, in a sense, a notion of past tense. Once that demand is in the market and a new time period begins, who is to say that the demand will continue? See Figure 5.2.

Often times you may hear a trader say something like, "Wow, that was really a bearish bar. There were over 100,000 sellers in five minutes and that is five times the normal amount of sellers." What the trader does not understand is that there were also a lot of

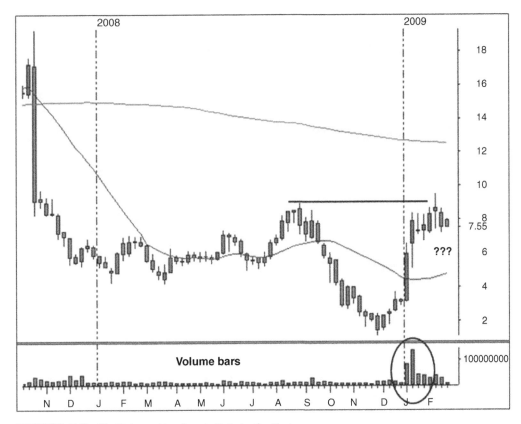

FIGURE 5.2 Big Volume May Speak Only to the Past
Chart courtesy of Mastertrader.com.

buyers. If the stock initially dropped, it is assumed that the move was created by a seller or sellers. However, the question we want to know is not whether or not there was a big seller. We want to know if there will continue to be big sellers. If the stock returns to its prior price, it does not matter how much volume occurred during the initial move down because whatever volume in selling was created was equaled by the number of buyers. The question we have to answer now is where we are going from here.

A common misuse of volume is to assume that movements in price cannot continue unless they are happening on large or increasing volume (see Figure 5.3). This is the converse of a true statement, but converse statements are not true. There are times when a larger volume surge will indicate a new move is underway. However, the reverse of that, that a new move beginning cannot be real without increased volume, is false. Traders who waited for volume and did not react to price may be missing some of the best moves. Good traders will enter the trade when the price pattern indicates and the volume that steps in after they do will help take good traders to their targets. This is something we will talk about more shortly.

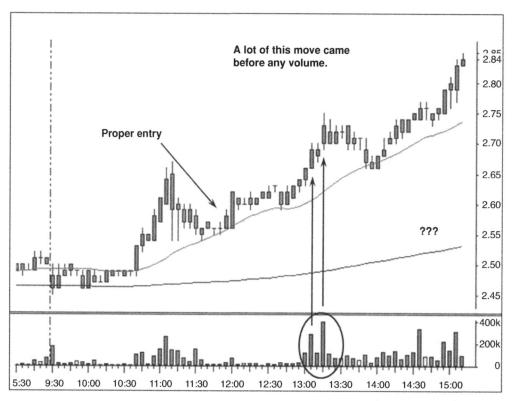

FIGURE 5.3 Waiting for Big Volume Is Not the Answer
Chart courtesy of Mastertrader.com.

One of the most misconstrued concepts regarding volume is so popular that there are actually scans written to find them. Traders look for these situations and feel that they have gold mines, but in reality, they have nothing. This discussion is about block trades. Sometimes prices will be going along and, all of a sudden, a trade will occur well outside the market. For a trade to occur outside the market, it means it happens outside of the current bid and offer scenario that is set up on the Level II screen (the Level II screen is a screen that tracks the real-time bids and offers for any particular stock or issue). Let's say, for example, a stock is being bid for at 32.10, and being offered at 32.14. If a trade were to suddenly go off at 32.30, there is one of two possibilities that caused this to happen. First, there could simply be a mistake. They do happen. If it is a mistake, it will likely be one single trade that is showing the typical volume for one trade. The trade may have 100 shares or perhaps 1,000 shares. If one trade occurs that far out of the market and then returns to the normal price on the next tick, it is simply a mistake and can be ignored. The charts will usually correct these mistakes as soon as they can.

However, if that trade at 32.30 occurred on significant volume, it probably was not a bad tick. It likely was a block trade. The difference is that in this case, a trade likely did occur at 32.30. Many traders look to this as a sign of extreme bullishness because a large volume traded above the current market price means somebody must be willing to really pay up for the stock. This thinking is very flawed. I will explain how these things happen and you will see why they really have no affect on your ability to make money on the stock.

In a block trade what happens is that a market maker may have a large order to buy a stock. If this occurs, he is probably working the order all day long trying to get it filled without driving the price of the stock higher. There may come a point in time when he has a little bit of stock left to purchase, perhaps let's say 150,000 shares out of a 1 million share order. At that point, he may call up one of his market maker friends and simply say, "Look, I still have to buy 150,000 of XYZ. What are you willing to sell it to me for?" The two market makers will agree on a price that will be above the market and the trade will go through and hit the tape. While many traders get excited about this, the truth of it is that most of the time this will be the last transaction of that big order. Perhaps a stock was moving up all day due to this big order, but this will usually bring an end to the buying, not the beginning. Therefore, while big volume on an out-of-the-market trade may prove to be a block trade rather than a bad tick, that does not mean the stock is likely to go higher in the future.

USING VOLUME PROPERLY

There are truly only two uses of volume that are really important to know and understand. In addition, of these two, only one can really make you money. The other one can sometimes make you money and is very important to know and understand. Before we get to those two, let's take a look at some of the other uses of volume that are nice to know, but don't necessarily make you money.

After a strong move up or after a new breakout, it is nice to see the pullback, that is to say the retracement, or the consolidation following the big move, to occur on reduced volume. The idea is that strong buying pressure has caused the new move up, and the only selling there should be is that of profit-taking from the buyers that caused the move up. If we see new selling begin that outpaces the volume that occurred on the rally, you have to question the rally. As always, the same would be true for a retracement rally after a strong move down in the downtrend. Remember, throughout this book, the bearish patterns deserve the same comments as bullish patterns, even if I do not mention them separately. See Figure 5.4.

In other words, volume should be decreasing when prices are moving against the underlying trend in the market. This indicates that the price trend is still strong and traders are holding off as prices move against the previous trend. As prices move back into an area of support, for example, we would like to see volume decreasing on the pullback. This tells us that few traders want to abandon their position and new demand will resume the up-move in price. At that point, volume is telling us to start watching for a changing of the guard. Once prices move into an area of support or resistance I like to

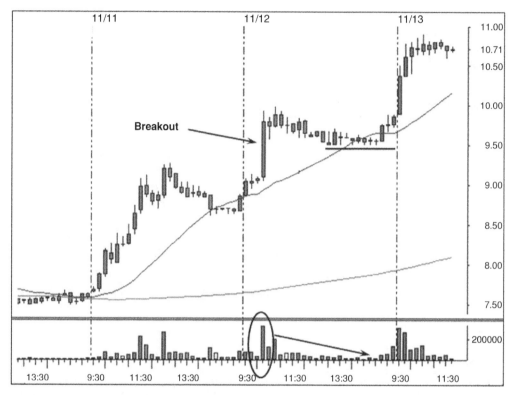

FIGURE 5.4 Volume Decreasing on a Bullish Pullback
Chart courtesy of Mastertrader.com.

see volume increase as well. This tells me that interest in the stock is increasing at the place where it should.

While this is nice to see, like everything in technical analysis you must take it with a grain of salt. There are times, such as what we call at Pristine, a transition from stage one to stage two, where a longtime sideways pattern goes into an uptrend. It is possible that these types of breakouts have limited volume on the initial rally, and can sometimes be sold heavily after the first attempt to move higher. This isn't uncommon and is contrary to the idea that breakouts have to, or should, happen on high volume. The reason this happens is based on trader psychology, as all patterns are. Because the stock was moving sideways for a long time, there are many prior positions that are being held by long traders who have been growing impatient and will sell the initial rallies. Therefore, even this rule about light volume on a pullback is not always applicable. Once in a nice established uptrend, new breakouts and continued moves up should occur on bigger volume than the resulting pullbacks. Once you start to see heavy volume on the pullbacks, it could be a signal that the rally may be ending and transitioning to a sideways or downward pattern. An example of this is shown in Figure 5.5.

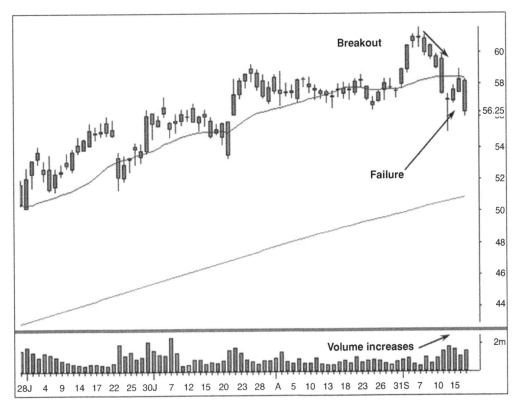

FIGURE 5.5 Volume Can Be Tricky
Chart courtesy of Mastertrader.com.

THE PRIMARY USES OF VOLUME

Now that we have removed some of the fallacies and some of the less important uses of volume, I will spend the rest of this chapter looking at the two primary uses of volume as I see it. These two uses of volume are by far the most important, and the only ones that can perhaps help you make money. As I said, many of the other uses are nice to know, but I usually will not take or negate a pattern because of them. The first of these two uses of volume is in the category of large volume that ignites a new move. Here we are talking about trends that are challenged or actually change on a single bar that occurs on heavy volume. We are talking about downtrends that have a very high-volume reversal bar, or more accurately a sideways trend that breaks into a new uptrend as result of the single breakout. These high-volume bars signal an ignition of the new move. This is especially true when it occurs after a long time of reduced volume. As you can see in Figure 5.6, the more asleep the stock has been, the more likely that a significant and substantial move will follow an initial high-volume breakout bar.

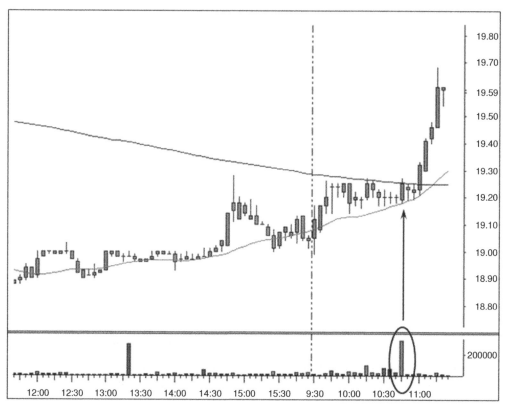

FIGURE 5.6 Volume Igniting a New Move on a New Breakout
Chart courtesy of Mastertrader.com.

Examples of this type of breakout volume can be found in several places. It is much preferable to see this volume occurring when an existing uptrend rests for a while and then begins a new uptrend on big volume. That is because all of that volume is going into a current trend that simply took a rest. When a downtrend has a single reversal bar on heavy volume, it is usually meaningful but sometimes can be tricky. Sometimes heavy short covering can come in to make a temporary bump that may not have follow through. In these cases, I prefer to see a retest of the prior lows to make sure that that large volume bar is going to follow through. See Figure 5.7.

This type of volume is called "professional (or committed) volume" in a general sense. We also call this heavy volume on new breakouts: "High-volume igniting a new move." A special note about this type of volume: It does not always make you money. The reason is that the volume is coming in after the point of entry. In other words, when a pattern forms, you need to take the pattern based on price whether the volume is there or not. Once the pattern is under way, you may see that exceptional volume is coming in. This confirms it as a good trade and may encourage you to add to the position at the appropriate time. However, the initial entry cannot wait for volume. To do so would be

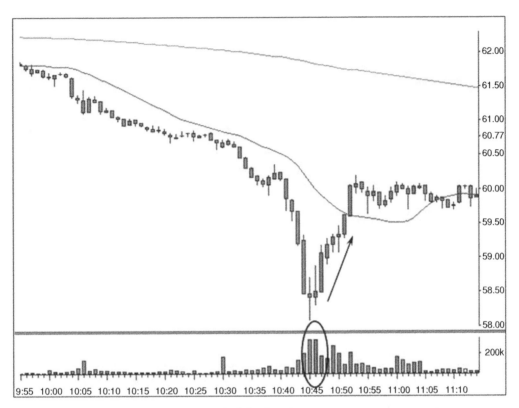

FIGURE 5.7 Volume Igniting a Reversal of the Trend
Chart courtesy of Mastertrader.com.

to sacrifice many good trades. Remember, we are reading charts and understanding the patterns better and in doing so we know when to enter trades. When the rest of the public figures it out, the big volume comes in. However, I want to be in the trade at that point, and let the big volume help carry me to my target.

The second type of volume is known as "novice volume." This second use of volume is also what we call "high volume ending a current move." Here we are talking about stock that has been down for many, many bars. After it appears that the stock can drop no more, the stock then drops sharply and does so on heavy volume—much heavier than the last several bars. This volume is sometimes also called "exhaustion" or "climactic volume." Regardless of what you call it, this type of volume shows that the end of the current move is at hand. See Figure 5.8. If the last bar down is a large wide range bar on heavy volume, and it comes after a string of extended red bars, odds are that prices are ready for a reversal.

Every chart communicates a picture of traders' actions and emotions. To bring this point home as it relates to this type of volume, think of a time that you have been long a stock that was going against you and was dropping. With each move lower the pressure and the pain of the increasing loss builds. As it becomes more and more obvious to you

FIGURE 5.8 Novice Volume Ending an Extended Move
Chart courtesy of Mastertrader.com.

and others that the stock it is not going to bounce, those long reach the point where they cry "Uncle!" and they will sell. All of a sudden, where a $200 loss was unacceptable to take, a $2,000 loss is easy to press the sell button on. That moment in time is where the majority sell together, causing a huge increase in volume. It's amazing how this often happens right at prior price support. Why would the majority sell at the obvious place where prices are likely to stabilize? Emotion takes over from being objective about what is happening, even if you were aware of the concept of support at the time. If you are new to trading and technical analysis you may be thinking why anyone would do that. However, I can assure you that you will experience it and understand it afterward. Part of the learning process of technical trading is living the chart to fully understand the patterns. There is no way around it.

This experience and understanding of this type of volume is exceptionally useful to us because it is giving us a heads-up before the next move is about to happen. This type of volume increase will often precede a turn and tells us an opportunity should be at hand soon. After this type of volume, if it is truly exceptional, the next buy setup may be an appropriate time to enter. See Figure 5.9.

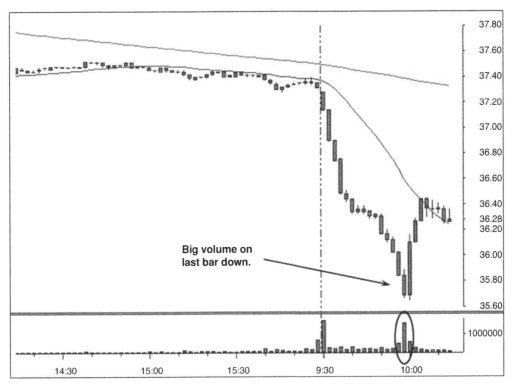

FIGURE 5.9 Novice Volume Gives a Heads-Up to the Only Entry
Chart courtesy of Mastertrader.com.

While it may be advantageous for us to wait for a retest of the turning point, patterns like this sometimes will not retest. They may simply trade higher after what is called a V-bottom and it pays to be in the first move.

There are different levels of volume that we often try to identify and associate with the different setups. When you look at the volume bars at the bottom of your chart, the normal size bars are what we simply call "average volume" for that stock or market at the time. You can actually see the average if you like by putting a moving average onto the volume bars. I typically do not do that; I simply eyeball the recent volume bars to see what an average would be. This is not rocket science and simply taking a look for exceptional bars is the best way to go. Don't make all this too complicated, it should be kept simple. When we have a bar that breaks above the high of the last six to eight volume bars, view it as above average volume. When that volume bar becomes more than twice the height of the average of the last six to eight bars, we can call that "climactic volume" or "committed volume." Climactic volume comes after an extended move and number of bars, and committed volume would happen just before or with a buy or sell setup triggering. These are very loose definitions and should not be taken strictly,

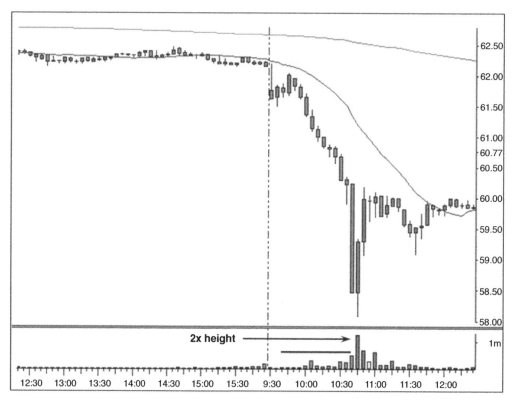

FIGURE 5.10 What Climactic Volume Looks Like
Chart courtesy of Mastertrader.com.

but they give you a guide as to what type of volume numbers we are looking for. See Figure 5.10 for an example of climactic volume.

By the way, I like to watch for committed volume that occurs prior to a reversal pattern forming. In this example, the stock has moved into the area of support. As the COG pattern forms, volume picks up as more traders step into the trade. This is volume that is committed to the trade and is trying to push prices in the intended direction of the trade. As shown in Figure 5.11, combined with the actual formation of the pattern, completing this type of volume can give prices an explosive push in the direction of our trading position.

Another way to look at this is to say that there are only three types of volume that we consider and we classify them as novice, professional, or continuation. The two we just described above are named novice and professional types of volume. Continuation volume can be difficult to read and understand and may give many false readings. Basically, anything that is not novice or professional could be considered continuation. This type of volume is not very useful for making money, although it may be useful for discussion when sitting around the water cooler.

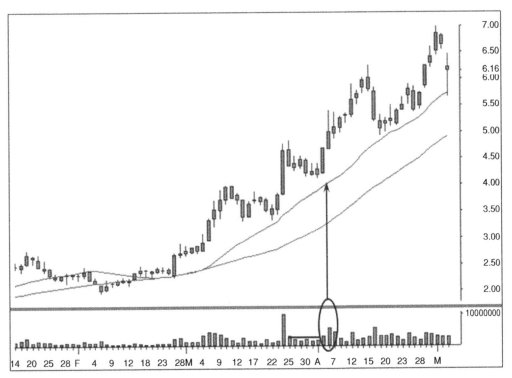

FIGURE 5.11 A COG with Increased Volume
Chart courtesy of Mastertrader.com.

Visuals of Different Kinds of Volume

Here are several examples to illustrate our discussion about volume. The chart in Figure 5.12 shows an example of a high-volume bar that ends a down move on the pullback that is happening inside of the bigger move up. This high-volume on the last part of the pullback indicates that the stock is ready to reverse and resume its move upward again. This volume is particularly useful to us for helping find the correct bar to ignite a new Pristine Buy Setup in an uptrend.

In Figure 5.13 we see an example of heavy volume that is ending an extended move to the downside. The large volume on that large bar at the end of the move indicates that the end of the move down is likely near, and we can expect to see a reversal in prices. This is a good example of novice volume that is ending a novice move at this point. While the initial move was strong and for real, it is now overextended and we are seeing the type of exhaustion that indicates that the people still selling on this last bar are novice sellers.

Figure 5.14 is an example of professional volume. This is volume coming in to ignite a new move upward. This change of direction happened on a gap in this case, but all the volume coming in are a combination of new buyers that are igniting this new move

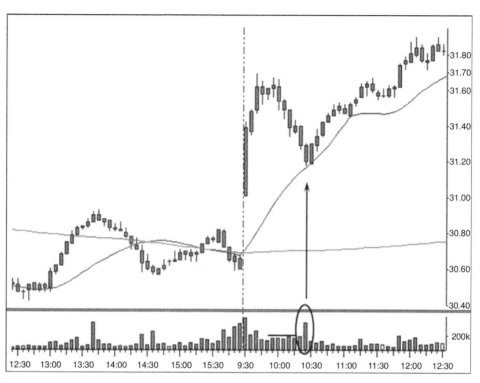

FIGURE 5.12 High Volume Shows the Pullback Is Ending
Chart courtesy of Mastertrader.com.

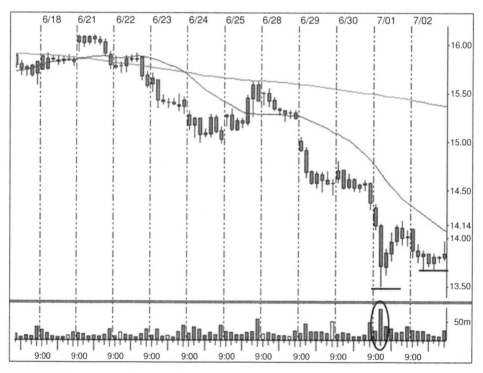

FIGURE 5.13 Novice Volume Ends the Move
Chart courtesy of Mastertrader.com.

FIGURE 5.14 Professional Volume Ignites a New Move
Chart courtesy of Mastertrader.com.

to the upside, with a combination of the old short-sellers who are now buyers as they need to exit at this point due to the sudden change in direction.

Here is an example of continuation volume in Figure 5.15. While, as we said, this is not particularly helpful, you would like to see diminishing volume as the stock is resting in a current trend. The pullbacks or consolidations that happen in an uptrend should occur on decreasing volume, which indicates that there is still good interest in the stock to move to the upside.

Volume increases should occur in the direction of the prevailing trend. Volume decreases should occur against the direction of the prevailing trend. When prices move into the areas of support or resistance, a volume increase acts as confirmation that these areas are acting as support or resistance. Volume increases while the price continues within a prevailing trend is a warning of potential reversal. Look at the following chart.

Figure 5.16 gives you some idea of how to use price volume in conjunction with price, to find the best trades. If you look to the far left at point number one, you can see an almost ideal condition. Trading volumes are rising as prices move up. This tells us a growing number of traders are enthusiastic about the stock as the demand is constant. As prices move up and consolidate, we can see at point 2 that volume expands as the size

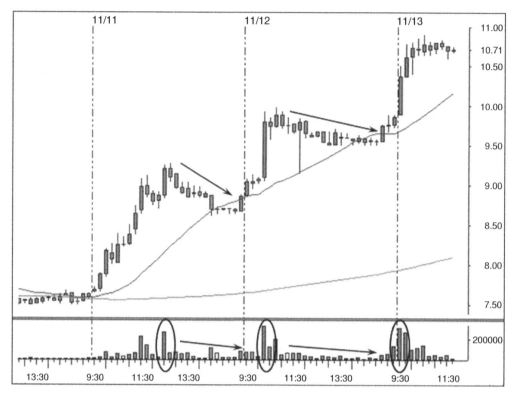

FIGURE 5.15 Continuation Volume
Chart courtesy of Mastertrader.com.

of the price bars is contracting. Prices are also moving back up to the resistance area at the high of the prior up move. More traders are in the stock but the number of buyers and sellers are matching up pretty well. This is a clear danger sign and indeed, we see a reversal pattern form and prices fall.

Now, at point 3, you can see a volume spike followed by a narrow body bar signaling that the price decline is likely to slow. As you can see, prices do slow, although no clear reversal pattern forms. As the down move continues, we get climactic volume as the trend accelerates. More traders are jumping on the seller's bandwagon and pushing prices lower very quickly. At point 4, you can see that we get a final volume spike on a narrow range bar indicating once again that the attitude of traders toward the stock is changing. We get a wide range bar that pushes well above the prior bar indicating that demand has once again taken control of the price action.

In Figure 5.17, we can see another good example of reading volume and price. As you can see, at the far left of the chart, prices are moving down but volumes are fairly low. At point 1 on the chart, you can see that we get committed volume into the chart as the Pristine Buy Setup forms. This ignites a rally as the sellers are done and buyers have regained control of the price. After prices run up, we get a topping tail bar and prices

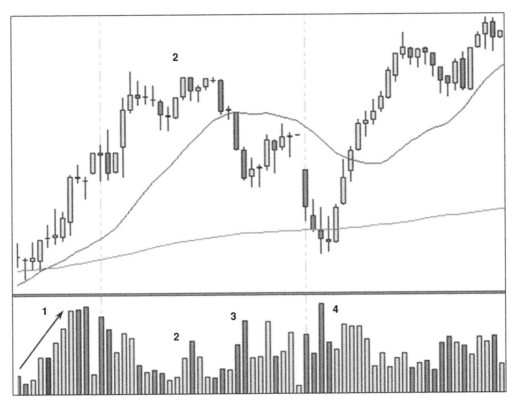

FIGURE 5.16 Multiple Uses of Volume
Chart courtesy of Mastertrader.com.

begin to pull back toward the 20-period MA. Look at what is happening with volume, however; as we move toward the MA at point 2 in Figure 5.17, volume is decreasing. There are probably not going to be enough sellers to push prices through the support point. Indeed, we see a Pristine Buy Setup occur on a spike in volume at point 3. A new source of committed volume has come into the stock and it takes off to the upside. The price increases on higher volume until it reaches the area of the 200-period MA. As we consolidate at that level, probably due to the actions of more subjective traders, we can see that once again volumes decrease. Not that many traders are interested in getting out of their position. As the two moving averages converge, we know that we can expect to see an increase in volatility. We get in when we get a bullish candle that closes right on the high at point 4, and we see prices resume moving higher.

In Figure 5.18, we have a serious increase in volume without a breakout. This can often show that the current trend is ending. This base is occurring in an uptrend but the increased volume that occurred did not result in a breakout. This is an indication that perhaps this breakout will no longer work, the uptrend is over, and we may be seeing prices below the base soon.

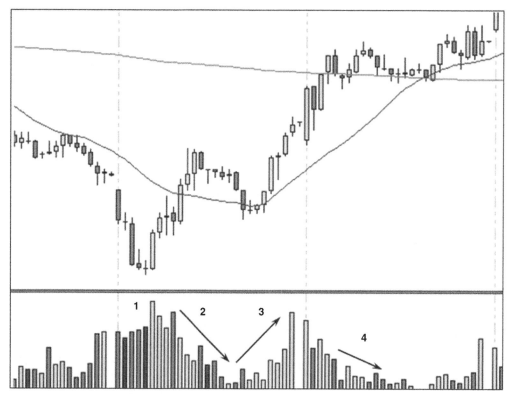

FIGURE 5.17 Volume Complements the Price Pattern
Chart courtesy of Mastertrader.com.

In other words, on occasion we will see volume increasing as prices contract within a trend. When I see trading volumes rising as the size of the bars are getting smaller this tells me that a reversal could be coming. Think about what is happening when we see this. If the trend was still strong and likely to continue, the new volume would be pushing prices further in the prevailing direction. The price bars would be getting taller, not shorter. A higher volume within a tighter price range indicates that traders are starting to bet against the trend and we could see prices reverse direction soon. That by itself, of course, is not enough to justify a trade but it does tell me to watch the price action closely for a change.

VOLUME AS IT RELATES TO TRADABILITY

What we have been discussing so far has been the practical use of volume in order to understand how to complement our chart-reading abilities. This is the technical use of volume. In addition to this, we need to discuss volume as it relates to tradability. Volume

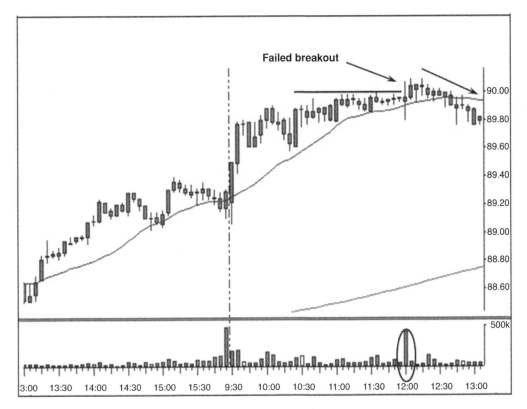

FIGURE 5.18 Increased Volume Fails to Ignite the Breakout Attempt
Chart courtesy of Mastertrader.com.

will also relate to how fluidly a stock moves, and how easy it is to enter and exit. For those traders who are looking only for long-term patterns, such as on a weekly and daily chart, the total volume has less effect. The reason is that if you are going to hold the stock for days or for weeks, your exact entry point is not as critical. If you need to pay a nickel or a dime, or even a little more in order to enter or exit the trade, it has less effect as you are likely going for a bigger move.

However, for traders that are entering on intraday patterns, it is essential that we get good entries and exits. We cannot be throwing away ten or fifteen cents getting into a stock. Many stocks trade on such light volume, that they are very difficult to enter and exit. Even if it appears easy to enter, or even if you made a relatively easy entry, the issue is not the entry when things are good. The issue is going to be how you get out when things go bad. When a stock surges to the downside and we have several sellers, or when a stock breaks a significant support level, the selling pressure on a light volume stock may drive it down so fast it causes heavy losses.

To help avoid trading stocks that are simply too thin, you can look for the total volume the stock is trading as a guideline. You should begin to note things like charts, such as Figure 5.19, that have gaps on the intraday pattern. Charts do not gap on intraday

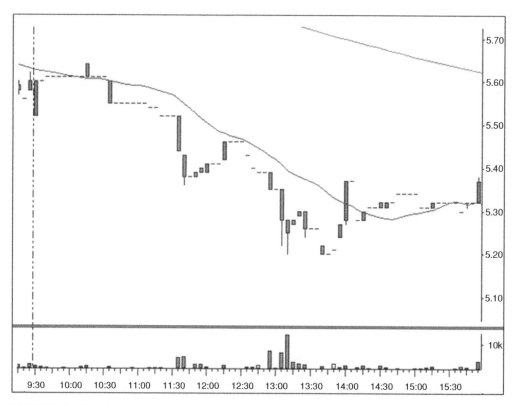

FIGURE 5.19 Thin Volume Can Lead to Spotty Charts
Chart courtesy of Mastertrader.com.

patterns; this only happens when volume is so thin that the price literally changes from one bar to the next due to a wide spread between the bid and the offer.

Another side note about volume; volume in general tells us about the magnitude of interest that occurs when a particular pattern happens. In other words, a very good pattern that never gets volume at any point, may fail due to the fact that the pattern is not as good as we think it is, because it never attracts buyers or sellers.

Volume is a useful tool in our trading but keep in mind that it is just a tool. The way price reacts to volume can give us valuable information, but it is price that determines the trade. We know that if volume is expanding as price bars are contracting, we should be watching for a reversal. We are not going to trade on this information until we actually get a buy or sell setup. Expanding volume during a climatic move of several bars may be a signal that most traders have made their move and direction could change. There is no change however until we get an actual signal and hopefully new committed volume to push prices in our intended direction.

We should also look at volume in multiple time frames. A chart like Figure 5.20 that shows low daily volume but is showing rising volumes in a shorter-term time frame can

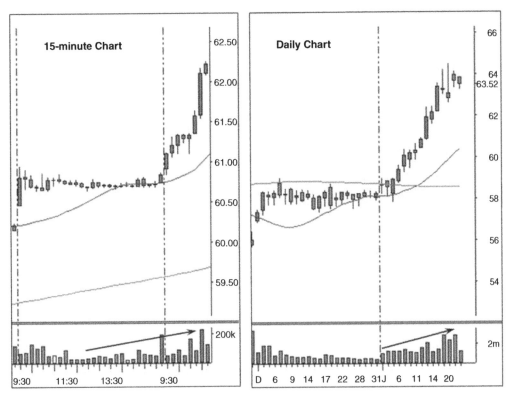

FIGURE 5.20 Multiple Time Frames Can Put Volume in Perspective
Chart courtesy of Mastertrader.com.

tell us that a change is on the way. A chart where volume is rising across all time frames can be an indication of a powerful trading signal.

IN SUMMARY

Remember that volume in general is never a reason to place a trade. The candlesticks are the reason to place a trade, when the proper pattern occurs. Many trades can be confirmed as being better trades when volume comes in, however many of these trades will be entered too late if you wait for volume. Novice volume moves help us not only get confirmation of the ending of a move, but also can signal us to the proper entry that is still yet to come. Price patterns still rule, but volume can add some real meat to the bones of any strategy that is setting up.

Next we talk about what happens after a move, and how the location of the move and the pullback can tell us much about future prices. The topic is retracements.

CHAPTER 6

Retracement Analysis

Using Retracement Analysis to
Continue Your Move

When we discuss retracements in technical analysis, we are talking about how much a strong move up or down gives back on the countermove. We are talking about the pullback, the countermove, or (and you may have heard the term) Fibonacci. We may be looking at various things such as the steepness of the pullback, the angle of retracement, the percentage of the decline or rally, or we may talk about the precision or the sloppiness of the pullback. But no matter the analysis used, the goal is the same: A stock has moved a certain amount in one direction, and we want to see what happens next.

THE CONCEPT OF RETRACEMENTS

Let's say a stock has moved to the upside. If the bulls are in control, and if that move was serious, there should be a limit to how much the stock gives back of the move that just happened. This is the bottom line to retracement analysis and it's that simple.

Like anything else in technical analysis, this is one concept or tool to use in conjunction with all the other technical features we are discussing in this book. It is very rare that any trade would be played due completely to one technical component. It is not so rare, however, that we may negate a trade due to one technical component being way out of line. Notice, though, that when one technical component gets out of line, it will usually spill over into other technical areas, as well. For example, when the retracement becomes too steep, at some point it challenges the uptrend. It may also violate areas of support. Therefore, you do have to look at the whole picture but, many times, one technical component being out of line may put the whole trade in question. Lastly, to this point, in regard to when we talk about subjectivity and objectivity, many people want to put retracements into the category of objective. However, they are not. Once again,

FIGURE 6.1 The Retracement of a Bullish Move
Chart courtesy of Mastertrader.com.

the price bars and what is actually happening are most important. When we discuss the concept of Fibonacci, you will see why many people feel that this is an objective occurrence because of the precision that Fibonacci attempts to use. However, the truth of it is that most buyers will not enter positions because a certain line exists on a chart or somebody said that this retracement meets a Fibonacci level. That being said, Fibonacci (FIB) enthusiasts are likely to do just that, with a stop based on another FIB level.

Before I explain the objective use of retracements, I want you to understand how subjective, misleading, and confusing the idea of Fibonacci retracements can be if used, as most do, as it relates to trading. Once you are beyond the Fibonacci hocus-pocus you can use the concept of retracements in your trading in a simple, common sense way.

Leonardo Pisano Bigollo

Leonardo Pisano Bigollo, also known as Leonardo of Pisa, or Leonardo Pisano, or Leonardo Bonacci, or Leonardo Fibonacci, or, most commonly, simply Fibonacci, was an Italian mathematician. He was considered by some to be the most talented western mathematician of the Middle Ages. What he is best known for is the Fibonacci Sequence of numbers wherein the last two numbers added together provide the next number in the sequence: 1, 1, 2, 3, 5, 8, 13, 21, 34, 55, and so on. From this sequence, came the ratio of .618 and others that are pointed to as the perfect measurements seen in everything such as flowers, the Parthenon, and even the perfect face. Names associated with these measurements are the Golden Ratio, the Golden Rectangle, and the Golden Section.

There are a couple of things we can deduce from these numbers and names. First, they are very exact numbers and we know that markets do not respond well to exact numbers. Traders are attracted to the exactness since it provides a sense of knowing what will happen at a number. We all want to know what will happen. This is human nature of course, but it works against us when it comes to trading. There is no sure thing in trading and this analysis gives traders that use it a false sense of knowing. Second, the very nature of his work implies that these are subjective numbers when it comes to the stock market. The mystique of the analysis and names used works well to sell secret or proprietary support and resistance numbers in the market to the less knowledgeable.

Since the exactness of these numbers is subjective I do not use them in my trading. There is no actual support or resistance at a FIB retracement level. They are just lines that traders have picked to hang their hats on, based on drawing lines between two points hoping that a strong stock should stop falling here. Some traders take the FIB theory to an even higher level of subjectivity by drawing levels from various highs and lows in hopes of finding points where the retracement levels from those different highs and lows will overlap.

This in theory is supposed to provide an even stronger reference point of support or resistance. The idea of locating support or resistance and measuring its strength is not only subjective; I'll go so far as to say that it's ridiculous. If I haven't yet made you have second thoughts on the validity of Fibonacci as an analysis tool, think of these kinds of questions that must be answered when using this type of tool:

- When you draw Fibonacci lines, which highs and lows do you use as reference?
- How many highs and lows?
- What about the highs and lows from a higher time frame?
- Should the lines be drawn from the extremes of the bars, the bodies of the candles, or the closes?

The thought of drawing from different points that would move the retracement lines and, as such, support and resistance, should be enough to realize that the whole concept is a black hole of confusion just waiting for those new to technical trading. This isn't to say that I avoided a short stay in the dark side myself, but I found my way out.

I do understand that traders have these exact numbers plotted out on their charts and that is a reason to be aware of them. As a matter of fact, most every trading platform that I know of has the ability to draw these Fibonacci retracement levels built into the system. That means these numbers are widely used by many traders, especially on futures contracts, currencies, and broader market indices. And, as such, they do become self-fulfilling prophecies. Now that you know this we can move on without the air of mystery.

TO RETRACE OR NOT TO RETRACE?

Before we begin talking about retracements, we need to see how retracements fit into the big picture. Again, the big concept here is discussing what happens after a big rally or a big decline. To keep it simple, I will continue to discuss a big rally. After a big rally, the stock or market will run out of buyers, which will cause the prices to stop. Running out of buyers may be a temporary occurrence, or a more permanent one. We never know at the time it happens, we can only infer what might happen by looking at different time frames and the whole technical picture. But for now let's talk about what can possibly happen after a stock gets tired from moving up and needs to rest.

There are two ways in which a stock can rest after a strong move up. We call this resting "consolidation" when discussing a stock or a market. Stocks can consolidate in two different ways. First, they consolidate through time; second, they can consolidate, or correct, through price.

When a stock consolidates through time, it means that it is not going through a price retracement. It means that after the rally, we may not have enough new buyers to keep the issue moving higher, but there are sufficient buyers camped out under the current price of the stock so it is not able to drop. Buyers are still there and willing to buy the stock at any price lower than where it currently is, but they are not willing to chase the stock higher. This is the highest level of bullishness for a stock after a strong move up. You will typically see stocks like this going sideways very near the high achieved on the last rally. Figure 6.2 is an example of a stock that is consolidating through time, rather than through price.

Note that this only happens when the current buyers have decided that they will not chase the price higher, but they are willing to buy any price lower than the current one. If the stock is not quite as strong, those who begin taking profits by creating sell orders do not have buyers beneath them to support the stock and prices begin to decline. We will see prices continue to fall until a combination of two events occurs. First, the profit takers have to get exhausted so that the selling ends. Second, the prices must decline to a level that new buyers are willing to step in and purchase the stock. When a combination of these two events occurs, it means that the buyers finally outnumber the sellers again, demand becomes greater than supply, and the stock sets a retracement level at some point before moving higher again.

Note also, that the stock could really do anything in between these two occurrences. It is not uncommon to see stocks do one or the other, because there seems to be a sort of snowball effect: Some stocks simply do not drop and they consolidate. However, if selling does begin, it seems to promote new selling and a full retracement occurs to an appropriate level. Prices can also fall in between and make it difficult to ascertain if they are going to continue to pull back, or if they will begin moving up at some point. I cannot tell you exactly what will happen. The point is to follow what *is* happening. There will be times that the price movement will not fall into our plan of how it should happen. That's okay and it's why we have a plan. There are times that the market (which is the sum of

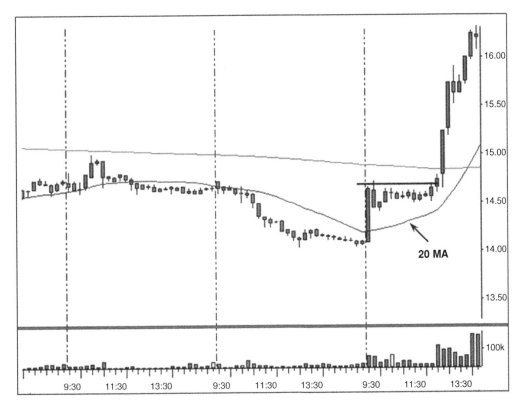

FIGURE 6.2 A Stock Consolidates through Price
Chart courtesy of Mastertrader.com.

all traders) is confused and retracements will be erratic. Recognizing this will keep us out the choppy action.

To keep your thinking straight, you may want to look at stocks that consolidate through time near the highs of the rally as being zero retracements. These are the strongest stocks that are creating a new level to start an advance from. When stocks do begin to correct through price, the issue then becomes how much is too much before we are no longer interested in playing the stock long.

RETRACEMENTS IMPLY A TREND

Notice that we are talking about retracements as something that occurs after solid moves in one direction. Therefore, by definition, you may imply that the concept of retracements has less meaning when prices are in a sloppy or sideways type of pattern. When no group is in control, there is no point in knowing how well they are in control. Figure 6.3 shows the basic concept of retracement.

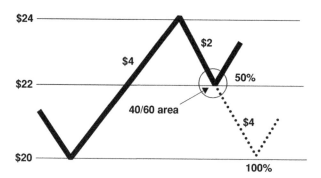

FIGURE 6.3 The Concept of a Bullish Retracement
Chart courtesy of Mastertrader.com.

When prices are in an uptrend, we expect that rallies will make new highs beyond the last pivot high, or beyond where the last rally stalled. When that new high is formed, it is the amount of the next pullback that we are concerned about in retracement analysis. Notice in Figure 6.4 there is no trend therefore there is no concept of retracing from the last rally. Rallies that occur when prices are declining will simply leave behind a new pivot and set a new low, which will be the basis of a downtrend. It is the rallies in

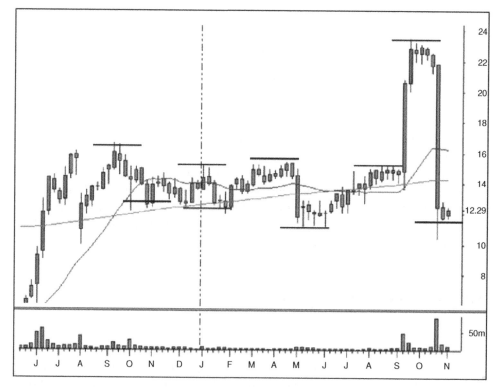

FIGURE 6.4 Retracement Analysis Only Exists Inside the Trend
Chart courtesy of Mastertrader.com.

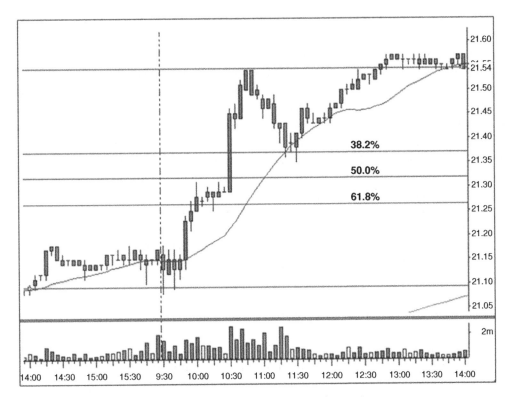

FIGURE 6.5 Measuring the Exact Retracement Levels per Fibonacci
Chart courtesy of Mastertrader.com.

downtrends that we want to measure retracements on, not the declines. This should be obvious, but many traders who only think bullishly may start to get confused here about downtrends.

So what kind of retracement levels are we looking for and what do they imply about the entry on the pullback or the likelihood of the trend continuing? We take a look at this issue in Figure 6.5, starting with the concept of Fibonacci.

As I explained, I do not like the concept of Fibonacci retracements as an exact form of analysis of support and resistance. We can simply round off these numbers to 40 percent, 50 percent, and 60 percent. Once we do this, we can make some deductions about the current pullback and what it implies about the next move in the stock. At the outset of this chapter I said if the bulls are in control, and if that move was serious, there should be a limit to how much the stock gives back of the move that just happened. Again, that's the bottom line to retracement analysis.

So let's assume we have a bullish uptrend in place and we are discussing the pullback inside of that uptrend. First, anything that retraces 40 percent or less and begins moving higher would be considered to be very bullish, as buyers are aggressively stepping in early to get into the stock. As a matter of fact, if the new rally begins well above the 40 percent level, we have to be certain that we have other things in place that assure us that the rally is for real. A continued move higher from a very shallow retracement may initially fail and come back to a lower level, but still above our major support area. A lower high and lower low that forms while still above an area of major support is tradable. This is an advanced technical pattern and one I suggest you study.

The 50 percent level is the average that we would expect most stocks to pull back to before finding buyers. This is the comfort zone where we often see profit taking from the recent move up come to an end. We do not want to see people taking profits too late in the pullback as it implies they are not as confident as the trend suggests. We also do want to see buyers step in before the stock retraces too far because it indicates there is a lack of buyers. The 50 percent area is about the midpoint and typically works on most stocks experiencing pullbacks in uptrends.

Note that as we begin to get significantly below 50 percent of the pullback (say, to something greater than 60 percent), we have to begin to question the ability of the stock to rally again above the old high. Normal profit taking should not involve selling the stock that close to the point of the original breakout. We also should be finding buyers at this level or higher if there are any buyers left in the picture. Therefore, stocks that retrace back more than 60 percent are more likely to form rallies that fail to go to new highs and may even begin a new downtrend on the bigger time frame.

Remember that there are always going to be sellers at prior highs. If prices have to travel too far to get there (for example, having retraced 75 percent and now moving back to the prior high), the odds of more sellers showing up at that high are greater. The reasons being, first, the size of the retracement will make traders already long doubt the stock's ability to move beyond the high because of the weakness, so some will sell there based on that. Second, those that bought at the reversal after the deeper retracement will have a reasonable profit to sell at the prior high. The thinking or analysis being that the more traders that have similar beliefs about a reference point of resistance, the greater the odds that reference point will have an effect on prices and their ability to move beyond it. Patterns are always reflections of the prior actions and possible actions of traders (see Figure 6.6).

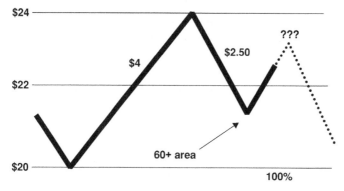

FIGURE 6.6 The Bigger Pullback Questions the Stock's Ability to Make a New High
Chart courtesy of Mastertrader.com.

CONTINUING TO KEEP IT OBJECTIVE

As I have discussed above, retracement analysis is largely a subjective tool. There are no buyers that always live at a 38.2, 50, or 61.8 percent retracement. However, like all technical tools, there is a degree of self-fulfilling prophecy at work. As a self-fulfilling prophecy, retracements may be one of the better ones. Every charting platform has the ability to automatically draw these retracement levels, as well as the fact that virtually every trader has retracement concepts in mind. What tends to work well is when these subjective measures line up with objective measures.

Just like our discussion about moving averages, the same applies to retracement levels. When a 40 to 50 percent retracement level can land on a minor price support area, we have a subjective area that makes sense because it lines up with an objective area. When retracement levels meet at price support it can lead to a significant rally. If you also think back on our discussion about moving averages, you can use it as yet another item that can line up in the picture. In other words, a strong rally that pulls back to both a minor support level and a moving average, and that is in the 40 to 50 percent retracement level, has the greatest success of moving higher once the initial move begins.

These are a lot of indications that, somewhere in the middle of the pullback from the prior rally, buyers will begin to dominate sellers once again. The more traders with the same tools or similar tools that line up together will increase the odds of a reference point holding. In other words, the more traders focused on the same area, even for different reasons, will act together at that area. For the most part, technical analysis really is one big self-fulfilling prophecy. Realizing this puts it in the proper perspective and removes the mystery many associate with it. A nice example of these technical occurrences lining up is shown in Figure 6.7.

WHAT LIES BEYOND 60 PERCENT?

We are about to explore what happens when prices retrace even more than 60 percent, and how this relates to a double bottom. This discussion can confuse many traders but, once you read this, it should clarify your thinking quite a bit.

You have probably noticed that there are several technical patterns that do not seem to work well even though you see them talked about in various places. Figure 6.8 shows a picture of a retracement that goes beyond 60 percent and the likelihood that the next rally will fail. As retracement comes back more than 60 percent and approaches 70, 80, 90 percent, the same concept applies. The extended pullback has weakened or possibly killed the uptrend. While a bounce may be due, it is likely that the bounce will not go very far and will roll over to a new low. Remember, if the bounce that occurs does not go to a new high, we have ended the uptrend. As we pull back further and further, and get close to a 100 percent retracement, the odds become lower and lower that the stock

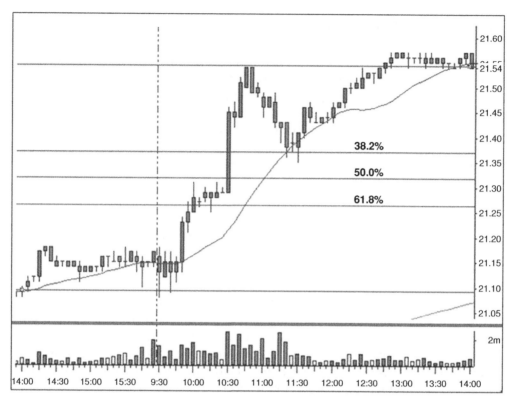

FIGURE 6.7 The 50 Percent Pullback Area Lines Up with Support
Chart courtesy of Mastertrader.com.

will be able to rally to new highs. The lower prices go, the more likely the next rally will stall quickly and may even begin a new downtrend.

It is interesting that as we get to the weakest form of all, we get all the way back to 100 percent retracement. That sets up a chart pattern that many traders see as being a double bottom, which most traders consider bullish. This is in fact, a double bottom, and the truth is that double bottoms are not bullish. Well, at least many of them are not. There are situations where double bottoms can be bullish and be played as longs. However, because traders do not recognize the difference between double bottoms and 100 percent retracements as a whole, they tend to take the trades that fail often and then wonder why.

Remember the starting point: If prices are in an uptrend, a double bottom is actually a weakening of that uptrend. It is 100 percent retracement of the prior rally, which we did not want to see go back more than 60 percent. It is likely that that decline will find support at the prior low and give a bounce. However, this bounce will likely be short-lived and the better trade may be to short the next rally. Refer back to the explanation earlier about a deeper retracement and sellers at the prior high. With a 100 percent retracement

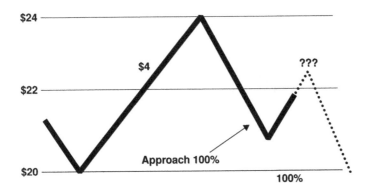

FIGURE 6.8 Larger Retracements Are Even More Bearish
Chart courtesy of Mastertrader.com.

its price may not even get to the prior high. A double bottom bounce is shown in Figure 6.9.

Again, it depends on how all this is setting up. Having this conversation just regarding retracements cannot analyze all of the things that go into determining whether a double bottom will be an effective double bottom that can be traded higher or if it will only produce a technical bounce that will eventually go lower.

It suffices to say, that when prices are in an uptrend, a double bottom is a 100 percent retracement and is considered weakness as to that trend. Yes, a bounce may happen at the support level of the prior bottom. However, this bounce is more likely not to continue the current trend.

However, when prices are in a downtrend it can be a different situation. The double bottom in a downtrend actually stops the downtrend as prices begin to move sideways. In this case, a double bottom can be bullish. Likewise in a sideways pattern, a double bottom can become a triple bottom and so on, and a sideways base likely develops. Playing

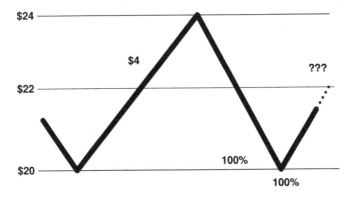

FIGURE 6.9 The Reaction to the Double Bottom Creates a Bounce
Chart courtesy of Mastertrader.com.

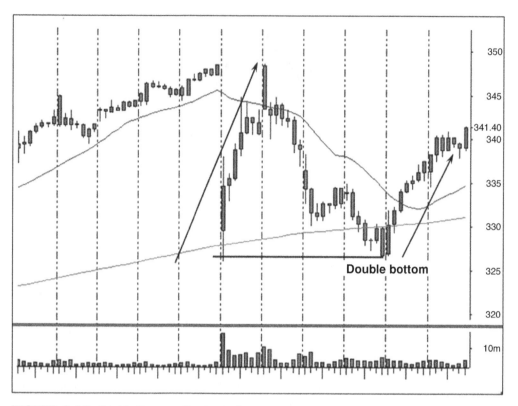

FIGURE 6.10 Double Bottoms Can Be Tricky Areas
Chart courtesy of Mastertrader.com.

the bottoms in this case can also be bullish. (However, keep in mind, it is very difficult to play the first one as a double bottom, or, better said, it is less reliable since you do not know if a base has formed yet. See Figure 6.10.)

In general, the best time to play double bottoms is when you are retesting a prior area of great significance. This can be a prior area from which a substantial rally developed that ended a prior downtrend, or when any high-volume decline or climactic decline ended at the prior low.

RETRACEMENT LEVELS IN DOWNTRENDS

We have been discussing the implications of certain retracement levels when stocks are in uptrends. Naturally, when prices are in downtrends, everything we discussed applies equally as well. When stocks are falling and prices are declining, that pullback, which is the counter rally, will fall into the 40, 50, or 60 percent retracement levels as we discussed. Everything stays the same. Take a look at Figure 6.11, which is simply the reverse of Figure 6.3 detailing retracements in uptrends.

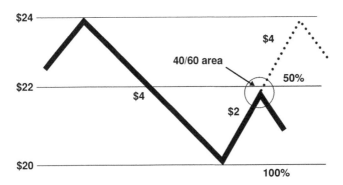

FIGURE 6.11 Retracements in a Downtrend
Chart courtesy of Mastertrader.com.

Regarding terminology, the words retracement and pullback are non-directional in meaning. That means that when prices rally they will correct to the downside and we call that a retracement or pullback. When prices fall and they correct by rallying to the upside, we also call that a retracement or pullback.

Just as with uptrends, when a downtrend retraces 100 percent back to the prior high, a pattern that many call a double top, it is actually a sign of strength in many cases, not weakness. While a double top high may stall the stock temporarily, a downtrend in stock that rallies back 100 percent to form a double top high is actually strong enough to challenge the downtrend and, in many cases, should be respected. Everything discussed so far applies here as well (meaning, the same concepts apply when stocks are falling).

A SPECIAL RETRACEMENT PATTERN

Double tops and double bottoms can be very deceptive in nature. There is one time, however, that the double top or double bottom is a clear indication of a price reversal and can be played. The only problem is that with that extra confirmation comes a late entry. I am referring to what I call "W-" or "M-type" patterns. The reason these are so reliable is that the double top that becomes an M pattern gets confirmation quickly by breaking the trend shortly after the double top forms. Take a look at Figure 6.12.

As the double top begins to form in Figure 6.12 we cannot be sure that the top will hold (when looking at the right side of the M in this case). It is possible that it will stall only for a short time and then proceed higher. However, once prices trade below the last low, which is the middle of the M, we not only have confirmed a double top high, but we have actually broken the uptrend which confirms that the double top high will likely be in place for a while.

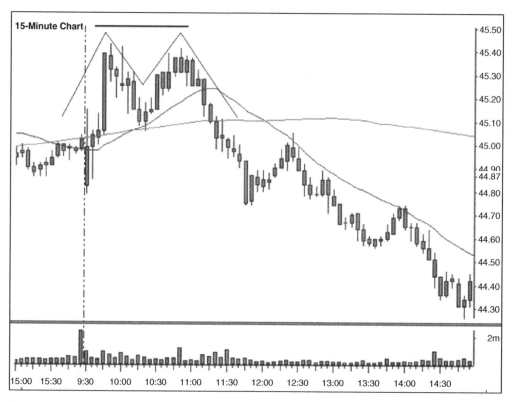

FIGURE 6.12 The M Formation
Chart courtesy of Mastertrader.com.

You may ask what good this is because it is such a late entry. First, while it is late entry, it is the most secure or high odds entry that the move will follow through. In addition, while it is a late entry on this time frame, it is possible that a trader might be playing a larger time frame and simply looking to a smaller time frame to get confirmation of the top being in place. So while this may look like a late entry on this time frame, for a trader playing a larger time frame with a bias of a larger move, the entry may be just fine as shown in Figure 6.13.

Figure 6.13 shows a sell setup occurring at resistance on the 60-minute chart where the trader is uncertain that the stock will hold this resistance level. Therefore, instead of shorting as a sell setup forms on the 60-minute chart shown in figure 6.13, the trader waits for the confirmation of the retest and the M pattern to develop as shown on the 15-minute chart in figure 6.12. As the smaller time frame (15-minute chart) trades under the middle of the M, this confirms his entry on the bigger time frame (60-minute chart) giving a more reliable entry.

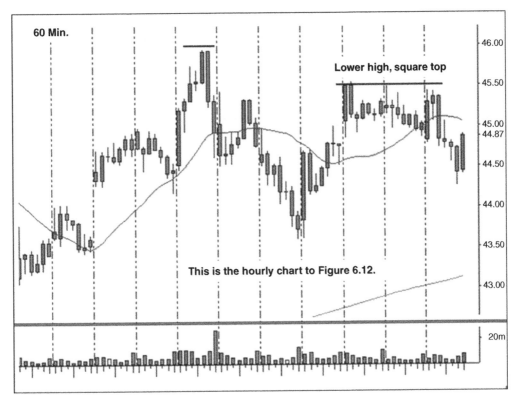

FIGURE 6.13 An M Top Confirms the Entry from a Bigger Time Frame
Chart courtesy of Mastertrader.com.

RETRACEMENT LEVELS IN SIDEWAYS TRENDS

If stocks are not in any type of trend and are just wandering aimlessly, then retracement levels do not matter. However, sometimes stocks fall into a very nice wide sideways pattern. When stocks repeatedly hit similar highs or similar lows (please review the discussion of major support and major resistance in Chapter 3) they are consistently doing 100 percent retracements. In this case, however, because the stock is not trending up or down, the 100 percent retracement is exactly what is expected. Once a significant support or resistance level is setup, we expect to see 100 percent retracements from the top to the bottom and back to the top of the base repeatedly. So, the rule of thumb in an orderly sideways pattern is to expect 100 percent retracements from the top to the bottom of the base. Figure 6.14 shows this example with consistent 100 percent retracements in a sideways trend.

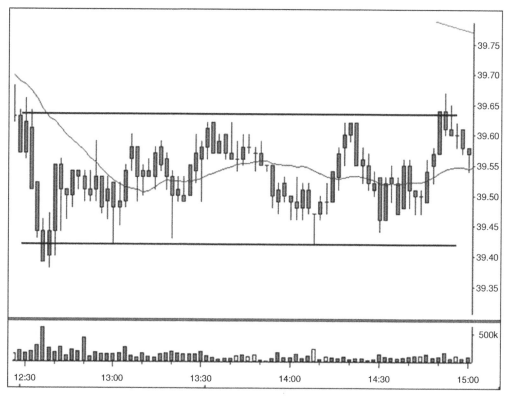

FIGURE 6.14 100 Percent Retracements Are Expected in Sideways Patterns
Chart courtesy of Mastertrader.com.

WHAT LIES BEYOND 100 PERCENT?

A funny thing happens when prices go beyond the 100 percent level. This phenomenon is best observed in wide sideways patterns as just discussed. When prices are traveling between the top and bottom of the base, the bottom of the base can often be a very loose area. If the stock travels a good distance to get from the top to the bottom of the base, and then falls an additional amount below what appears to be the bottom of the base, many novice traders will short this as a break of support. However, this is a very low odds trade after the stock has already dropped the entire distance from the top of the base to the bottom of the base. This is one of the worst entry points for a trade that there is. The influx of short-sellers below the base are usually proven wrong and as the stock begins to come back into the base, the normal buyers of support coupled with the new short-sellers who need to cover, usually drive the stock back up significantly into the base again. From here, one of two things can happen. This could truly be the start of a breakdown of the base, but those who shorted below the base find themselves with a very bad entry. It also can be that the slop going below the bottom of the base simply was just

FIGURE 6.15 Many Traders View This as a Breakdown
Chart courtesy of Mastertrader.com.

that, slop, and the stock will target the top of the base again. This frustrates many new traders repeatedly (see Figure 6.15) and is actually one of the biggest mistakes traders can make, which is to short what appears to be a break of support after the stock has already dropped a considerable distance.

Whether the stock has only a temporary rebound, or whether the stock is actually going back to the top of the base, buying the stock on the changing of the guard bar can be one of the most reliable plays in trading. Naturally, there is a limit to how far the stock drops before you have to consider the fact that it truly had a severe breakdown (meaning, stocks that have a quick hard fall below a base and then begin a very quick and immediate rebound).

I call this concept the 110 percent retracement play, due to the fact that the stock has actually retraced beyond that 100 percent level. It is a bit of a paradox because the greater the retracement, the weaker the stock. Nevertheless, at some point the rule snaps as a stock is overextended and a rebound becomes almost a sure thing. If you watch for this event, you will see it happen time and time again. Yet most traders will be on the wrong side of this trade most of the time because they fail to see this pattern even when it routinely happens. It usually comes from following a set of rules believed to be accurate and when the rules do not work, traders continue to assume they will work the next time and do not adjust accordingly.

Where Did the Retracement End?

Another issue to note when discussing retracements is whether or not the excessive retracement also violates other technical focal points on the chart. Figure 6.16 shows the retracement was more than 50 percent, giving us a heads up as to the possibility that the stock is not as bullish as we think. However, notice that in order for prices to retrace greater than 50 percent, they traveled through a complete void and did not violate any other technical feature.

Compare this to Figure 6.17 where the retracement was also greater than 50 percent, and prices had to battle their way through a minor support area and the moving average in order to violate this 50 percent level. This would give extra cause to be concerned

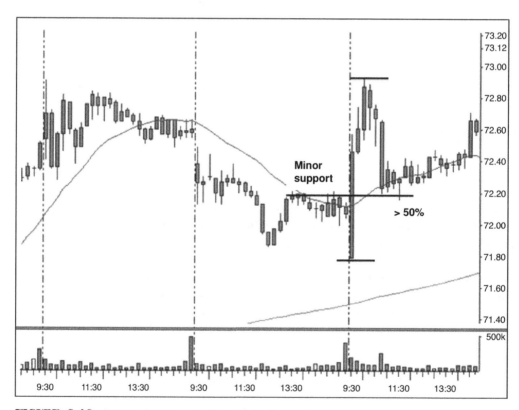

FIGURE 6.16 A Large Retracement Stays above Support
Chart courtesy of Mastertrader.com.

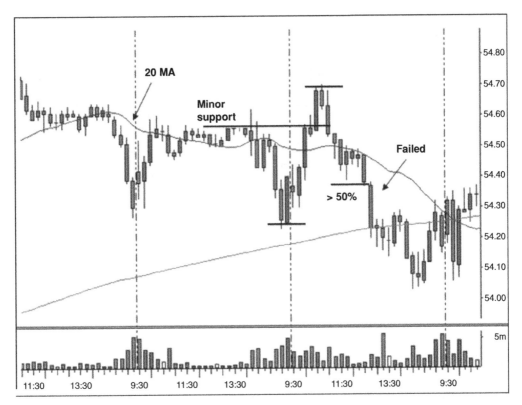

FIGURE 6.17 A Large Retracement That Violates Other Technical Areas
Chart courtesy of Mastertrader.com.

because not only did the subjective price retracement area not hold, but the objective areas of price support also were violated. It simply reemphasizes the more things you have working for you in an area, the more likely a play will work. Also, the more things that you violate in a certain area, the more likely the play will fail.

THE BIGGER PICTURE

Another great use of retracement concepts for the more advanced trader is noticing the relationship of retracements as they occur throughout time frames. Retracements that go beyond expected levels can be looked at carefully after the stocks have a bullish run. However, to gain a better insight as to how bearish those retracements are, it is necessary to look at the bigger time frames and see what is happening in the big picture.

In the left half of Figure 6.18, we have a stock that made a significant run and retraced almost 100 percent of the distance of a breakout that we presume to be a new

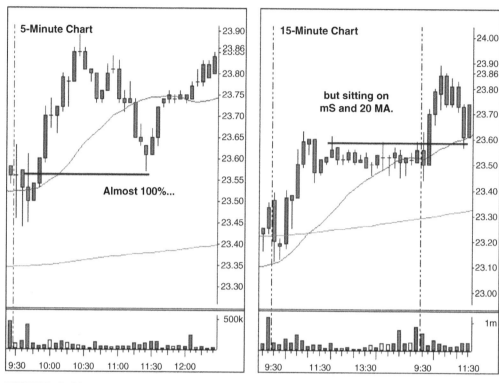

FIGURE 6.18 A Look at Two Different Time Frames
Chart courtesy of Mastertrader.com.

uptrend. This should be considered somewhat bearish. However if you look at the bigger time frame in the right half of Figure 6.18, you will notice that the bigger time frame actually does experience a new breakout from a considerably long consolidation. Since this is a new breakout, the initial steep retracement at the start of a new uptrend is a frequent occurrence and does not always end the bullishness of the stock. By looking at the bigger time frame, we see that a new breakout often gets initial selling the first time, but follows through to the upside despite the initial selling. After the move is underway, the retracements should be within the bullish area and controlled.

Figure 6.19 shows the contrary by depicting a stock that had excessive pullback. However, as we look at the bigger time frame, we see that it is extended to the point that it is almost climactic. This extended pullback forms a big topping tail in the bigger time frame and, after the extended move, prices that have this top must be respected as being a short-term top. In this case, we would not be interested in buying the excessive pullback because the smaller time frame warns against it and the bigger time frame is telling us it is the correct way to go. You can find examples like these repeatedly on charts.

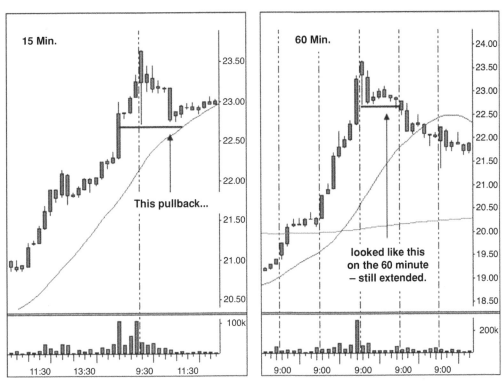

FIGURE 6.19 Another Look at Two Different Time Frames
Chart courtesy of Mastertrader.com.

IN SUMMARY

Retracement analysis is one of the tools used to objectively determine strength or weakness and the likelihood of continuing the initial move. Retracement analysis is subjective when trying to find the exact area of reversal by using only retracement analysis and nothing else. It becomes a much higher odds concept, even as a subjective one, when coupled with objective forms of support and resistance.

The concept of retracement analysis across multiple time frames is one of the small parts involved in analyzing different time frames and we discuss multiple time frame analysis in the next chapter. Please note that it is one of the most important chapters in this book and can help you understand why many trades you have been looking at may not be functioning as you feel they should. For now, however, if you can understand and realize that retracements can have different meanings depending upon where the bigger picture is, it will serve you well. Then, the concepts in Chapter 7 will deepen your understanding of all the technical issues we have discussed.

Bar-by-Bar Analysis

Each Bar Tells Us Something

Trading, or understanding the markets, is really not about absolutes. Each time period in the market is like a fingerprint; it is unique and will never be reproduced exactly. Trading is not about guarantees. Many aspiring traders spend a good deal of their initial time looking for the Holy Grail to guarantee the success of all future trades. No such Grail exists, at least not in the form that most traders are looking for. If there was one, I would have found it by now. Trading is not about exactness, although we all start out seeking to gain certainty that our trades will work.

Many traders new to the market carry the habits of prior professions with them and continuously look for the precision that comes from accounting or engineering or a similar profession. The market does not tolerate this type of approach. Trading is about understanding probabilities. The only way to really get an edge in the market—all that I do in the market and all that we teach at Pristine—is to find patterns that have high probabilities of a certain outcome.

So far, the chapters in this book deal with finding certain occurrences on charts and understanding that, once the proper setup is in place, there is a higher probability that a certain series of events will follow. The further in the future we try to extrapolate those probabilities, the less accurate they will be. Another way to state this is that the highest degree of probability exists at the moment a trade is entered, when it is entered in the proper fashion. Every minute, hour, or day after that moment brings lesser probabilities as time marches forward.

That is the reason for bar-by-bar analysis, which is the focus of this chapter. What we are doing is continually updating the probabilities of success as the trader's progress. This analysis does not change anything that we have discussed up to this point. What it does is offer you a tool to continue to analyze the likelihood of success of the current trade, or the continuation of the current trend. This tool will also tell you when the likelihood of success is fading.

OBJECTIVITY IS STILL THE GOAL

Let's use bar-by-bar analysis to analyze the likelihood of the success of a current trade. We are talking about a trader who is in a position and trying to determine if it is still a good position. Understand that this process should not be overused. If you have done your research and entered a trade properly, based on your knowledge and your plan for the current trade, it is not appropriate to doubt that trade only minutes later when it is part of a trading plan. Meaning, it wasn't an impulsive trade that was entered because prices started to move and you decided to jump on. However, as time progresses and we begin to see that the odds are shifting, there are times when circumstances change. Perhaps we looked at the trade slightly incorrectly at the beginning and are now seeing it more clearly. Perhaps the trend has changed in the broader markets or the stock begins to trade a bit more erratically. This makes us think the trade is no longer the same trade as when we first looked at it.

Hence the term, bar-by-bar analysis. We are going to look at analyzing each new bar that forms and discuss the relevance it has on the existing pattern. This information is useful beyond analyzing an open position. By the same analysis, it is also very useful to simply analyze the ongoing trend in any stock or market. Here, we may be looking at entering the position based on the likelihood that the trend will continue. We are not in the trade yet, but we are looking for the best entry point. Some trends are very strong and are clearly playable. Some trends are tentative or in the early stages of developing and need to be confirmed. This bar-by-bar analysis can help us decide when we want to play the lesser trends, and can also help us to see when the strong trends may be ending or faltering.

Many of the prior chapters discussed the proper use of technical tools. Traders use many tools incorrectly because they are used in a subjective way, rather than in an objective way, when looking at prices. Bar-by-bar analysis is a little different. Its very nature exists just so traders can have an objective view of what is going on in the moment as it relates to the past. Once traders put money into the market, their perceptions tend to change to justify the position they are currently holding. Their view or bias can become vulnerable to being clouded about what is actually happening when they have money at risk. Bar-by-bar analysis is designed to help force a trader to maintain an objective view of their position at all times. Its intent is to focus on what is actually happening now, rather than what has happened in the past, or what the trader wishes to be happening. Once you learn this concept of bar-by-bar analysis it becomes virtually impossible to rationalize what is happening in the moment. If you have had difficulty taking stops, you're going to find that this tool will help you greatly.

A QUICK REVIEW OF INDIVIDUAL BARS

In Chapter 2, we discussed the use of candlesticks on our charts. Let's now focus on some of the key individual candles we will need to know for bar-by-bar analysis. The key

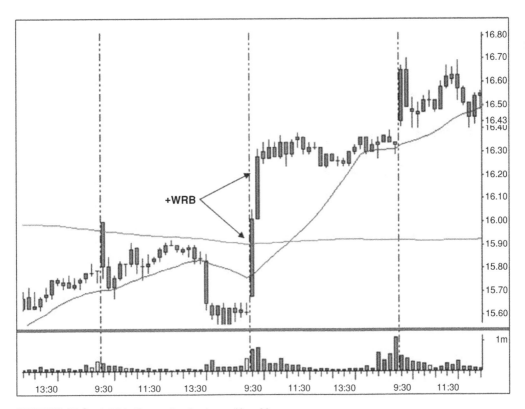

FIGURE 7.1 A Wide Range Bar Ignites a New Move
Chart courtesy of Mastertrader.com.

individual candles we need to understand are the Bullish Wide Range Bar (+ WRB), The Bearish Wide Range Bar (−WRB), The Narrow Range Bar (NRB), The Bullish Changing of the Guard (+ COG), The Bearish Changing of the Guard (− COG), The Bottoming Tail (BT) and The Topping Tail (TT).

As you may recall, the wide range bars are range expansion bars that show an increasing dominance of either buyers or sellers. They can show great commitment to a new move, or can begin to show exhaustion to an old move. They, in general, are showing increases in momentum. The expectation is that wide range bars, following periods of inactivity, will begin new moves that will continue in the move of the wide range bar. Figure 7.1 shows an example of a bullish wide range bar showing commitment to a new move.

On the other hand, narrow range bars show slowing momentum. A slowing of momentum in and of itself does not give us a clear idea what is going to happen next. Strong moves often rest by slowing in momentum before continuing their move. After a strong momentum move, prices can reverse, and the precursor to prices reversing is usually a slowing the momentum as shown by a narrow range bar. Figure 7.2 shows a narrow range bar that allows the stock to rest before continuing higher.

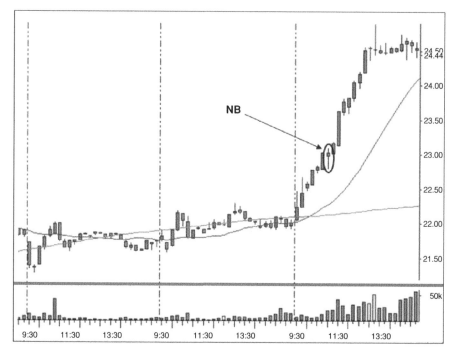

FIGURE 7.2 Narrow Range Bar Slows Momentum before the Stock Continues Higher
Chart courtesy of Mastertrader.com.

Changing of the guard bars can have special significance. As you recall they show a change of momentum on the current time frame. If the COG bar is happening in the proper area, we will expect follow-through in the direction of the COG. When the COG bar happens in the proper area and it totally fails, that tells us that prices will likely continue for a period of time in the original direction (counter to the COG direction). In the next section we will be discussing how to evaluate patterns as they follow up on a COG bar. Figure 7.3 shows a bullish COG bar with follow up to the upside.

Last, candles with tails are treated similarly to COG bars. When prices form a bottoming tail in the correct area, we expect follow-through on the following bars to the upside. If the bottoming tail forms in the proper area and it fails on subsequent bars, we expect a continued move in the failure direction. Figure 7.4 shows a bottoming tail bar with follow-through on the subsequent bars.

HOW THE BARS INTERACT

We now know the implications of any single bar. Now we want to look at how bars interact and how they either meet or fail the expectations of the current move. To better understand that concept, I will be using two-bar combinations to see how they interact

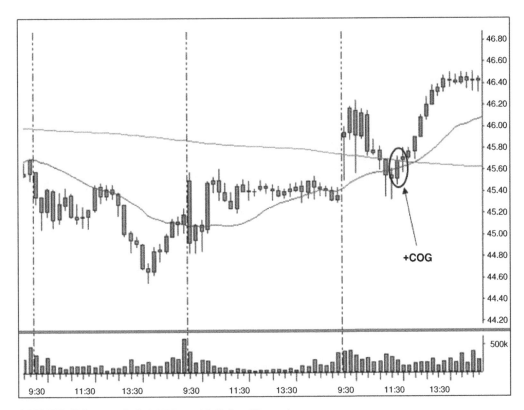

FIGURE 7.3 A Bullish COG Bar with Follow-Through
Chart courtesy of Mastertrader.com.

with each other. For this discussion I will discuss bullish bars, but the same concept applies in reverse to bearish bars. Figure 7.5 shows three different combinations of inter-actions between two bars.

In the first combination, we show a bullish green bar (dark shading) with the second bar closing relatively bullishly as well. We will define the term relatively bullishly as closing anywhere above bar number one or an intrusion of less than 40 percent into bar number one. In other words, after a bullish first bar, at least 60 percent of the bullish first bar is remaining. Naturally, the most bullish combination would be to have the second bar green and closing well above the high of the first bar.

In the second combination, we see a second bar that has intruded about halfway into bar number one. This is considered neutral, as half the bar has been engulfed and half of the original bullish bar still remains. You will notice that we are discussing once again the concept of bullishness remaining, just as we were doing when we were discussing retracements in multiple bar patterns. It is the same concept: If bar number one is truly bullish, we should find buyers before the bar is completely reversed.

In the third combination, we are interested in seeing if that second bar, which has encroached upon the first bar, is more than 60 percent or has nearly engulfed the

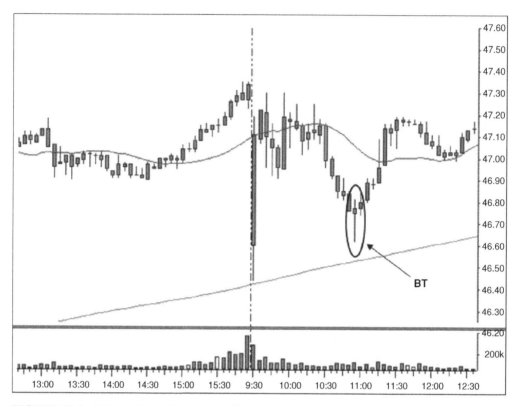

FIGURE 7.4 A Bottoming Tail Bar with Follow-Through
Chart courtesy of Mastertrader.com.

first bar. The more the first bar is engulfed, the more bearish it becomes. In this case, the bar was totally engulfed. Here the expectation for continued bullish movement is greatly decreased, as all the bulls in the first bar have been proven wrong. You will find many names for these different two-bar combinations in Japanese candlestick language, and in general technical language. This last pattern is the most commonly known. When the second bar totally engulfs the first bar it is called a bearish engulfing bar. We sometimes use other terms for this combination such as a Bearish 180 bar or a Bull Trap. The names

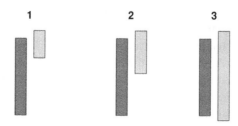

FIGURE 7.5 Bullish Two-Bar Combinations
Chart courtesy of Mastertrader.com.

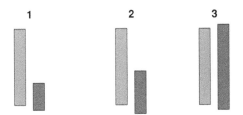

FIGURE 7.6 Bearish Two-Bar Combinations
Chart courtesy of Mastertrader.com.

do not matter, but understand that the implication of the pattern does matter. The bar-by-bar method moves you beyond candle or pattern names. Whatever is happening, you will understand it without names that others may or may not have associated with them.

Let's take a look at these same three combinations from the bearish side in Figure 7.6.

Here we see bar number one in the first combo as a bearish bar and the expectation is that we will see bearish follow-through to the downside. If the second bar is able to close below the first bar, or remove less than 40 percent of the first bar, we expect to see a continued downward movement in prices. If the second bar is able to close between 40 to 60 percent of the way into bar number one, the expectations for continued downward movement in prices are neutral. If bar number two removes more than 60 percent of our number one, or totally engulfs it, as shown in Figure 7.6, the bearishness of bar number one has been largely removed and the expectation for lower prices is greatly diminished.

You can now begin to see that by looking at how the individual bars form and how they interact from one bar to the next, we begin to get a feel for the likelihood of prices continuing to move in the desired direction.

Now let's analyze an ongoing Pristine Buy Setup. Assuming we have a chart that is in an uptrend, and after the last rally it has gone to new highs, the pullback sets up a proper Pristine Buy Setup in a support area. We have a bullish COG that forms, and we enter the trade over the bullish COG bar. An example of such a setup is shown in Figure 7.7.

The setup is in place and we enter as we trade above the bullish COG bar. Let's say the bar that we used for entry closes strong as shown in Figure 7.8.

Assuming we enter this trade and want prices to continue higher, the bar-by-bar analysis so far is showing us what we want to see. With the entry bar closing near the high, even though it is a narrow bar, it has not encroached upon the COG bar and has moved in the correct direction. Everything is still good for the trade moving higher.

Let's say the first bar after the entry bar, that is the second bar of the trade, closes very bullishly as shown in Figure 7.9. Naturally, with this setup, everything still looks bullish and we have no expectations for the trade to reverse. Do take note however that this wide green bar is the third green bar and the short-term pattern may be getting extended. This means it would not be unreasonable to see a neutral or slightly bearish bar form without any damage to the pattern. This is what happens in Figure 7.10.

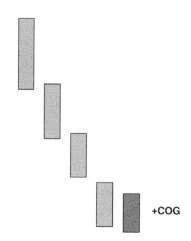

FIGURE 7.7 A Pristine Buy Setup Showing a Bullish COG Bar
Chart courtesy of Mastertrader.com.

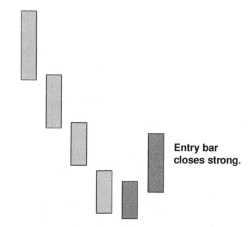

FIGURE 7.8 The Entry Bar Closes
Chart courtesy of Mastertrader.com.

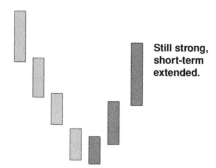

FIGURE 7.9 Bar Number Two Closes Strong
Chart courtesy of Mastertrader.com.

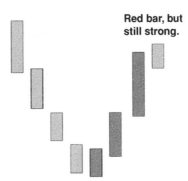

FIGURE 7.10 Bar Number Three Closes Red
Chart courtesy of Mastertrader.com.

In Figure 7.10, we are seeing a red bar for the first time in the pattern. Naturally, if you are long this position, you would prefer not to see any red at all. However, that is not the question at hand. Most trades, even the best of them, will not move directly from point A to point B without taking a rest. The question we are trying to answer here is, what is an acceptable rest for a stock on its journey from the entry to the target? A red bar is being shown here and while it is a significant red bar, it is simply a reaction to the strong move the stock had to the upside so far. Notice that it has encroached only about 25 percent into the prior bar and is therefore not considered threatening. However, imagine if that bar has a long topping tail on it. See how bar-by-bar can change your view based on what is happening?

If the next bar continues a downward movement and begins to erase most of the wide green bar, the expectations of the stock continuing on to make a new high without a much more serious decline first, becomes very limited. You can see this example in Figure 7.11.

FIGURE 7.11 Another Red Bar Begins to Damage the Pattern
Chart courtesy of Mastertrader.com.

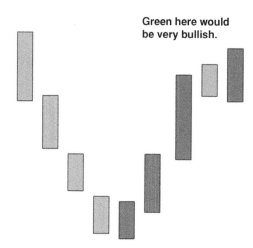

FIGURE 7.12 A Green Bar Keeps the Trend Going
Chart courtesy of Mastertrader.com.

Compare that to the expectations that would happen if the fourth bar were a green bar that erased the prior red bar. This example is shown in Figure 7.12.

Whenever we see a red bar get erased by green bars, it is a very bullish sign in our bar-by-bar analysis. Ignoring red is what you always want to see when expecting the prices to move higher. One way to view the concept of a bar-by-bar analysis on the bullish side is to see how much respect red bars command. The red bars become significant when they start growing in size and/or when they are not immediately erased by green bars. Then we know that the bears are getting better control of the stock. If red bars are temporary and are erased quickly, we know that the bulls are still in charge and this is what we want to see if we are expecting prices to go higher.

When red bars are being erased or ignored, what is happening is that traders focused on pullback patterns in a smaller time frame are buying the stock as it pulls back, or it could even be those scalpers reading time and sales. As demand begins to overcome the supply that is causing the pullback, the momentum shifts back to the upside and the red bar is erased and followed by a green bar. To those only viewing the higher time frame this simply looks like a red bar ignored (RBI). We will discuss this further when we talk about multiple time frames. For now, just view RBIs as a bullish sign and what should happen in an uptrend when buyers are in control.

Let's go back and take a look at a different scenario for the third bar. Figure 7.13 shows bar number three being much more bearish than the one we showed previously.

Here the prior wide green bar has been largely negated by the next bar, and this is changing our expectations. As we discussed, if more than half of a significant bar is erased, it begins to change the odds of prices being able to continue higher. Figure 7.13 shows a pattern that is likely going to stall or continue lower over the next couple of bars. If that last red bar was to be erased on the next bar, that would be a very bullish

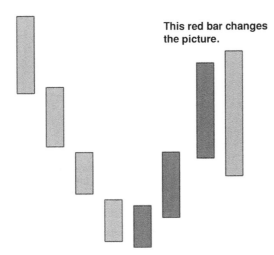

This red bar changes the picture.

FIGURE 7.13 A Solid Red Bar Changes the Pattern
Chart courtesy of Mastertrader.com.

sign but a low odds event that it would occur. In other words, it is not likely to happen, but if it did, it would be very bullish again.

You should now have a good understanding of the likelihood of follow-through to any series of bars. However, you may still be asking, for what purpose to use this information? We are currently looking at these bars as if they were in a vacuum. In a vacuum, all we can do is take this information and make intelligent comments about it as we have just done. However, where the beauty of this can really come into play is when you see the whole price pattern developing in front of you.

For example, let's look at that green bar that we have shown to be a wide green bar in our example and say it advanced into a very significant resistance area. Since this was a wide bar and occurring after two prior bars up, we may very well use this green bar to take profits as it has run into a resistance area.

If we are not at a target but close enough that our plan says that we need to protect profits, let's take a look at a way to do that. What if after the wide green bar we form a small red bar as in Figure 7.14. The next bar begins to turn green when we trade to more than half the red bar, we may want to raise our stop to the low of the red bar, as it becomes a sort of line in the sand. Either that red bar will be a stalling bar, and prices will continue higher, or if this new move up on the current green bar fails, we will see prices going lower so we know it is time to take profits on long positions.

ADDITIONAL THOUGHTS

The concept of using bar-by-bar analysis must be taken in perspective with the strategy being played, the time frame being used, and one's trading plan. Many traders tend to over-manage their plays, and sometimes using bar-by-bar analysis can be an excuse

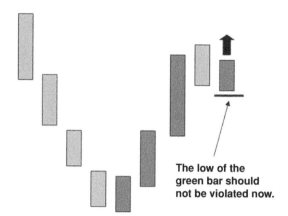

FIGURE 7.14 A Small Red Bar Becomes a Line in the Sand
Chart courtesy of Mastertrader.com.

to step in and exit a trade early. Here are some rules of thumb to keep in mind when applying bar-by-bar analysis.

First, only use bar-by-bar analysis on the relevant time frame. In other words, if you are taking your strategy and setting targets based on a 15-minute chart, use the 15-minute chart to do your analysis. If you study a one-minute chart, you will always find an excuse to exit the trade. Remember, no stock moves from point A to point B without pulling back or resting along the way. We only want to note if the rest the stock is taking is excessive or trying to tell us something.

Second, you must take into account the strategy being played and the potential target for the stock. The larger the target you are expecting, the more you must be tolerant of pullbacks and consolidations along the way. This goes hand-in-hand with playing the correct time frame as well, but, simply understand: large moves will sometimes require larger pullbacks that may be totally acceptable to bigger patterns.

The decisions of when and how to use bar-by-bar analysis should really be worked into your trading plan and be something that is a precursor to your trading activity. You must have an exact plan of what you consider to be acceptable or not acceptable for a stock's behavior on the way to its intended target. If you wait until the middle of the trade, in the middle the trading day, and do not have your bar-by-bar analysis well thought out, you will find yourself exiting many trades that were probably better left unattended. You may also miss good opportunities to save profits by not understanding what the right time was to get out.

Lastly, we have discussed the concept of bar-by-bar from the point of view of having already been in a trade. You can and should read bar-by-bar on a stock or market that you have not entered to assess what has happened. This will give you a clear view of how prices have traded and guide your bias accordingly. From that point of view, each new bar as it forms may be an entry point (for example, if you are looking to trade a breakout of a stock in an uptrend based on your prior bar-by-bar analysis). A bottoming tail bar just formed, the tail of that bar is under the last several bars, and prices have closed above the opening price and near the high of the bar. What should you do? Right, it's time to buy! You've come to that conclusion with nothing more than price data. No other indicators needed.

IN SUMMARY

Remember that the goal of bar-by-bar analysis is to keep your mind focused on what is actually happening to prices, not what you hope will happen to prices. A funny thing happens when we are involved in a trade. We begin to lose our objectivity and begin to analyze the pattern based on what we hope, or what we fear, will happen. This means that some traders may stay in a trade that is no longer working hoping to hang on to their original trade without taking a loser. Some traders may experience anxiety over needing to take profits and come up with any excuse that they can to exit a trade. The idea here is to use a simple objective method to determine if the trade is still meeting your requirements to hold the position, or if one of various management concepts should be introduced. Those concepts may include exiting the entire trade, raising or lowering a stop for all or part of the trade, or taking partial profits at that time. Management options will be discussed later in this book.

You may discover one last issue in using bar-by-bar analysis: you may have an accurate grasp of bar-by-bar analysis and know what the proper action is to take, but you may not take the action. Traders who can properly analyze patterns but hesitate to do what is needed, lack the discipline to be good traders and this alone may hinder their career. As you use this tool and the other information in this book your confidence in what you see on the chart will grow.

Bar-by-bar analysis can be a very powerful concept that keeps you focused on what is actually happening with prices. It is part of what I use in my everyday trading to read the moment rather than getting stuck in the past analysis or to not project the future. The future is the unknown and we are playing the odds that what is happening will continue.

There is so much focus in this business of trading on trying to predict what will happen with methods like Elliot Wave, Gann, Cycles and general indicator use. If you are there or have been there, I hope that you are beginning to see the light and a new way.

Price patterns for individual stocks are all unique, but there is one common thread that binds them all together. They all make up the stock market and when money is coming into the market, and the market prices are rising, this naturally puts pressure on most stocks to rise. It is known as the "tide that lifts all boats," and, naturally, it is also true for stocks having a bias to fall when money is leaving the market.

Up until now, we have focused on an in-depth look at price bars and price patterns but, coming up in Chapter 8, we will look at additional pieces of information that will help us tell if the price action of the stock market can be trusted, or if the trend may be close to changing. We will look at the concept of market internals. This concept helps us in such a way, it's as if we were taking an x-ray of the market.

Market Internals

Examining the Direction
of the Market

This chapter is about using market internals. Market internals are a set of tools or gauges that we use to get a better look into the likely direction, continued direction or likelihood of the market reversing. More accurately, they are helping us to determine the veracity of the current trend that exists. In this chapter, we also look at Inter-Market Analysis and how it can affect your long-term view of the market. Before we have this discussion about looking into the internals of the market, though, perhaps we should talk about why we care about the market in the first place.

Many traders like to trade the market itself. I'm one of them, since it offers trading based on pure technical information. The market can be traded in a variety of ways. There are symbols that are known as ETFs, which stands for Exchange Traded Funds. These symbols include QQQ, SPY, QLD, QID, SSO, SDS, DXD, DDM, and many others. They let you trade the entire market they represent by simply trading one symbol. An example of that is shown in Figure 8.1. Many of them allow you to short the market by going long the ETF. This is known as an inverse ETF where the ETF moves up as the market moves down. Many of the ETFs also represent a leverage amount of two or three times the underlying issue. That means that there are symbols that you can trade long that would allow you to be three times short the QQQ or SPY. Many traders also prefer to trade the E-mini futures contracts for some of the markets. These provide additional leverage and offer tax advantages as well. There are many E-mini future contracts available, the most commonly traded are known as the NQ, the ES, or the YM. These are the abbreviated letters that stand for the NASDAQ 100, the S&P 500, and the Dow Industrial markets. A typical futures contract for example would look like NQ Z0. The NQ stands for the NASDAQ 100, and in the Z0 means that it expires in December of the year 2010.

Regardless of what instrument is used to trade the market, traders who trade the market must understand the movement of the market as their primary job. Throughout this book, you notice that as I discuss the movement of prices, I frequently refer to them

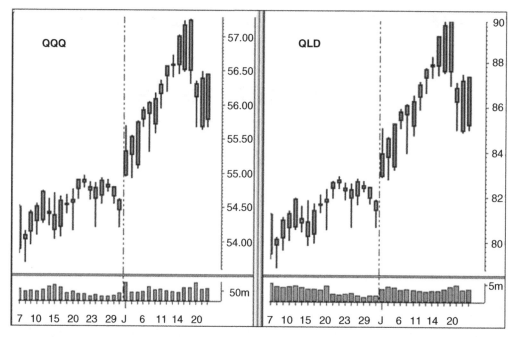

FIGURE 8.1 Comparison between the QQQ and the QLD
Chart courtesy of Mastertrader.com.

as either a stock or market. We really do not care in terms of technical analysis using the Pristine Method whether a set of prices represents an individual stock or the collection of stocks known as a particular market. Therefore, for those who want to trade the market, it is imperative that you understand the market.

However, even for those traders who prefer to trade individual stocks, the market should not be ignored. The market can be looked at as the "tide that raises all boats." Trading against a strong trend in the market will be a lower-odds trade regardless of the trend of the particular stock. For days in which the market is not trending strongly, this concept is less important. The individual stock trend is always most important; however, it is always best to trade in the direction of the market when possible. This will give the best results. This may be stating the obvious, but many traders miss this important point. See Figure 8.2.

So it becomes imperative when trading, regardless of what we are trading, that we have an understanding of where the underlying market is likely going. To analyze the underlying market, we simply apply the Pristine Method to the price pattern of the market as we have to all tradable instruments. Because the market is so commonly traded, there have been many indicators that have been created to look at the market. Many of these are worthless, as are most of the technical indicators that are put on charts. However, market internals bring us information that is useful to help us determine the strength of the underlying trend that the market is currently showing, or if it is waning.

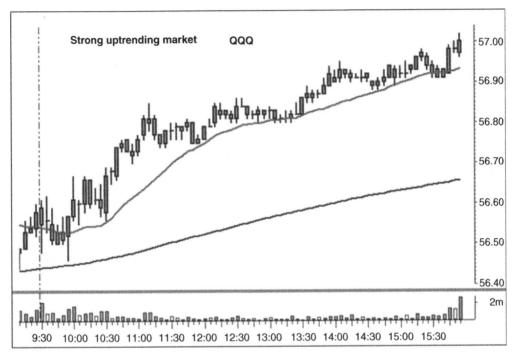

FIGURE 8.2 Always Play with the Market When It Is Trending Strong
Chart courtesy of Mastertrader.com.

DETERMINING PRICE MOVEMENT

It is important at this point to understand a basic question about trading. The question is, "What makes prices go up"? While there may be a whole variety of answers that are at least partially correct, the true answer is that prices move up because there are more potential buyers than potential sellers. This may sound a little comical to some of you, but it is a basic truth that has to be understood. This is the only thing that makes prices move up. When there is more demand for a stock than there is supply of that stock, prices move up. This is a concept that exists throughout the economic structure of the world. There may be good earnings on a particular stock, there may be great news about a particular stock, the stock may have just discovered a great new cure for some disease, but if more people are selling the stock than buying it, the stock price will decline. This is why we focus on prices and why we focus on living in the moment and not making suppositions about what commentators or news may bring to the stock price.

The next issue gets a little tricky. If the price pattern is all that matters, then why do we need market internals? One answer is that perhaps we do not need them. As with everything else I have taught you in this book, price is king and is all that really matters. The question we are getting at here is, what about when price is not giving us a clear answer? We want to take a long trade, we want the market to be behind us, and we are not sure if this trend is likely to continue or not. One way to look at this issue is to go back to the question of what makes prices rise. There truly could be two answers to this question. Prices rise when there are more potential buyers than sellers; but they will also rise when there are fewer potential sellers than buyers. This may sound like semantics, but herein lies the reason for market internals.

Picture a very bullish stock with buyers who are tripping over each other to try to buy the stock. There are plenty of sellers who are willing to sell, but the buyers simply outnumber them and continue to drive prices up all day. A constant battle is going on between buyers and sellers, and the buyers simply have the numbers over the sellers. Picture another instance when prices are going up, and it is simply because the very few buyers that are out there do not have any sellers from which to buy. In other words, the sellers are not interested in selling at this particular price. As sellers back away from their offers, buyers are forced to chase them even though the actual number of buyers may be few. The trend may be up, but will not be sustainable. If you can picture this as pushing a string rather than the normal pulling of a string, it may help you understand where market internals can come in to help give us an indication of the actual strength of the rally that's underway. An example of unquestionable strength by the bulls is shown in Figure 8.3.

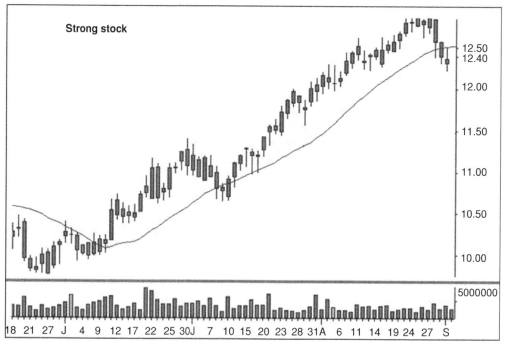

FIGURE 8.3 A Very Strong Trend Where Buyers Are Relentless
Chart courtesy of Mastertrader.com.

WHEN TO BE DIFFERENT

Before we walk through the handful of market internals that I like to refer to, realize that some of these market internals operate on the concept of taking a contrarian view. A contrarian view is when you are going against the majority. When we talk about following trends, we are following the majority. We are following the big money. This is what we normally do. However, when things get to the extreme, they can give us an indication that a turn may be coming. It is similar to the concept of a climactic sell setup. At some point, a stock will simply run out of potential buyers at that particular price. When it does, prices cannot advance.

For example, what if we were able to survey all the big fund managers every week, and asked them one simple question: "Are you bullish or bearish for the long term of the market"? There would naturally be a wide variety of responses and those responses would vary somewhat due to the current state of the market. However, what if as time went on a huge percentage of these people surveyed started to say "Bullish"? At first glance you may think, "Well, if they are bullish than I should be too." However, this is really a backward-looking survey. Once their long-term view of the market is clearly bullish, it means that they are fully invested in the market. Why would anybody say that they are bearish if they had all their money in the market? Therefore, when this number begins to rise to an extreme reading of bullishness, we know that all the big money is in the market, and therefore there is little money left to fuel the market in the future. There actually is a survey that does ask just that question. Naturally, nothing is perfect, but it is one of the indicators we can use to get a feel for the potential of the market to continue a trend, once the trend is well underway.

FAVORITE MARKET INTERNALS

The most common market internal indicators that I use during the trading day are known as the TICK and TRIN readings. I keep these on my main screen all day and refer to them on a regular basis. These two readings are available for both the NASDAQ market and for the NYSE. Let's discuss the TICK first. However, I only use the NYSE TICK. The NASDAQ TICK for me is redundant information, it updates slower than the NYSE, and the NYSE is more widely followed.

The TICK

TICK readings can theoretically be done for any market or for any group of stocks. However, information is commonly only available for TICK readings on the NASDAQ market (NAS) and for the New York stock market (NYSE). They are also available for the Dow 30, but since the Dow 30 is only 30 stocks, we do not typically study or use this market as an indicator of the broader market. Futures traders can find the DOW TICK, which is called TIKI, helpful if used as a buddy system with the NYSE TICK. (This is something covered in detail in a class we teach at Pristine about trading Futures and you can see the preface for more information on Pristine.)

There is also an issue with using the NASDAQ TICK. Here, we have the reverse problem. The NASDAQ TICK takes its readings on all the stocks in the entire NASDAQ. After the NASDAQ 100 (the top 100 capitalized NASDAQ stocks), all the remaining stocks make up only a small percentage of the total capitalization and volume of the NASDAQ exchange. Since TICK readings are comprised of the entire market, they are frequently not an accurate picture of the true movement of the stocks that matter. Therefore, the only reading we really refer to is the NYSE TICK.

What the TICK actually measures is the difference between the number of stocks trading on an uptick or on a downtick at any moment on the NYSE. When traders sell a stock at a price below the price of the preceding transaction it causes a downtick. When traders buy a stock at a price above the price of the preceding transaction it causes an uptick. By comparing the total number of stocks trading on upticks to those trading on downticks, we can get a value for how aggressive buyers and sellers are at any moment or the lack thereof, and how that aggressiveness may change throughout the day by tracking the TICK readings on a chart.

On an intraday basis, I view the NYSE TICK on a bar chart. Years ago I used a candlestick format just like any other chart I looked at. In time, I decided to use a bar chart since all I was interested in was the value it was at and its turning points, not the patterns it formed. That isn't to say that a TICK chart will not form patterns that suggest a turn. But I'm not trading the TICK, and thinking about patterns causes over analysis. If you like using a candle chart, and many traders do, that's fine. It's really more of a personal preference.

I keep the TICK on a 5-minute chart and a 2-minute chart. The 5-minute will show more overlapping bars and where the TICK bars are spending the majority of the time. The 2-minute shows more swing highs and lows, rather than overlapping bars. I place horizontal lines at plus and minus 1,000 and 600 levels. Plus and minus 1,000 are extreme alert areas and I do set audible alerts at those values as well. Sometime you will not be looking at the TICK and the alert will make you aware of the extreme reading. TICKS moving between plus and minus 600 consistently are considered neutral and often a reason not to trade since there is no significant power in either direction. Figure 8.4 shows the NYSE TICK.

Once we have the TICK being charted throughout the day, here are the common uses we have when looking at this chart. Generally, the TICK is looked at on an intraday basis, but the closing TICK can give a heads-up of a daily short-term turn when it closes at an extreme and hasn't done that for a long time within a trend. First, we want to look at where the extreme highs and lows are falling, and thereby, whether the average is above or below zero. Second, we want to see what the trend of the TICK is. Third, we want to look for a possible divergence in the TICK readings and the market's trend. Let's take a quick look at each one of these.

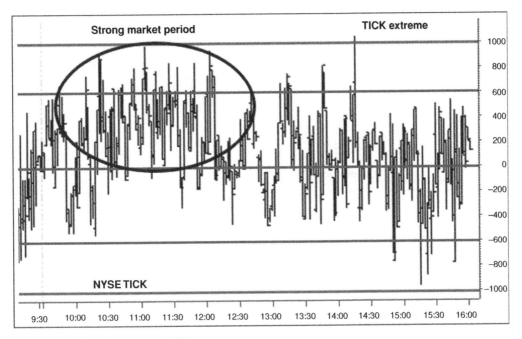

FIGURE 8.4 The New York TICK
Chart courtesy of Mastertrader.com.

The TICK readings will typically fall between +1,000 and –1,000; however, they are not limited to 1,000 as they can go significantly beyond those numbers, although readings like that are considered somewhat extreme. In a bear market, you will see –1,000 TICKS and below almost on a daily basis. That's one way of being aware of a bear market environment, other than the obvious downtrend, of course. As a day progresses, one of the things we want to note is how high the TICK readings are compared to how low they are. If the TICK readings are hitting +900 on the positive side, and are staying above –300 on the bearish side, those are very bullish readings. Anytime the average between the high and the low of the day is above zero, it is somewhat bullish. When the TICKS stay at a high level and above zero, the odds are good that the market and strong stocks will trend higher with shallow pullbacks. You will notice for part of the trading day shown in Figure 8.4, the TICK held above zero for a significant period of time, showing a bullish close to the market was likely to come.

Second, the TICK readings will rally and fall many times throughout the trading day. Some may look at that and think, "Can sense be made of these wild oscillations"? Oh yes! This is one of the most valuable tools an intraday trader has. Frankly, if I could only have one internal gauge it would be the NYSE TICK.

The next indication we want to gather from the TICK readings is whether they continue to form higher lows and higher highs as the day progresses. In other words, if

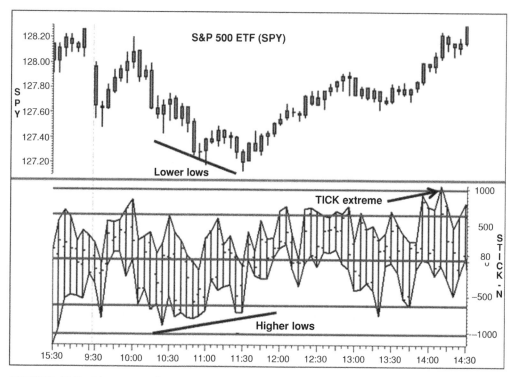

FIGURE 8.5 Divergence of the NYSE TICK
Chart courtesy of Mastertrader.com.

the TICK maintains somewhat of an uptrend during the day, that's bullish. The reverse is true if the TICK begins to show signs of a downtrend intraday. The TICK typically doesn't trend, but when it does make note of it.

Last, we can examine the higher highs and higher lows that are being set, and compare them to the actual chart of the market. For example in Figure 8.5, you can see that just before the low of the day, the TICK actually made a higher low at the same time the market made its lowest low. This is an indication that the market trend may be changing. It's not uncommon to see this midday when the market has been trending most of the morning. The message here is that while the market is continuing its trend, there are an increasing number of stocks that are not. If you trade the broader market indices with SPY, QQQ, or the E-minis this provides a valuable piece of information about the underlying strength or the lack thereof. Use it.

By using these three concepts of the TICK, it helps us to confirm or deny a bullish or bearish price pattern in the market. The TICK can also be used to help with the timing of trades. Once the TICK has confirmed a bullish market environment, we want to favor long positions. While you may think that is obvious, the use of market internals like the TICK forces you to align your bias with that of the market. Your opinion should be whatever the market's is. Internals guide you in that direction.

You will note that once the TICK rallies to extreme highs near +1,000, it will typically pullback for a period of time. It is best not to enter new long trades when the TICK is at extreme high readings. Rather, let the TICK retrace and watch your stock's reaction. For example, if the TICK retraces from +1,000 down to zero and your stock bases sideways, it's showing strength to the other stocks that are trading on downticks. Odds are high that stock is going to breakout and move higher as the TICK turns higher from the zero area. The strategy is to identify the strong stocks when the TICK is at extreme high readings, and then wait for the proper pullback and setup entry when the TICK hits its lows. This is providing that the TICK is still maintaining a bullish overall bias. Likewise, it is not advisable to enter new short trades when the TICK is at extreme low readings. This little bit of timing can help many trades. Again, set the alerts at plus and minus 1,000. If that alarm goes off and you were ready to enter a trade, reconsider. You might be chasing to get into a position at the worst possible time.

The TRIN

The TRIN is an acronym that derives from the phrase "short term TRading INdex." It is in the category of being a "breadth indicator." It is also sometimes referred to as the "Arms Index," named after Richard W. Arms, the person who developed the indicator in 1967. Again, like any indicator, the TRIN can be calculated on any index or group of stocks. However, it is most commonly obtained for the NYSE and for the NASDAQ. Because this particular indicator does use volume as a key component of the formula, we are very interested in the NASDAQ readings. You remember when we were discussing the TICK, we said that we would have to largely ignore the NASDAQ TICK readings because it encompassed all the NASDAQ stocks of which many were very small or nonexistent issues. Since every TICK is given the same weight, the NASDAQ TICK often does not give useful information. When discussing the TRIN, it is a volume weighted indicator so the NASDAQ readings once again become relevant. In addition, TRIN readings are available for just the NASDAQ 100 (see Figure 8.6).

The TRIN readings are actually calculated by dividing the advance-decline ratio by the advance-decline volume ratio (see Figure 8.7). If that sounds a little confusing, let's back up a minute and take a simpler approach to how the TRIN readings are calculated and this will also show you why it is such a valuable new piece of information. Perhaps you have heard of the more common indicator that is typically discussed, the advance-decline line. The A-D line simply shows the number of advancing stocks minus the number of declining stocks, and that value is added to the prior. This continues continuously, which plots the line. If there are an equal number of advancers as compared to decliners, the advance-decline line will be 0. The A-D line is a very commonly quoted statistic on the market, you may even hear it mentioned on CNBC during the trading day.

The problem with the A-D line is that it does not in any way incorporate volume. In other words, you may have a situation where there are many stocks advancing on very thin volume, yet the market is being driven by the very heavy volume that is declining the stocks that are falling. The A-D line may show a positive number, yet the majority

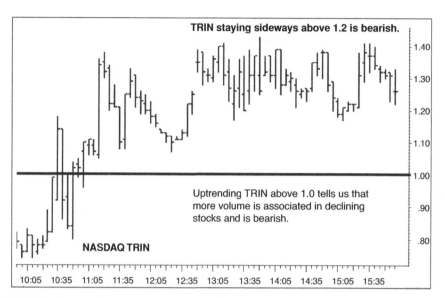

FIGURE 8.6 The NASDAQ TRIN
Chart courtesy of Mastertrader.com.

of the money in the market is actually going to the declining issues. This can lead to a misleading interpretation of the A-D line that day.

What the TRIN does is take the advancing stocks and divide them by the declining stocks and put it in the numerator of the new equation. In the denominator, we have the ratio of the volume that is actually going into the advancers, as compared to the volume that is going into the decliners. That way, if the A-D line is 1.2, and the advancing volume as compared to the declining volume is also 1.2 to 1, the TRIN will be 1.0. However, if the A-D line is 1.2, and the advancing volume as compared to declining volume is only 1.0, the TRIN reading will be 1.2 / 1 or 1.2.

When looking at the TRIN readings it can be a little confusing, because the ratio is simply set up in a way in which numbers rising above 1.0 are becoming more bearish and numbers under 1.0 are becoming more bullish. We typically view rising prices as bullish and falling bearish. It is just the way the equation works. If the advancing volume is not keeping up with the advance-decline ratio, that is actually a bearish thing, and, as it is becoming more bearish, the number is growing over 1.0, as shown in the preceding example.

When using the TRIN there are primarily two things to look at. As with the TICK, we are going to graph it on a 5-minute basis for the intraday pattern. Then, we are going to

$$\frac{\text{Advancing Issues / Declining Issues}}{\text{Advancing Volume / Declining Volume}}$$

FIGURE 8.7 The Formula for the TRIN
Chart courtesy of Mastertrader.com.

note whether the TRIN as an absolute number is living above or below the neutral area of 1.0, and we are going to pay special attention to whether or not the trend of the TRIN is up or down for the day. Trends that are above 1.0 and trending higher are very bearish. The higher the TRIN trends, the more bearish it is.

While the TRIN can trend higher and higher, the historical intraday extreme for the vast majority of days is between 1.5 and 2.0. I have alerts set at these levels to be aware if the TRIN hits them. It's not necessary to be staring at the TRIN all the time. Just be aware of its general level and direction. Let your charting software monitor the TRIN and the TICK for extremes. You only need to glance at them every now and then. Also, while we are primarily interested in the trend of the TRIN, a sideways TRIN at say 1.4 is very bearish. This means that volume is consistently flowing into declining stocks. Combine that with bearish TICKS under zero, and shorting stocks or the market should be like shooting fish in a barrel. That being said, stay aware of extreme negative TICK readings of –1,000. Countertrend moves can be fast and violent even in such a bearish environment. Once the TRIN starts to trend lower and the TICKS turn positive, look for stocks that have shown relative strength to the selling pressure or those that have had a climactic drop and are setting patterns signaling a rebound.

Trends that are below 1.0 and that are trending lower are very bullish. Ideally, the TICKS will be well above the zero line with a few +1,000 readings to confirm the bullish environment. These are the clear-cut examples and when both the NASDAQ and NYSE TRIN show the same extreme bullish or bearish readings, they should be taken very seriously. Figure 8.8 shows a bullish example of the TRIN.

The TRIN may not always trend. It may move sideways. Your job is to be aware of the level of that sideways movement. Sideways at .50 and lower is very bullish as there is

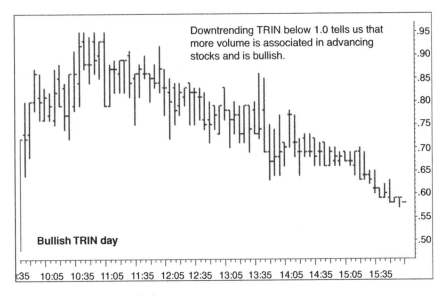

FIGURE 8.8 A Day with a Bullish TRIN
Chart courtesy of Mastertrader.com.

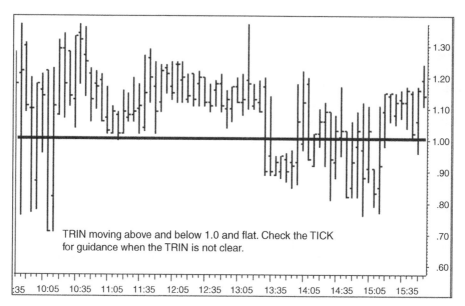

TRIN moving above and below 1.0 and flat. Check the TICK for guidance when the TRIN is not clear.

FIGURE 8.9   The Picture of the TRIN Is Not So Clear
Chart courtesy of Mastertrader.com.

much more volume associated with advancing stocks. Now check the TICKS. You should see many more TICKS above zero and hitting the higher levels above +600.

What may be a more confusing situation, which is susceptible to more interpretation, is when the TRIN is above 1.0 but declining. Here we have some ambiguity in reading the TRIN. The actual numbers are bearish, however the trend is showing a bullish pattern by heading down (remember that the TRIN readings are reversed to what you may normally think, high readings are bearish and low readings are bullish).

In this situation, we need to be more cautious and understand that we have an environment that is bearish at the moment, but is improving to be more bullish. We need to see more information, such as how far the TRIN declines before actually reversing and how far it rallies. If the trend continues down, we need to be very cautious about taking bearish positions even though the number is still above 1.0. Figure 8.9 shows an example of this. Again, this is where the TICK helps clear any confusion. If the TRIN is declining (becoming more bullish as volume is increasing in advancing stocks) and the TICK is not showing a reading at least above +600, be suspect of longs. When the TRIN is declining from above 1.0 and the TICKS are pushing toward +800 and greater, you're dealing with a more reliable signal of a changing environment.

Naturally, the exact same situation exists in reverse when the TRIN is below 1.0 and in an uptrend. While the absolute number of the TRIN is currently bullish, the uptrend must be examined and caution must be had on the long side until a clear situation develops. In both of these situations, we must look for the strength of the trend that exists and make note when it falters, if it does. For example, when the TRIN is below 1.0 and an uptrend exists, if that uptrend fails we know it will be bullish again. Until then, caution must be used because the uptrend could continue to drive the TRIN above 1.0 and higher, where a more bearish situation would exist across the board. At this point you know to check your TICK to see if it's giving negative readings that confirm the TRIN's uptrend. If the TICKS are not moving below –600, don't be so quick to jump to the bearish side.

Over time, you will see many relationships between the TICK and the TRIN in different market environments and you will get a feel for them. The TRIN moves more slowly than the TICK. That's good since we want an internal that gives us a general intermediate-term bias intraday, but will change as the market does. The TICK moves much faster and, while it too can provide an overall bias, it also provides a bias and extremes on a very short-term basis. Learn to use these two gauges together and they will keep your bias aligned with the market's bias, not what you think the market's bias should be.

In addition to these very powerful uses of the TRIN on an intraday basis, we also have a use for the TRIN on the bigger time frame. By plotting a daily chart of the five- and ten-period moving averages of NYSE TRIN, we can use this as a guideline to determine a longer-term overbought or oversold condition of the market (see Figure 8.10).

Figure 8.10 shows a general guideline on the upside of a TRIN reading of 1.2, and on the downside, a TRIN reading of 0.8. Once the 5- and 10-day moving averages get above

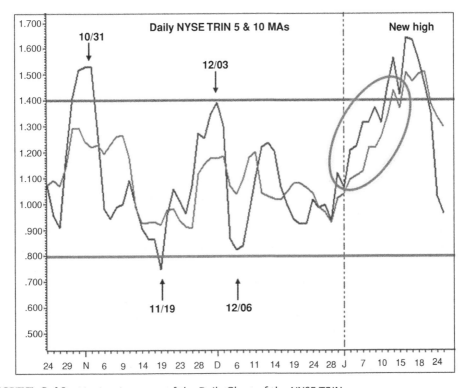

FIGURE 8.10 Moving Averages of the Daily Chart of the NYSE TRIN
Chart courtesy of Mastertrader.com.

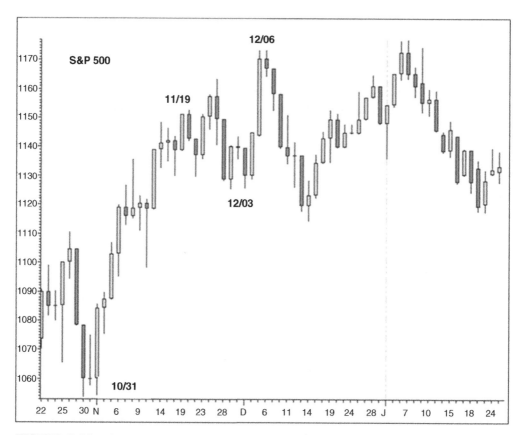

FIGURE 8.11 The S&P 500—Compare to Figure 8.10
Chart courtesy of Mastertrader.com.

or below these numbers, we are at extreme readings and prices should be watched for
reversal. In addition to using these exact numbers, notice if the chart has followed a
certain level over a period of time. This is the level that should be used, or a break of that
level will be considered extreme. You will notice in the chart that is shown, the upper
level of the TRIN is closer to 1.4 to 1.5. This was a more bearish time in the market. You
will notice that when the levels hit new highs in mid-January, the prices did not make
new highs, and then they began a significant selloff. You can see the corresponding price
data to the TRIN readings of Figure 8.10, in Figure 8.11.

Market internals, such as moving averages of the TRIN (there are others), actually
provide historical readings of overbought and oversold points in the market. It is signaling when an extreme amount of volume is associated with advancing or declining
stocks and when a short-term reversal occurred in the past. This is valuable information for swing and intermediate-term traders that tells them when the odds of a turn are
increasing. Price oscillators like RSI, Stochastic, and others are based on the market-
chart view alone. They are misleading and actually useless as overbought or oversold

indicators, since they provide no insight to what is happening within the underlying broader market compared to historical extremes over years. For more discussion of market internals and additional materials for purchase, please visit Pristine.com.

The VIX

Another favorite market internal I like to use is the volatility index, or as it is more commonly abbreviated, the VIX. The VIX is measuring the implied volatility of the call and put options in the market. The VIX is actually measuring the volatility of the options in the S&P 500, while there is another volatility index known as the VXN that is measuring the volatility of the call and put options in the NASDAQ 100 market. These volatility indexes are actually sentiment gauges and used in a contrary way, as we discussed earlier.

While there may be differences from time to time between the VIX and the VXN, I generally use the VIX. I will continue to discuss the VIX throughout this chapter, though you may care to occasionally compare the two.

Without getting into the technicalities of what implied volatility means in a put or call option, suffice it to say that this reading gives us a look into the anxiousness or the complacency with which the traders are viewing the market. The VIX is generally used as an inverse market indicator. When the VIX is trending lower, volatility is decreasing and confidence that the markets can move higher is growing. When the VIX moves to an extremely low level though, the odds of a market pullback is increasing. Extremely low will be relative to what it was in the most recent past. There have been times when a value of 20 was low and others where it was 10. Markets change—just read the chart of the VIX as you would any other chart. The difference is when the VIX reaches support it has bearish implications and when it reaches resistance it has bullish ones.

As markets pullback, whether it's from within an uptrend or in a downtrend, you want to see the VIX move higher. In an uptrend this shows that there's still a healthy amount of fear that the trend may not continue. This is a good sign, and increases the odds that the trend will move higher. When the VIX does not advance during market pullbacks it's an indication of complacency in the market. When this has happened in the past, markets have continued to decline until the VIX did move higher. There has to be skepticism and fear in the markets for an uptrend to continue. When the market is in a downtrend the VIX will be trending higher. If not, you can be sure that the downtrend will continue. As the trend continues, fear of it and a market crash grows. The VIX provides us a measure of skepticism and fear in the markets that will guide us to trends that are continuing and extremes in sentiment.

When measuring fear properly, the increase in the VIX will be accompanied by a continued drop in market prices. Figure 8.12 is showing a daily chart of the VIX at an extreme reading, which, when coupled with candlestick knowledge, tells us this is the likely turning point in the market. Candle patterns on the daily time frame are useful for determining turning points. Just like a stock. The meaning is just opposite since the VIX is more inverse to the broader markets.

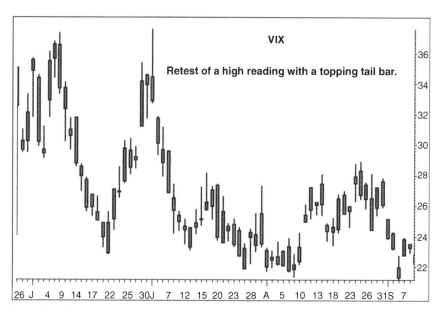

FIGURE 8.12 The VIX at an Extreme Level
Chart courtesy of Mastertrader.com.

The VIX is most useful when it shows extreme readings, to help us pick long-term turning points in the market. What constitutes an extreme reading of the VIX is something that is very much subject to change. Numbers from years ago that were considered to be extreme got blown away in recent years. Extreme will continue to be a relative concept to the VIX, but very sharp increases that challenge prior extreme highs or lows are what we are looking to see. Remember price is always king, and extreme readings in the VIX simply give us a heads-up to look for price patterns to change. Always wait for price patterns to confirm the move. Figure 8.13 shows an excellent example of price that reversed to the upside due to the VIX hitting the prior high, and also an area of complacency that drove prices lower.

The VIX is also useful as an intraday sentiment gauge. I view it on a 5-minute time frame with a 20-period moving average. When it's trending higher, sentiment is bearish and is increasing. When declining, sentiment is bullish and increasing. Follow its trend and be aware of prior turning points. I use a bar chart intraday, as I do with the TRIN. I'm not interested in candle patterns here, just the trend and value it's at.

Some think that the TRIN and VIX are the same since they both move inverse to the market. They are not. The VIX is a sentiment gauge and the TRIN is a breadth gauge. Market internals analysis must done with both breadth and sentiment gauges.

The Put-Call Ratio

Finally, let's talk about the put-call ratio, or more commonly annotated as the P/C ratio. Like the volatility indexes, the P/C ratio is another inverse sentiment market internal. It

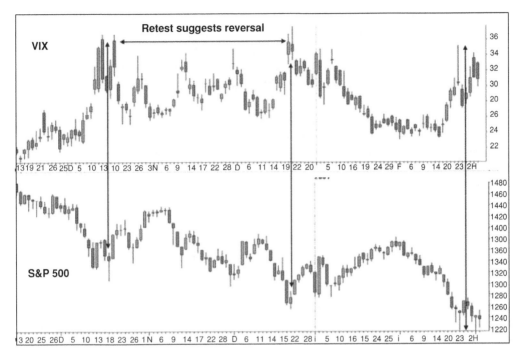

FIGURE 8.13 The VIX Compared to the S&P 500
Chart courtesy of Mastertrader.com.

moves up as bearish sentiment increases or down as bullish sentiment increases. A P/C ratio is created simply by dividing the total volume of puts (bearish bets) by the total volume of calls (bullish bets). However, it is not quite that simple in this case. There are four types of P/C ratios available. There is a P/C ratio that measures the put and call activity on indices, which is mostly hedging, and known as the Index P/C ratio. This P/C ratio historically stays high and I have found it to have little to no value.

There is also an Equity P/C ratio that measures the put and call activity on individual stocks. It tends to reflect individual investor sentiment, that is to say the sentiment of the little guy or dumb money. This isn't to say that there aren't dumb big guys that trade equity options. Whoever is trading these options, historically, they have been an excellent contrarian gauge. When they load up on call options, it has preceded a market high and when they load up on puts, it has preceded a market low. So it pays to know what these traders are doing.

There is also a Total P/C ratio that measures the total of both Index and Equity P/C ratios together. This P/C ratio moves closely with the Equity ratio, but not exactly. If it did it we wouldn't need it. Many times, either Total or Equity ratio will hit an extreme, but not the other. So we monitor both. When they both agree the odds are even higher that a turn is near.

Now here is where it can get a little confusing. When you look at the charts, the OEX P/C ratio appears to be saying something different than the Total and Equity P/C ratios.

It often moves in the opposite direction of the other two and here is what is happening. The OEX P/C ratio is where the smart money is trading options. These traders are typically right on their market directional bets. Of course, this is why we want to monitor them. The ideal signal comes when the dumb money is on one side and the smart money on the other. The dumb money is loaded with puts and the smart money is buying calls and vice versa.

The numbers we use as a general guideline are .80 for excessive bearishness sentiment and .50 for excessive bullish sentiment. In other words, when the five- and ten-day averages get over .80, this shows a very high level of put to call activity. This means there is high bearish speculation, and we know that this means the bottom is likely near. Naturally, we wait for price confirmation.

On the contrary, when the five- and ten-day averages of the P/C ratio gets as low as .50 or below, we know that there is very little put speculation and more call buying. It's time to start being bearish in the market as a contrarian. Figure 8.14 shows an example of the five- and ten-day moving averages of the P/C ratios and how they can show market turning points.

Market internals, whether used for intraday or end-of-day analysis, should always combine breadth and sentiment gauges. We want to know when breadth internals are signaling an extreme, combined with sentiment signaling that traders are totally committed at that extreme.

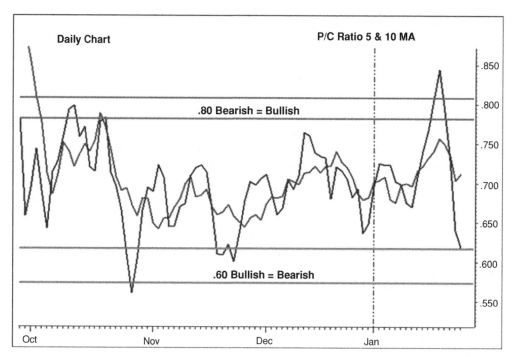

FIGURE 8.14 The P/C Ratio Showing Turning Points
Chart courtesy of Mastertrader.com.

A QUICK OVERVIEW OF INTERMARKET ANALYSIS

To truly understand the markets you must have an understanding of technical analysis, market internals, and intermarket analysis. I call this the three-legged stool of understanding the markets. Intermarket analysis is another large subject that I could fill an entire book with. Again, feel free to visit Pristine.com if you are interested in additional materials delving into this subject.

For purposes of this book, though, let's discuss how intermarket analysis is the technical trader's fundamentals. If you want a read on the economy's health look to the bond and commodity markets. When the economy is growing and businesses are doing well, demand for money and commodities will increase. As that happens, medium to long-term interest rates will rise and so will the cost of goods. This in turn will cause some inflation and the fear of it getting out of control. Now the balancing of growth happening too fast or just right happens. If the economy is expanding too fast, the Federal Reserve will raise short-term interest rates, which begins to tighten the money supply and narrow the spread between long- and short-term rates. This can give the stock market a short-term bump, but the initial increase in short-term interest rates is actually a positive signal that reinforces what the markets have already told us.

The ebb and flow of this balancing act can go on for quite some time and whether the Fed gets it right or goes too far is anyone's guess. Your job is to read the tea leaves; but what are they? A major one is the spread between long- and short-term interest rates. When they are wide, and it became that way because it was preceded by a downturn in the economy and the Fed had been lowering interest rates, money is being pumped into the system. In time, that flows into the banks and then into the hands of businesses and individuals. This all takes time of course, and eventually it assumes that businesses are going to do well and make profits, so stock prices will go up.

This is the theory of course, and you have to look for clues that it's happening. For example, if business is good or improving the price of Federal Express (FDX) should move up. Why? Because the cost of moving goods, information, and services quickly are relatively low compared to the cost of moving them slowly. Another is Home Depot (HD). If the economy is expanding, home building will increase, people will make improvements to their homes, and Home Depots' profits will rise.

As the spread tightens, so does the supply of money. But what is too much? If the yields invert where short-term rates move above long-term ones, history tells us that a recession is not far off and stocks are in for a correction. With that in mind, now look to see if commodity prices begin to decline. If they do it will confirm the coming contraction before it happens. The markets anticipate the future and it will be reflected in the charts. You have to know where to look.

Another clue to look at in this case would be the direction of retailing stocks. If the Fed's actions have become too restrictive, it will show up in the price of those stocks. As the economy contracts—and the markets will anticipate this before it happens—the price of retailers will begin to fall. Keep the Retailing Index on your list to review at least once each week. The same will happen to transportation stocks when the economy begins to contract. Before the bear market started in 2000, the Transportation Index started dropping long before the broader markets did.

This is a basic insight into intermarket analysis, but as you study more of it you will realize that you don't have to be an economist to understand the big picture of what is happening (or I should say, what is going to happen). The study of intermarket analysis will give you guidance for the price of equities, currencies, gold, oil, and the stocks related to them. The study will take time, but if you're serious about the markets you won't mind at all. In fact, you should enjoy the time you spend looking for these relationships and how to take advantage of them. Reading this book will help you to learn how to do it on your own and be independent of others' opinions.

IN SUMMARY

Many traders who like to trade equities (stocks) will often find stocks that move on their own, and pay little attention to the market. However it is not always easy to find those stocks and you often don't know you have found one until it's too late. The bottom line is that if you are long a market stock, you probably have a vested interest in the market going up. This is why traders should always have a view on what the market is doing and where it may be going. Knowing the market internals will help achieve that bias.

Naturally, if you trade the market itself, your only edge in the market is to have another look into the market, and that is exactly what market internals are for—like an X-ray to determine if that strength or weakness is likely going to hold. Next, in Chapter 9, we look at another topic that goes beyond the candlesticks: the concept of relative strength.

Relative Strength

Relative Strength Defined

Relative strength is the visual comparison of one stock to another, or the stock as compared to its sector, or the market in general. It can also be one sector compared to another sector or one sector compared to the broader market. Any of these can also be compared to various market internals. Most of this chapter discusses the concept of relative strength but keep in mind that the information will also apply in the exact same manner for relative weakness.

Most often, when discussing relative strength, we are looking at a stock as it relates to the market in general; a visual pattern in which the particular stock shoulders a stronger pattern than the market does. Note we are not talking about a technical indicator that is in some charting packages and known as the Relative Strength Indicator (RSI), a name that is completely misleading since the indicator does not show relative strength at all. RSI is just another indicator that is widely followed since it's in every charting program. But as I've said before this and other indicators aren't needed and are best left to the chart artists.

The comparison charts in Figure 9.1 give you an idea of the visual picture we are looking for to view relative strength. Similar to much of technical analysis, there is no exact definition for relative strength. Technically, any stock that shows the slightest degree of a stronger rally or the slightest degree of a lesser decline would be considered relative strength to some extent. However, we are not interested in every small showing of superior strength. We are looking for the instances where the relative strength is so clear that the stock is showing a tendency to "be on its own page." This is used to indicate that the stock has in a sense, deviated from the market, is simply in its own world, and will not be affected much by the market. Initially, it is not easy to make a call that a stock is definitively devoid from the market. However, as time goes on, the more a stock tends to show its own pattern and disregard the moves of the market, the more likely it will be on its own page and showing true relative strength.

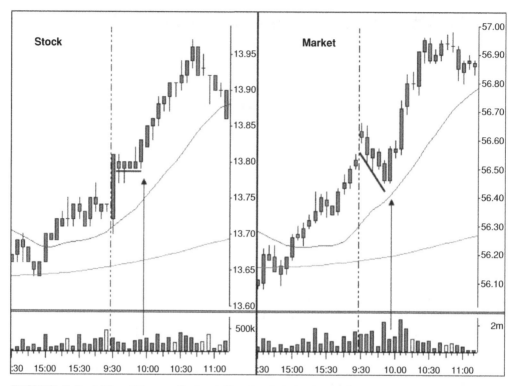

FIGURE 9.1 A Visual Picture of a Stock Showing Relative Strength
Chart courtesy of Mastertrader.com.

IDENTIFYING DIFFERENT TYPES OF RELATIVE STRENGTH

The reasons why we say a stock has relative strength can vary from a very subjective chart that can show every penny of technical relative strength, to a very subjective visual view of two charts side-by-side.

The first way of viewing relative strength (and most objective way of all) is to show a chart that actually takes the price of the stock and divides it by the price of the market or index to which it is being compared. This generates a single line and we know whenever that line is rising, the stock is showing superior performance to the market. Whenever the line is declining, the stock is showing inferior performance to the market. Figure 9.2 shows a relative strength line that is calculated based on Figure 9.1.

Using the dividing method for charting relative strength has a couple of advantages. First, as I already stated, it is objective in nature. No one can argue that the stock has relative strength or relative weakness because the decision has been reduced to the slope of a single line. This has the advantage of finding strong relative strength plays: any charts that are set up to show this divide-by method can be quickly scanned.

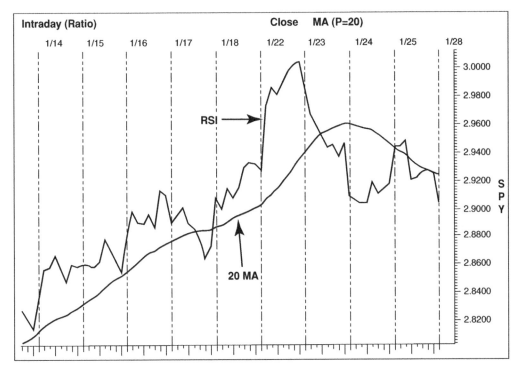

FIGURE 9.2 A Single Line Relative Strength with a 20 MA
Chart courtesy of Mastertrader.com.

This method also has a serious drawback. This drawback will begin to touch on a significant concept that we will discuss further in this chapter. It is introduced here and perhaps you can see the concept fairly quickly. A stock that shows relative strength may simply mean that the stock is declining at a slower rate than the market. Obviously, this is not the type of relative strength we want to uncover, or at least not to trade. The problem with using the divide-by method is that all relative strength looks the same on the final chart. If the market is falling, but a stock is simply falling at a 10 percent slower rate, the divide-by chart will look the same as if the market was rallying and the stock was outperforming the market by 10 percent. This can be a serious problem because, as you will see, we are not really interested in stocks that are showing the former type of relative strength. Due to this severe limitation, I do not use this type of chart to help identify relative strength. It may be a good educational tool for you when starting off, but eventually you will need to evolve to a better system of finding stocks which you actually want to trade.

The next method is the simplest and most basic one. It is also the most objective, but it can lead to some other methods of analyzing relative strength. This method is simply to visually compare two charts. Take a look again at Figure 9.1 and Figure 9.2 and you get the visual presented in Figure 9.3.

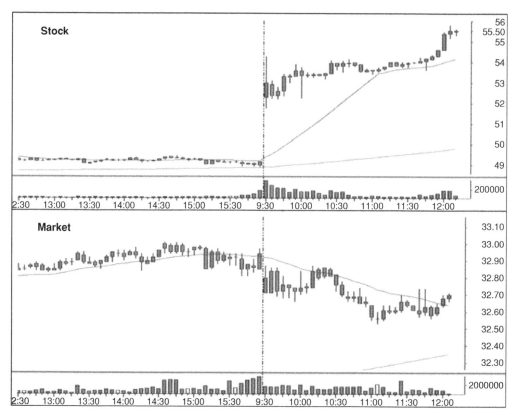

FIGURE 9.3 A Visual Comparison of Two Charts
Chart courtesy of Mastertrader.com.

By stacking the charts vertically it is much easier to see a bar-by-bar comparison of what the two price patterns are doing. When inspecting these two charts, first note the candlesticks that are forming the trends involved in both charts. Figure 9.4 shows the relationship between the high and low pivots on both charts.

Note that when you identify the pivots, you can see the flow of the higher highs and higher lows. Note how higher highs react in comparison to the prior high in both charts. Do the same with the higher lows. Note the difference between lows that are forming slightly higher lows, as compared with those that are forming significantly higher lows. This is just a more detailed way of taking a very close look at the exact trends that are occurring as a chart develops. When the chart of the stock is showing significant higher highs, and showing them sooner than the chart of the market, this is good relative strength. When the chart of the stock also begins to form higher lows, and more significant higher lows than the chart of the market, this is also good relative strength.

Another thing to look for when comparing the two charts is the quality of the bars that form. Here we are looking at a nice tight pattern developing as compared to a very loose pattern. You will remember in Chapter 2, when discussing candles, we looked at

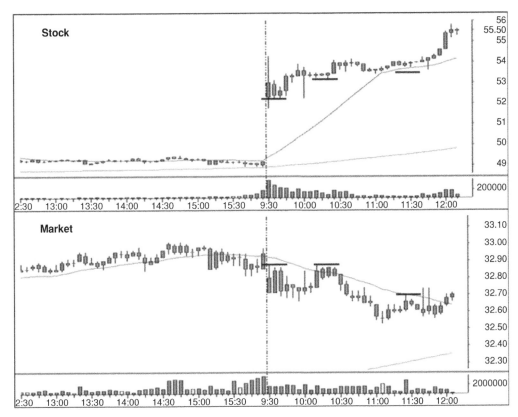

FIGURE 9.4 The Comparison Charts Marked with Pivots
Chart courtesy of Mastertrader.com.

many of the same things we see in Figure 9.4. As matter of fact, all of the things that we looked at thus far in determining a price pattern are coming into play to simply compare these two different price patterns to find out which is the superior one. Look again at the two charts as presented in Figure 9.5.

You will notice that the chart of the stock is showing a much more controlled and tighter pattern in the highlighted area. This means less indecision and more control by the bulls, leading to a better overall pattern, and a greater likelihood of the stock advancing further and sooner. The bottom line is that relative strength can also be measured by having tight, controlled patterns, especially while the stock is resting on its move up. Controlled, tight patterns communicate certainty in the trend and likelihood that the trend will continue.

Another way to view relative strength is to see how price patterns react to prior support and resistance areas. Again, we went over these concepts in Chapter 3, but now we are using that knowledge to compare these charts to see which has superior strength. If one chart is able to rally through a resistance area, while the other chart stalls at that resistance area, one has greater relative strength. Also, when prices drop to prior support

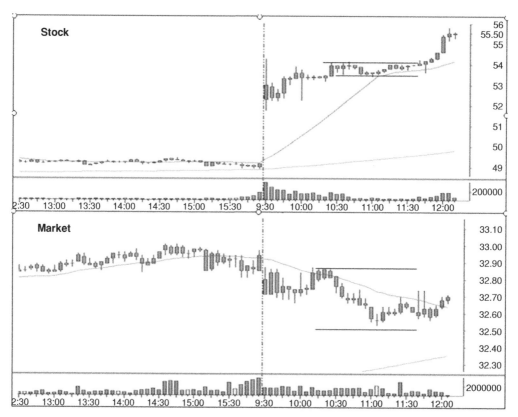

FIGURE 9.5 Compare the Quality of the Bars
Chart courtesy of Mastertrader.com.

areas, a chart that shows a more significant bounce from that support—as compared to one that simply sits on the support area—also shows signs of greater relative strength. In Figure 9.6, the stock is showing greater relative strength by pushing through a prior resistance area while the market has stalled in that area.

Let's now view relative strength by comparing the moving averages on the two charts in two different ways. First, by viewing the moving averages, we get a better feel for the actual strength of the trend. Second, we can also note the distance between price and the moving average on rallies and pullbacks. These two things together will give us a clear view of the relative strength of a stock compared to the market. Figure 9.7 compares the charts by looking at the price pattern and the moving averages.

When we look at moving averages to compare two charts, we see three things: the slope, position, and distance. First, we can get a good feel for the strength of the trend by the slope of the moving average. The steeper the slope (more vertical) the stronger the trend is in that particular price pattern. The flatter the slope (more horizontal) the weaker the trend is. Make sure that when you are comparing two charts, you have the charts scaled the same way. Usually this will be the case, but you could affect the look of the price pattern and the slope of the moving average by how the chart is scaled and

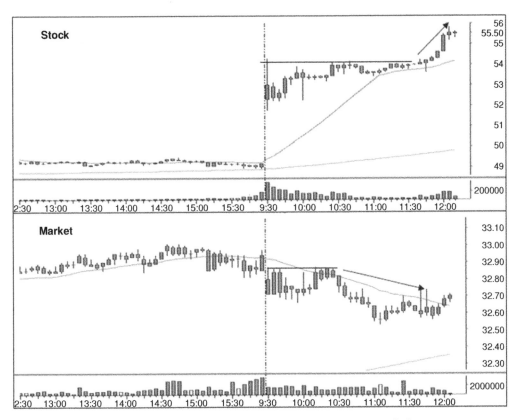

FIGURE 9.6 Relative Strength Viewed by How Resistance Areas Are Handled
Chart courtesy of Mastertrader.com.

sized. Make sure the comparison charts you are looking at are identical in terms of size and scale. To see an example of this, see Figure 9.8. These are identical charts that have simply been sized differently. You can see why when viewing trends you have to keep things very relative. A steep slope may not be so steep when viewing it on a differently scaled chart.

The second thing we want to see when looking at moving averages is the position of the price as compared to the moving average. As we discussed earlier, in a strong bullish trend the price will naturally be residing above the rising moving average. Sometimes prices may become strong, or an uptrend could even begin, although price has not yet established itself above the moving average. Look at how price reacts to the moving average on the rallies and pullbacks on both charts and you will be able to see the relative strength when it is there. You can see this difference in Figure 9.7.

Last, we can look at the distance between the price pattern and the moving average at the extremes. Whether the stock is way below the moving average or way above, the rallies and pullbacks can be measured in relationship to the moving average to view which chart has, or is developing, relative strength. Again you can see this difference in Figure 9.7.

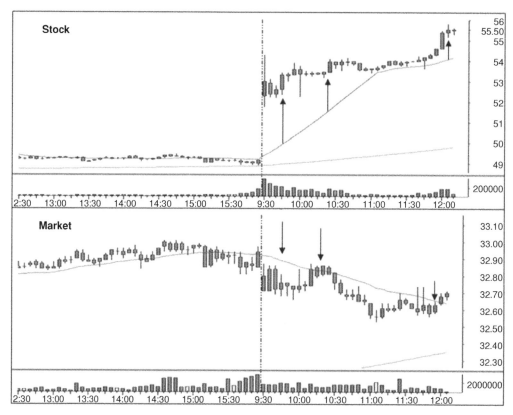

FIGURE 9.7 Using Moving Averages to Help Determine Relative Strength
Chart courtesy of Mastertrader.com.

IS RELATIVE STRENGTH ALWAYS GOOD?

Sometimes relative strength simply means that one price pattern is declining at a slower rate than another price pattern. Obviously, this does not necessarily make for a good play on the long side. This concept becomes a very important factor in deciding when you may want to actually play relative strength as one of your trades. Here's an example of when even extreme relative strength may not be good relative strength.

Let's say a stock is basing at the high of the day and the market is showing some signs of weakness. You may have identified this as a nice relative strength stock and you are watching it to see if it will be a possible long position. Let's say while you're watching the stock, the market begins to drop even more than it had before. What could you comment about the stock at this point? Well, obviously the stock is showing more relative strength. Moreover, this is a good thing if you want to be long. So the stock continues to base in a strong pattern near the high of the day. Then, the market begins to drop even more. The market accelerates down through today's low, through yesterday's low, and continues

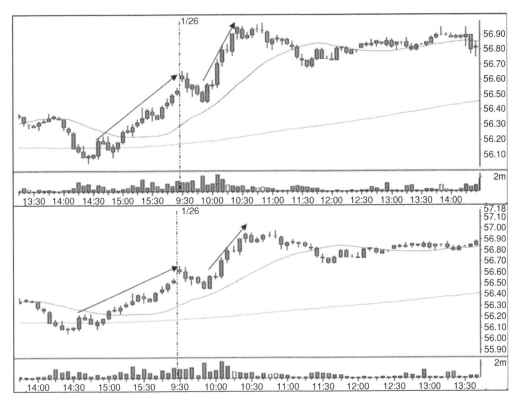

FIGURE 9.8 Be Sure Your Charts Are Scaled in Size Identically
Chart courtesy of Mastertrader.com.

to be extremely weak. Your stock is still basing at the high the day. Isn't the stock now showing the highest signs of relative strength? Shouldn't the stock be at the very top of your watch list for a long play? Maybe, but maybe not.

While this is happening, and we see the stock has great relative strength, isn't there also another concept that is flying in the face of taking the trade long? Remember our discussions about following the market—when the market is declining, is it not much less likely that any long play is going to work? Herein lies the problem; the more the market drops, the more our stock shows relative strength. However, the more the market drops, the more likely it is that all long patterns will eventually fail. The majority of traders just aren't likely to aggressively commit to get long at the moment. It isn't that they have changed their view on the stock, but they know that even the strongest stocks are likely to fall and get cheaper because of the weak market. Can you see why it's said that trading is so related to psychology? So all the stocks showing relative strength will begin to slowly fade away and follow the market. Eventually there will only be a couple of stocks left that hold relative strength throughout the weak market day. The odds are not good that your stock will be one of those very few select stocks by the end of the day. How do we resolve this issue?

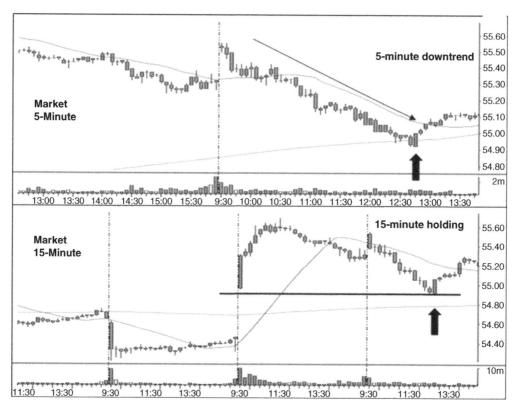

FIGURE 9.9 The Pullback in the Market Is Actually at Key Support
Chart courtesy of Mastertrader.com.

The way to resolve this is to determine just what market weakness is causing prices to decline. If the bigger picture of the market is in an uptrend, and the declines we are currently seeing are simply pullbacks to support areas, then all of the relative strength stocks are examples of good relative strength and all should be monitored for possible long plays when the price pattern dictates. If, however, the market is in a downtrend on all the relevant time frames, and is simply falling in a weak pattern with no support areas visible, then the stock in question is an example of bad relative strength, as it will likely fail to the weak market. Figure 9.9 shows an example of a weak market when viewed on a smaller time frame, but how that weakness is really a pullback to support on a bigger time frame. This makes the relative strength of the stock a playable situation at the right moment in time.

When this is what the market looks like and your stock is exhibiting relative strength that is exactly the type of pattern we want to see. As a matter fact, the perfect storm situation would be to have the market pulling back all morning on an intraday play, while forming what we call an hourly Pristine Buy Setup (PBS), while the stock in question is consolidating near the high of the day. Here we have a stock with

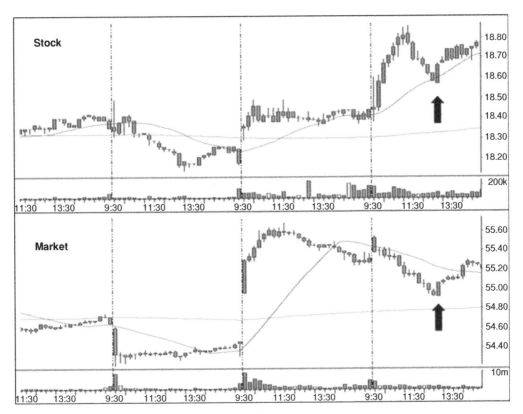

FIGURE 9.10 A Near Perfect Relative Strength Situation
Chart courtesy of Mastertrader.com.

relative strength to the market that is about to take off as the market completes an hourly PBS in an uptrend. This is the type of pattern that becomes a strategy without question (see Figure 9.10).

Even without the perfect market situation, as long as the market is not downtrending on the hourly or daily time frames, relative strength that goes beyond the first 30 to 60 minutes of the day is usually sufficient enough to gain serious attention to the intraday trader. While it is not a guarantee, any reasonable price pattern or break out that forms in conjunction with huge relative strength after the 10:30 reversal time is likely to be a winning play. Remember, all the same is also true in reverse for relative weakness. In other words, a stock that is consolidating near the lows of the day, while the market rallies to form a PSS on the hourly chart, is equally as good as a short.

These concepts apply to all time frames. If the market is pulling back for several days to find a support level in a daily uptrend, a stock consolidating on the daily chart without pulling back is going to be a good relative strength play when the market completes a PBS on the daily chart. You can find relative strength on daily chart patterns, as well as one- and two-minute charts. See Figure 9.11.

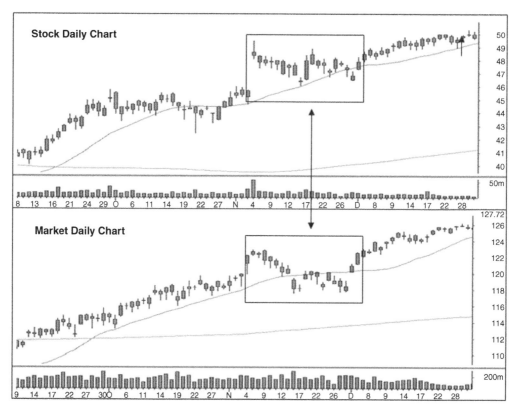

FIGURE 9.11 A Daily Chart Showing Relative Strength
Chart courtesy of Mastertrader.com.

RELATIVE STRENGTH AND WEAKNESS WITH MORNING GAPS

Another time we consider relative strength is first thing in the morning when analyzing stocks that gapped. Often the market and/or several stocks may gap up or down in the morning. Stocks that gap are of frequent focus to the intraday trader as they usually provide situations where the stock that is gapping is likely to be a mover and in focus for the day. When a stock gaps, one of the things we look for to determine if the gap is likely to continue in the same direction, or reverse, is the relative strength that the stock may have had in order to gap, and the resulting pattern after the gap.

Keep in mind that stocks that have serious gaps are more likely to be on their own page the entire day. This means that they are less likely to respond to market movements as other stocks. This is especially true for stocks that gap a significant amount. They will usually follow their own pattern the rest of the day, which may or may not be in tune with the market. However, we do want to take special note of any stock showing great relative strength and weakness. For example, when the market is gapping down a significant

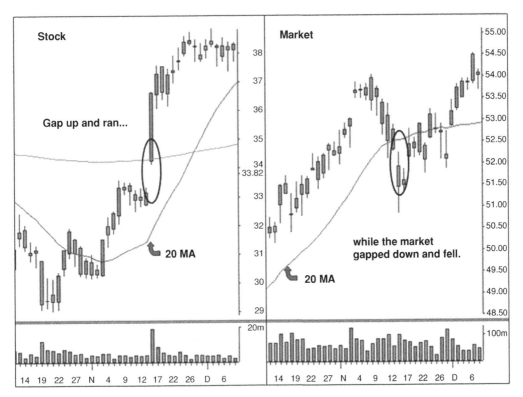

FIGURE 9.12 A Stock That Gapped Up While the Market Was Gapping Down
Chart courtesy of Mastertrader.com.

amount, it is interesting to note any stocks that are gapping up. Obviously, they are showing great relative strength at the time the market opens in order to gap up when the rest of the market is gapping down. That is no guarantee that they will continue higher however. As with all other concepts, price is king and we must analyze the price pattern of the stock that is gapping. However, it will be a bullish notation that the stock has gapped without the aid of the market. Figure 9.12 shows an example of a stock that gapped up on a day when the market gapped down and continued to display a bullish pattern all day.

In addition, we are interested in how the stock reacts after the gap. Regardless of whether or not the market gaps, if the stock continues to move up while the market is moving down the first few minutes of the day we know that the gap is resulting in some relative strength. Again, we have to analyze the price pattern to determine if there will actually be a bullish trade considered, but the relative strength will get it onto our focus list. Another example can be found when both the stock and the market gap up together. Perhaps the market comes down to fill the gap, but the stock only partially fills its gap and stops at a support level. These can be very good plays. The market has a greater tendency to fill the gaps, while individually strong stocks stay stronger and do not fill the gap. These, again, are good stocks to focus on for potential long plays. See Figure 9.13.

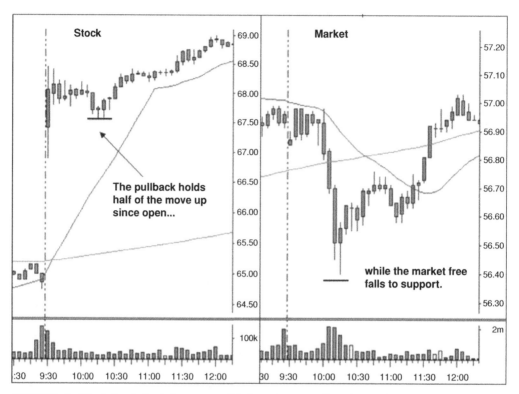

FIGURE 9.13 A Stock Finds Support Well Before the Gap Fill as the Market Fills the Gap
Chart courtesy of Mastertrader.com.

RELATIVE STRENGTH WITH SECTOR ANALYSIS

Up to this point, we have been discussing the relative strength of a particular stock as
compared to the market. For longer-term trading, it can also be an excellent idea to look
at the relative strength of certain sectors as compared to the market in general. This
idea also applies well on an intraday basis by finding the strongest sectors, and then
drilling down to find the strongest stocks in those particular sectors. Again, the same
exact concept can be used to find relative weakness, by drilling down to find the weakest
stock in a particular sector. See Figure 9.14.

When the market shows some weakness in the morning, or when pulling back inside
a daily uptrend, it can be very productive to look for the sectors that are staying strong.
As you can see in Figure 9.14, U.S. Oil Price Index (USO) was leading the charge higher,
while the Solar Stock Index (TAN) was suffering from sharp declines. Assuming that the
daily and hourly chart of the U.S. Oil Price Index (USO) and the Solar Stock Index (TAN)
did not negate the strength and weakness being shown, finding individual stocks showing
bullish patterns in the U.S. Oil Price Index, while also finding bearish patterns or weak
stocks in the Solar Stock Index, would be excellent ways to look for plays on this day.

Symbol	Gap Open	Chg. Open	Net. Chg. %	Range Today Pct.
USO	1.65	+1.33	+4.56	82.43
GLD	2.87	+2.31	+1.84	32.01
SEA		+.15	+.29	75.00
XLE	−.16	−.19	−.43	−35.00
XLP		−.31	−.96	−72.73
TBT		−.92	−1.03	−48.84
XLU	−.32	−.45	−1.34	−96.08
PPH	−.22	−1.00	−1.44	−94.74
IYR	−.79	−.89	−1.56	−72.93
MOO	−.07	−1.02	−1.65	−60.29
XLF	−.27	−.30	−1.75	−90.91
XLV		−.60	−1.80	−91.04
KOL		−.72	−1.94	−23.08
SMH	−.16	−.89	−2.08	−60.00
RTH		−2.04	−2.57	−71.77
IYT		−2.79	−2.82	−90.44
XHB	−.46	−.47	−2.84	−80.95
IBB		−3.06	−2.84	−97.42
TAN		−.27	−3.09	−86.21

FIGURE 9.14 A Ranking of the Sectors on the Day When the Market Was Showing Weakness in the Morning
Chart courtesy of Mastertrader.com.

What I mean by "assuming that the daily and hourly charts did not negate . . ." is that sometimes the strongest sector of the day is not enough information to assume there is bullishness. For example, assume that the U.S. Oil Price Index was in a daily downtrend. Perhaps we had a three- or four-day rally coming into minor resistance and into the declining 20-period moving average. This morning rally in the U.S. Oil Price Index may be exactly the rally that traders have been waiting for to get short the index. Therefore, it is not enough to simply see the sector at the high of the day. We need to see that relative strength or weakness confirming a bullish or bearish pattern on the daily or hourly chart.

RELATIVE STRENGTH TO MARKET INTERNALS

One last area to discuss regarding relative strength is when we are comparing the relative strength of the stock with a market internal as discussed in Chapter 8. In fact, as we discussed the use of market internals, one of the examples we gave was actually showing an example of the relative strength of the stock to the market internal. This concept can apply to virtually any market internal. The easiest way to explain this is to show an example (see Figure 9.15).

Both the TICK and the stock suffered a decline just before the noon hour. After that initial decline, the TICK fell very hard to make almost a climactic tight bottom just after noon. The stock actually formed a higher low during this period of time. This proved to be key, as the stock consolidated in a nice tight pattern and then led the way higher through the rest of the day.

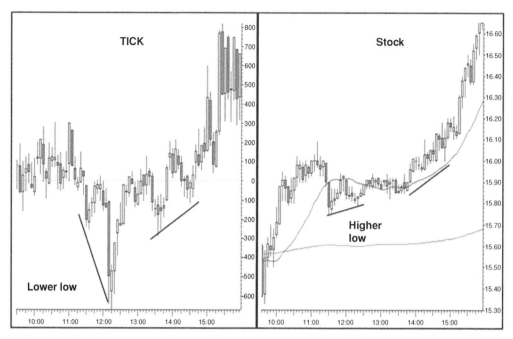

FIGURE 9.15 A Stock Showing Relative Strength of the TICK
Chart courtesy of Mastertrader.com.

A TICK divergence between it and the market can give a heads up to a turning point. For example, the S&P 500 may be trending higher and the TICKs making higher highs or at least equal highs at a higher level of 800 or above. However, on the last new high in the S&P 500 the TICK was only able to move up to 650. This tells us that there were less stocks trading on upticks on the new high than on the prior one. It's clear that there are more stocks that are weaker on this advance than the prior one. Knowing this, the odds of the uptrend at least going into a period of consolidation, and possibly breaking the short-term trend, are good.

IN SUMMARY

As with previous chapters, we try to gain every piece of evidence possible on our side for taking a trade, but the ultimate determination is the price pattern of the individual stock. That being said, stocks that are otherwise equal will generally prove to be a much higher probability for good trades when they are showing relative strength or weakness. Remember it is important that the stock be relatively strong to a strong market; or relatively weak to a weak market. Having relative strength in the declining market is not necessarily a bullish thing, unless you have confidence that the market is on a temporary pullback on a smaller time frame against a longer bullish time frame.

Simply put, the concept of relative strength is the analysis of comparing trends and price movement. Most concepts taught related to technical analysis have been made much too complex and this is most likely why so many struggle to understand them. Overly complicated, subjective explanations to understand price movement through the use of technical indicators is rampant in the trading education industry. After all, most of those teaching are just explaining what they have read and heard over the years, so it does go on and on and doesn't tend to change. A few years ago at a trading conference, a well-spoken educator was addressing a group in the exhibit hall. As I was walking by, someone in the group stopped me and asked, "What do you think about what he is saying?" Not commenting directly about the speaker, I said, "It's relatively easy to impress those that don't know trading by using complexity and confusion." You see, most of us starting out in the markets believe that we need complex indicators and concepts to understand how the markets work. This could not be further from the truth. However, it does sell a lot of proprietary indicators and systems.

Finding relative strength and weakness is always an excellent way to find watch list ideas, as long as their entries are timed so the price pattern and market internals indicate it is an appropriate trade. When the market is trending up, stocks showing relative strength with nice tight patterns can almost be played as strategies in and of themselves.

Next, we look at one of the most important clichés in trading: the trend is our friend. We can learn a lot more about trends than the fact that they are our friend and, in Chapter 10, we discuss which trends are stronger, which cannot be trusted, and which might be ready to stall or turn.

The Trend Is Your Friend

There Are Only Three Directions

There are many clichés you may hear when you enter the world of trading or investing. Many of these clichés make for very cute sayings but are often bad advice. However, some sayings, such as "the trend is your friend," are extremely accurate and good words to live by. The only problem is, the cliché does not come with instructions on exactly how to do it.

In reality, there are only three possible trends. This is because there are only three possible directions that prices can move. Prices can move up, they can move down, or they can move sideways. When any one of these trends is forming a tight quality pattern, it is very easy to identify the trend. However, sometimes the pattern can become so loose or whippy that they can become so hard to identify that traders tend to say that the price pattern is trendless. In reality, there is always a trend occurring in some time frame. Whether or not you want to take all of the extremely whippy trends and call them trendless or not is really a moot point. We only want to focus on the quality trends that are easily identified as going up, down or sideways.

It may seem like common sense to be following the trend. Most traders however, do not appreciate the absolute beauty that comes from following the trend. In a sense, it is one of the only times that we truly have an edge on the market. Therefore, it must be followed accurately and wisely. The problem is; what trend should we be following? On what time frame should we be looking? As a matter fact, sometimes it may not be clear if the market or stock is trending at all, or what direction the trend is in. Sloppy, whipsaw types of price patterns make this analysis very clouded. Even if you understand the basics about trend analysis, the question still arises as to when a trend can no longer be trusted. Or how about how to recognize when a trend may be changing?

WHAT MAKES A TREND?

In Chapter 2, we looked at candlesticks by studying individual bars and the various kinds of bars that formed based on various supply-demand relationships. We also noted that the high and low of individual bars is the first focal area of the supply-demand relationship. In other words, the high and low of each bar may represent points at which the balance between buyers and sellers has changed. Depending upon how the bars formed, there may or may not be a significant amount of supply or demand (resistance or support) in these areas. As bars come together, they form patterns on the chart that give us much more information. The next level of interpretation of the chart is when bars come together to form what we call "pivots." Pivots are the best indication of change in the supply demand relationship. Every time a pivot forms there has been a battle that has taken place and a change in power has occurred to some degree.

In this chapter, we look at many aspects of trend analysis; the first and most important aspect of which is pivots. Price is king, and pivots are a segment of a price pattern that has reversed due to the change in the supply-demand relationship at that moment. Price pivots are the basic building block that we need to understand in order to have a better comprehension of trend analysis. Once we define the various ways these pivots form, we can then determine the trend and trend changes in any time frame in an objective, consistent way everytime.

PIVOTS

Let's assume for a moment that prices are pulling back and they are forming a series of bars with lower highs and lower lows. Once we have at least two lower highs (LH) and two lower lows (LL), then the moment that a bar closes with a higher low there has been a disruption in the pattern. While the bears have been in control, for the first time they were not able to produce a bar with a lower low. If that bar closes with a higher low *and* a higher high, the pattern has formed what we call a low pivot. Understand at this point, we are not saying the trend is changing or there is any action to be taken. As a matter fact, pivots of this kind usually do not reverse the trend. However, we still need to notice this change and to understand its significance. See Figure 10.1.

It is very important to understand that the last bar must be closed. If the bar is not closed, it could still make a low below the prior bar. It is only when the bar closes that we know with certainty that this bar will have a higher low than the prior bar. As you can see, this pattern begins to form a V at the bottom. The V may not continue, but it has begun to form.

Pivots come in various strengths. The one we just looked at is one example of the weakest of all pivots, known as a minor pivot. We can get very detailed about ranking the pivots based on exactly how they form. For simplicity, we are going to discuss all pivots

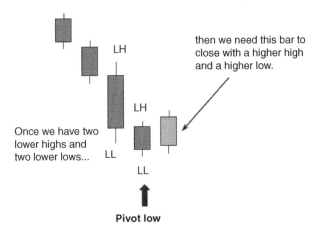

FIGURE 10.1 A Pivot Is Formed
Chart courtesy of Mastertrader.com.

as being either major or minor. The distinction needs to be made because we will expect different outcomes from major and minor pivots.

Here is another example of a minor pivot. The reason that Figure 10.1 has formed a minor pivot is because the lowest bar in the pattern has two higher lows and higher highs on one side, and has one higher low and one higher high on the other side. This is what makes a minor pivot. Note that the same relationship of having only one higher low on one side of the lowest bar can form in a different way. Notice in Figure 10.2 another example of a minor pivot that formed slightly differently.

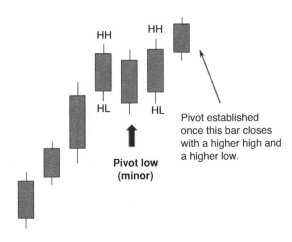

FIGURE 10.2 Another Form of a Minor Pivot
Chart courtesy of Mastertrader.com.

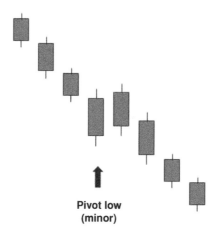

**Pivot low
(minor)**

FIGURE 10.3 The Minor Pivot Does Not Change the Trend
Chart courtesy of Mastertrader.com.

After that bar has closed and a minor pivot has formed, there are now two possibilities of what may occur to this price pattern. First, the pattern may continue lower which would mean that this minor pivot has "failed." I put "failed" in quotes because it is not necessarily a failure in terms of what our expectations were. Minor pivots are not significant and can simply be used to confirm that the down move will continue downward. You can see this occurrence in Figure 10.3.

The second option is that this minor pivot will be the beginning of a deeper V pattern that will become a major pivot. There are a couple of different ways that a minor pivot can become a major pivot. To keep your mind focused properly, it is always good not to become too hung up on very precise technical notions. We want to make things objective and that requires a good deal of specificity. However, we know that technical analysis cannot be that precise. The idea of a pivot becoming a major pivot that may actually reverse the move is focused on the visual concept of a deep V pattern forming. The minor pivots we have looked at so far are not in the category of having a deep V. When we have two bars with higher lows on each side of the lowest bar, we now have a stronger pivot. If the bars on both sides do not make consecutive higher lows, then the pivot is still weak enough that we consider it to be a minor pivot. Without consecutive higher lows, that deep V is not forming properly. Figure 10.4 is an example of another type of minor pivot. Here we have two higher lows on each side, but they are not consecutively higher, they are going more sideways and the lowest low does not really form a nice deep V.

If we now add another higher low on each side of the lowest bar, we have enough information to say that this low bar will likely be the low and a change is occurring so we will call this a major pivot. However, keep in mind, the broader notion of a deep V is still one that you should consider when looking at this pattern. Often times you can have three higher lows on each side, but moving sideways without really forming the deep V. To the extent prices are sideways rather than making a V, you should trust the pattern

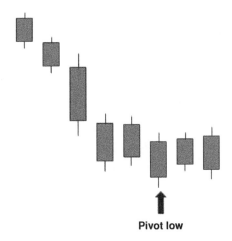

Pivot low

FIGURE 10.4 Another Example of a Minor Pivot
Chart courtesy of Mastertrader.com.

less to be a reversal-type pattern. Figure 10.5 shows an example of a major pivot that is being called major because it has three higher lows on each side.

Finally, the best pivots are formed when the higher lows on each side make consecutively higher lows. This pattern guarantees the deeper V formation. As long as we have two consecutively higher lows on both sides of the lowest bar we will consider this to be a major pivot. Naturally, the more bars on each side the better the pivot. Of course, at some point, it becomes a moot point to call it a pivot because the pattern has already reversed and little benefit can come from this information from the point of entering

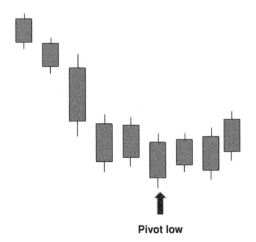

Pivot low

FIGURE 10.5 An Example of a Major Pivot
Chart courtesy of Mastertrader.com.

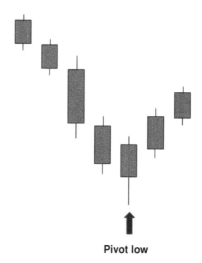

Pivot low

FIGURE 10.6 An Example of a Strong Major Pivot
Chart courtesy of Mastertrader.com.

a trade. Figure 10.6 shows an example of a major pivot due to the fact that it has two consecutive higher highs and higher lows on both sides of the low bar.

The purpose of identifying these pivots is to look at the type of pivot that has formed and to evaluate how well the deeper V-type pattern we have discussed has formed. The major pivots that form a nice V will be likely to reverse the trend of bars coming into the pivot, and they will have prices continuing in the direction that is formed once prices leave the pivot. In other words, when a low pivot forms, prices are falling into the pivot, and if the pivot formed is a major pivot, the likelihood is that prices will continue to rally after the pivot is established.

If however, the disruption in price forms only a minor pivot, the greater likelihood exists that prices will still continue lower. If there is a strong trend in place, the minor pivot may actually be used as a way to enter a short position to capture the move of prices falling. The stronger the minor pivot becomes, and the closer it comes to forming a major pivot, the more the trader should stand down from taking a trade and watch until more information develops. Figure 10.7 shows an example of how to use a minor pivot to capture the current downtrend. While Figure 10.7 shows a green candle, I want to reinforce the bar-by-bar concept. If that was a topping tail bar, it would tell us that sellers aggressively took the opportunity to sell into that minor move higher.

WHEN PIVOTS COME TOGETHER

When major pivots form, we expect that the short-term price pattern will reverse. That is what a pivot does; it takes the downward move and turns it back into an upward move.

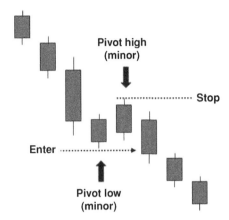

FIGURE 10.7 A Minor Pivot Only Temporarily Disrupts the Price Pattern
Chart courtesy of Mastertrader.com.

This is viewing things from the smaller time frame. The bigger concept of pivots is to see how pivots form one after another. If you mark off all the pivots that form, we can learn information about the bigger trend by how and where those pivots form. In an established uptrend for example, every low pivot that forms will form in an area that is higher in price than the prior low. This is known as a pivot forming a higher low. A consistent series of higher pivot lows is evidence of an uptrend being in place. This is the first notion of trend analysis. It is basic, but also perhaps the single most important part of trend analysis. Regardless of indicators, moving averages, fundamental analysis, or talking heads on TV, if prices continue to be bought at higher levels than previously, the pattern is bullish. This fact cannot be disputed. Figure 10.8 shows an uptrend that is in place due to the formation of the series of higher pivot lows.

Keep in mind that during most of this conversation we have been discussing the formation of low pivots. Remember, that the same exact concepts will apply to forming high pivots. High pivots will have a high bar with some combination of lower highs on both sides of the high bar. All the same rules apply. Figure 10.9 is an example of a major high pivot.

Remember that both types of pivots will form in uptrends, downtrends, and sideways trends. Uptrends will have both high and low pivots, downtrends will have both high and low pivots, and sideways trends will have both high and low pivots. It is where these pivots form in relation to each other that determine the downtrend, uptrend, or sideways trend forming.

Generally speaking, we want to see a series of at least two higher high pivots and two higher low pivots to say that an uptrend is in place. Remember, that most of the time the market, or any stock, is sloppy and generally sideways in nature. If you rely on any single higher low to determine a pattern is now an uptrend, you will be disappointed most of the time. Sloppy sideways patterns will temporarily form higher highs

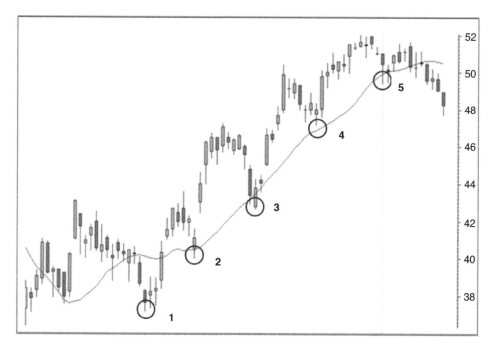

FIGURE 10.8 An Uptrend Based on Higher Pivot Lows
Chart courtesy of Mastertrader.com.

or higher lows that do not follow through. We increase the odds of finding a good up-trend when we wait until at least two higher high pivots and two higher low pivots have formed.

Likewise, we want to see a series of at least two lower high pivots and two lower low pivots to say a downtrend is in place. You may be wondering what type of

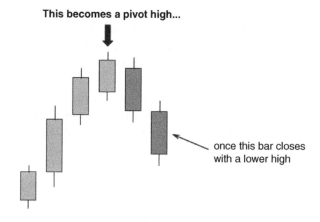

FIGURE 10.9 An Example of a High Pivot
Chart courtesy of Mastertrader.com.

FIGURE 10.10 A Downtrend in Place with Lower Pivot Highs
Chart courtesy of Mastertrader.com.

pivots are needed for these uptrends and downtrends. If you think about it, once a trend is in place, the pivots left behind will always be major. In a downtrend for example, there is no way that a lower pivot low can form without the prior lower high pivot being a major pivot. Think about it. It is only when the pivot is actually forming that we need to analyze at what point it is minor and what point it becomes major. Figure 10.10 shows a downtrend in place. Note how it works. Once you are challenging a prior low pivot, the prior lower high pivot has to meet one of the definitions of the major pivot. The only exception would be if one very large red bar formed as the first lower high bar.

A sideways trend will be forming when we have a series of at least two pivot highs that are in similar areas, and two pivot lows that are in similar areas. In other words, the pivots are not forming higher highs or lower highs; they are simply forming equal highs and equal lows. An example of a sideways trend is seen in Figure 10.11.

Even when we have established the trend, the next question that must be addressed is how long will this new trend last, and can it be trusted? Good trends tend to last a long time, but they are more difficult to form. Therefore, we want to err on the side of waiting until a pattern is well established. In order to help us determine when a pattern is well established, we will look to two subjective indicators: a trend line and a 20-period moving average.

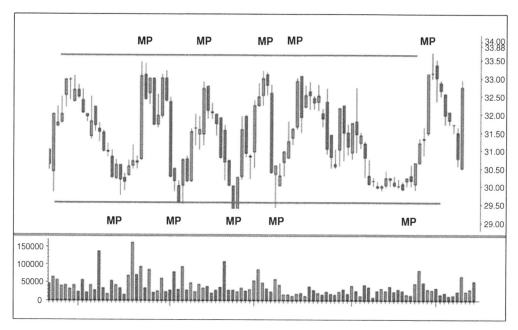

FIGURE 10.11 A Sideways Trend
Chart courtesy of Mastertrader.com.

SOME SUBJECTIVE GUIDANCE

I spoke of subjective indicators in Chapter 1 and I want to make it clear that they can have a proper place in trading. Too many traders focus on them incorrectly as being exact reliable areas and the basis to buy or sell. However, they do have a proper place in technical analysis. They can be one of many things that we look at to analyze a chart. There are two reasons for this. First of all, although subjective, they do have some basis in reality. For example, a 20-period moving average is the average of the last 20 bars. Mathematically, it is statistically true that price will not deviate a certain percentage from the moving average very often. These concepts are known mathematically as standard deviation analysis, and the Bell curve. I am sure you have heard of these concepts, as they do have a solid basis in math.

A 20-period moving average is best used for exactly that purpose: to note how the price aligns with the 20-period moving average, when it adheres to it, and when price becomes extended away from the moving average. The improper use, because it is the subjective use, is to assume that any time price touches the moving average it is automatically a buy. Well-established uptrends will have price patterns that stay above or very close to the 20-period moving average on pullbacks. The moving average will be on an incline, and prices will be staying above the moving average the majority of the time. When prices pullback to the moving average, they should be forming higher low pivots

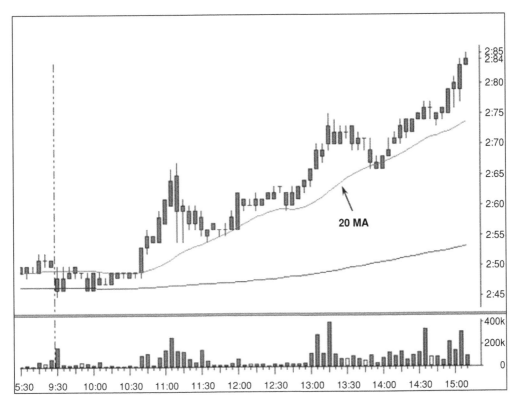

FIGURE 10.12 An Uptrend Adhering to the Rising 20 MA
Chart courtesy of Mastertrader.com.

in or around the area of the moving average. When this happens consistently, very nice looking, reliable uptrends develop. These are the ones where traders can focus on buying the pullbacks, as the pivots form. Figure 10.12 is an example of a nicely formed uptrend that is adhering to the rising 20-period moving average.

The same concept is true with a trend line. I very rarely use or refer to a trend line, because in very nice uptrends, the rising 20-period moving average often serves the purpose as a nice trend line. Sometimes, the uptrend is not steep enough to adhere to the moving average, yet prices are still consistently forming higher lows. We often see this pattern as the stock transitions from a sideways trend into an uptrend. It does not always burst immediately into a strong trend, sometimes a sideways pattern slowly turns into a slightly uptrending sideways pattern. In this case, the moving average often becomes intermixed with the price, but a fairly nice uptrend line can be drawn by connecting the lows of the low pivots that are consistently forming higher lows. See Figure 10.13.

So far in our trend analysis, we have discussed studying the pivots that form, the strength of these pivots, and their relationship to each other to see if prices are forming an uptrend with higher high and higher low pivots, or a downtrend with lower highs and lower low pivots, or simply a sideways mess that is not adhering to either uptrend or

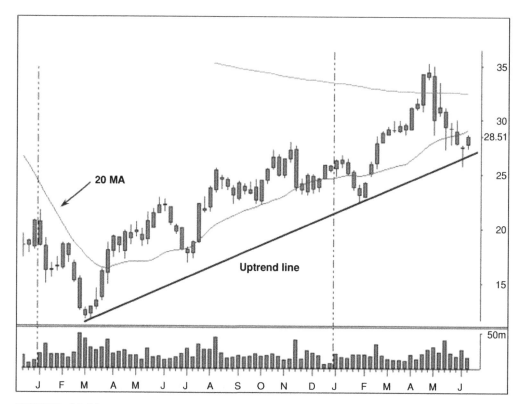

FIGURE 10.13 A More Gradual Uptrend That Follows an Uptrend Line
Chart courtesy of Mastertrader.com.

downtrend analysis. Once we have what appears to be an uptrend or a downtrend, we look at the moving average or trend line to see if the new trend is forming in a consistent reliable way. In addition to moving averages and trend lines, there is one other formation on the chart we want to look at to help establish the quality of this new trend: a clean pattern.

KEEPING IT CLEAN

A clean pattern is one in which we see the pullbacks in an uptrend develop in a nice orderly manner. When the stock is moving up, the pullbacks occur because of profit taking from those who are benefiting from the move up. This is an acceptable and natural occurrence that there will be prior buyers who will be meeting their profit goals and selling to take the profits. This could be short-term traders from just a couple bars prior, or long-term traders from many bars back. The issue is simply whether or not we continue to have enough buyers to absorb the profit-taking sellers, and can continue to move prices higher.

What we do not want to see is a pullback where these profit-takers do not have the opportunity to exit as they desire. We also do not want to see pullbacks that artificially attract buyers before they should be getting long. One example of a pullback that would be considered not clean, and that could make it more difficult for prices to rally, is when we have large topping tails or bottoming tails during a pullback. When a large topping tail forms, it means that many buyers jumped in on the way up, but because the tail forms, they are now holding a losing position. The same issue occurs with a bottoming tail. It shows a lot of buying to produce a bottoming tail. If prices trade lower and they trade underneath the bottoming tail, it shows that all of those buyers who created the bottoming tail, or created the green bar before the topping tail, are all currently underwater and may be wanting to sell their new position as it returns to breakeven rather than hold onto it for a longer duration. It also simply shows that prices were not ready to resume an uptrend, or they would have moved higher on either one of the rallies that created the topping or bottoming tail. It is evidence that there are still strong sellers. Figure 10.14 is an example of a pullback that struggled due to being sloppy because of the tails that formed.

Another issue is when prices gap down during a pullback. This can only happen on a daily chart or possibly on an intraday chart if you are playing the trend between

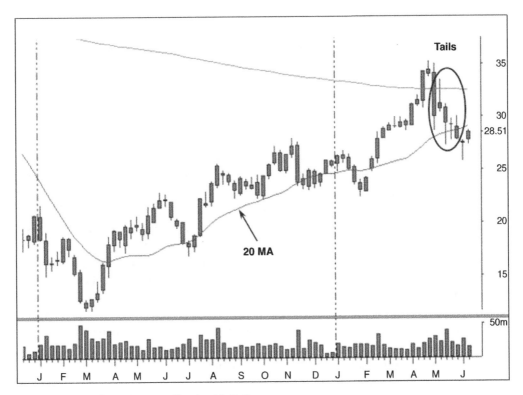

FIGURE 10.14 A Sloppy Pullback with Tails
Chart courtesy of Mastertrader.com.

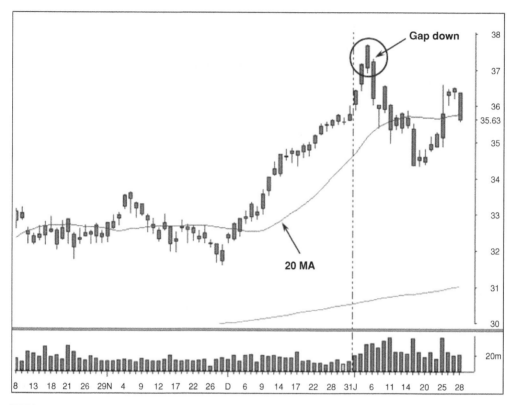

FIGURE 10.15 A Gap Down Occurs During a Pullback
Chart courtesy of Mastertrader.com.

trading days. The problem is that sellers who would like to take profits do not have the opportunity to do so. The price is trading at a certain level, and all of a sudden it opens at a much lower level. These traders will often hang on hoping for prices to come back to where they were so they can sell at the prior day's price range. When it does not happen, they become sellers on any rally and continue to drive prices lower. Figure 10.15 shows an example of a pullback that contains a gap down in the price pattern.

When prices gap down, this leaves a gap between the bars. When prices gap up but then continues to fall, the problem is just as severe. This creates overlapping bars, but the problem here is that a gap to higher prices was not bought by anyone with any additional demand behind it, rather it was used to sell, which shows that the buyers are still inferior to the sellers on this pullback. Remember the point is to time your long entry to the area where the buyers have once again overcome the sellers and will be able to continue to move prices higher on the bigger time frame. You can see an overlapping price pattern on the price pullback in Figure 10.16.

In addition to examining the quality of the pullback, we can look at the quality of the whole trend to see nice tight patterns. We want to see prices that do not get out of

FIGURE 10.16 Overlapping Bars Formed When a Gap Up Was Sold
Chart courtesy of Mastertrader.com.

control on the rallies or the pullbacks. The total range of the price pattern is contained in a narrow area, though the trend is very distinct. When the overall pattern is a high-quality pattern that is very clean and tight, it is much more likely that the current trend will continue whether that trend is up, down, or sideways. In Figures 10.17 and 10.18, you can see the difference between a tight, quality pattern, and a poor quality, whippy pattern.

There is one more aspect about the trend, or specifically the pullback inside of the trend, to discuss: the angle of the retracement. Do not get me wrong, just because the word angle is in that sentence, it does not mean we are going to pull out our protractors and begin to actually measuring angles. It is simply an indication to look at the visual of the charts. We want the pullback to come in an orderly manner and not all at once, straight down vertically. Very fast pullbacks do not offer the opportunity for all traders to exit at the levels they desire. In other words, if an uptrend suddenly has an extremely sharp decline that happens vertically, the speed of that decline may mean that traders are not able to exit when they want to. It also means that there were very few buyers. This again will build a backlog of traders who want to sell on the rally rather than participate in buying the next rally.

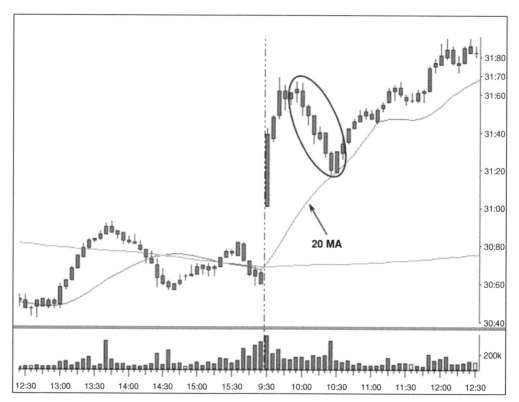

FIGURE 10.17 A Tight Quality Pattern
Chart courtesy of Mastertrader.com.

Figure 10.19 is an example of a very sharp pullback that may have a difficult time rallying without setting a new lower low first. The concept of setting a new lower low first to increase the odds of prices moving higher more easily is based on the new low, which causes additional traders to sell their positions, and in turn that reduces the supply (sellers) that would have shown up otherwise on a move higher.

CHECKING THE REACTION

There are a few more items on the chart that will help us determine the quality of a trend and thereby the likelihood that the trend will continue. The first of these additional items is to notice wide range bullish and wide range bearish bars that form. Let's say prices are in an uptrend. You should know that the uptrend should contain several bullish wide range bars. These are the types of bars that you likely did not see at all during the sideways or downtrend that preceded the uptrend. What you want to note about the bullish wide range bars is that in a quality uptrend this bullish move up will hold and

FIGURE 10.18 A Loose Whippy Pattern
Chart courtesy of Mastertrader.com.

maintain at least half of the bullish bar at all times. In other words, it could show the sign of a weakening trend if a bullish wide range bar were to be more than half negated. If prices were to close under a bullish wide range bar, it would seriously challenge the ability for the trend to continue. Figure 10.20 shows bullish wide range bars in an uptrend.

Likewise, in an uptrend, if a bearish wide range bar were to form, it should be totally negated very quickly if the uptrend is still strong. If a bearish wide range bar forms and prices continue to linger in the lower half of the red bar and eventually trade below the low of the red bar, this will seriously challenge the ability for the uptrend to continue.

Let's look at the same comments as they relate to a downtrend. First of all, you should note that the downtrend will likely contain several bearish wide range bars that were not prevalent in the prior uptrend or sideways trend. In a quality downtrend, the bearish wide range bars will be respected, as prices will stay in the lower half of the bearish bar. If a bearish wide range bar were negated, and prices were to close above the high of that bearish bar, it is a strong sign that the downtrend may be ending. When the range expands to the downside it creates an opportunity for aggressive short-term traders to play a countertrend move, and it also brings in profit-taking from those that

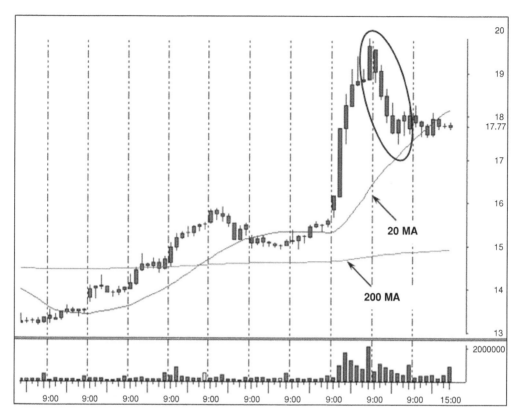

FIGURE 10.19 A Chart Showing a Very Steep Angle of Retracement
Chart courtesy of Mastertrader.com.

were short. If the downtrend is truly strong the supply will keep coming and prices will not be able to move up much. However, if prices are able to close above the high of the bearish wide range bar, it is signaling that the sellers (supply) are done, at least for now. You can see an example of a downtrend that is likely ending in Figure 10.21.

Likewise in the downtrend, if a bullish wide range bar were to form, it should be totally negated very quickly if the downtrend is still going to be strong. If a bullish wide range bar forms and prices continue to stay in the upper half of the green bar and eventually trade above the green bar, this will seriously challenge the ability for the downtrend to continue.

Another aspect we want to check is the reaction to prices as they approach support and resistance areas. In analyzing a trend, we want to look at how an uptrend will react to support and resistance areas. Likewise, we want to see how a downtrend will react both when it falls to prior support areas, and when it rallies back into prior resistance areas.

In a strong uptrend for this example, we should always see prices reversing from their pullbacks (forming higher pivot lows) at or near the prior highs of the uptrend.

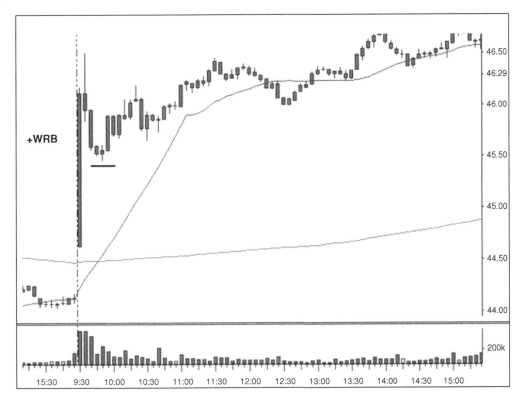

FIGURE 10.20 Bullish Wide Range Bars in an Uptrend
Chart courtesy of Mastertrader.com.

This is the minor support area we discussed in Chapter 4. Good quality uptrends will react to minor support levels. If prices are forced to return to lower areas, the uptrend itself is challenged. You can see an example of how a nicely uptrending stock reacts properly to its first minor support area in Figure 10.22.

As an uptrend begins to weaken, you will begin to see the pullbacks not respond as quickly to the minor support areas. As the trend continues to degrade, you will see the pullbacks actually begin to approach the prior lows. Once the pullback is retracing all the way back to the prior low, we are no longer making higher lows and therefore are no longer in an uptrend. You can use the same analogy on the rallies. When rallies fail to make significant new highs, this shows the trend is beginning to weaken. As those rallies stall at the prior highs, the uptrend once again has failed. The weakening process is shown in Figure 10.23.

What you are actually witnessing at this time is a transition in the trend of the stock. The stock is slowly transitioning from an uptrend, into a sideways trend. There are several ways a stock can transition, and this is one of the more common ways. The uptrend simply begins to weaken until it is heading sideways. If this process continues, you may eventually see the rallies fall short of prior highs, and the declines actually make

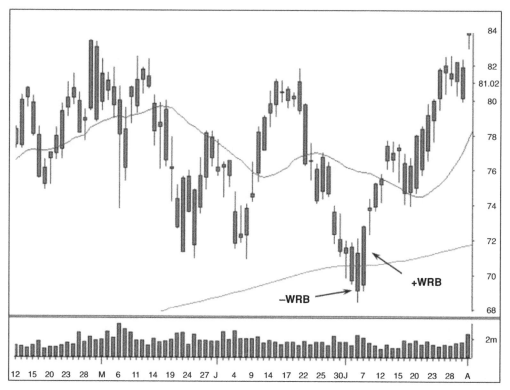

FIGURE 10.21 The Downtrend Is Likely Over
Chart courtesy of Mastertrader.com.

new lows. When this happens, we have a case where prices may have transitioned into a downtrend.

Now, it is time for an important reminder. The previous paragraphs regarding the transition seem simple to understand. However, remember, we are looking at only one aspect of the uptrend. Looking at pivots is looking at the price action and is the single most important thing to view. However, all aspects of the trend must be considered. For example, what about the case where we have a very strong uptrend, and price has extended far from the 20-period moving average? When a very small pullback forms a pivot that does not hold, does this mean the stock is suddenly weak? See Figure 10.24.

While the stock technically made a lower low based on pivots, this occurred well above the rising 20-period moving average. This is what we mean by needing to look at several aspects of the chart. In other words, to help keep things in perspective, the stock did break its trend but, because it happened above the 20 MA on a strong pattern, it is less likely the stock would continue to transition into a sideways trend or downtrend. If the stock broke its pivot (and therefore its trend) well beneath the 20-period moving average, it would be more likely to weaken, and possibly transition

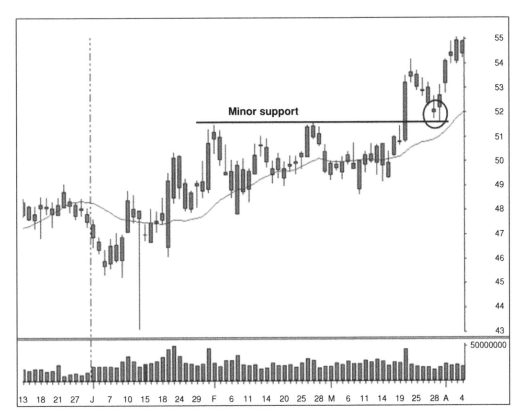

FIGURE 10.22 Prices in an Uptrend React to a Minor Support Area
Chart courtesy of Mastertrader.com.

into a downtrend. Breaking a pivot means the trend broke, but to figure what happens next, you need to factor in the location of the pivot break.

A Commonsense Test

At this point, I introduce you to one other test, perhaps the very first test you should do. It is a commonsense test that can be done at anytime and you should not take a position unless you can pass this commonsense test.

Despite all of the technical terms used in this chapter, sometimes the best indication of a trend is to pin the chart on the wall, step back 20 feet, and ask your 10-year-old son if the chart is pointing up or down. Sometimes we get a little too carried away with all of our precise ways to read charts, we miss the big picture. This is a good example of not seeing the forest for the trees. When you have extremely strong chart patterns, you want to find excuses to buy pullbacks, not to look for reasons why you think the trend is ending. Remember that the trend is your friend, and we always want to find an excuse to play with the trend, not to try to make a play against the trend. We do want to evaluate

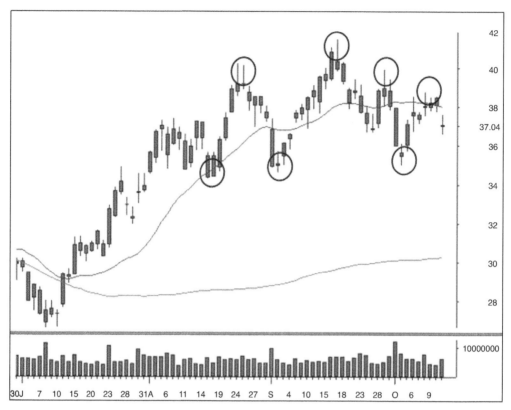

FIGURE 10.23 This Trend Is Weakening
Chart courtesy of Mastertrader.com.

when we feel the trend is ending, so that we can stand aside or wait for more information. However, do not take trades against the trend. If you cannot definitively say that there is a quality trend, do not try to play it. If you hang that chart on the wall and it is going up, at the very least, do not look to find a short position.

FINAL THOUGHTS

If you are an intraday trader, trends do continue from one day to the next. However, you need to allow for the fact that the first 30 minutes of the day can be a very volatile time in which stock prices may react to a variety of factors other than the balance between sellers and buyers. This means that trends from one day to the next may not conform perfectly to the parameters you expect them to. If the big picture of the trend is still up or down, continue to follow that pattern, but wait for the trend to fix itself before playing. Sometimes the trend will continue perfectly from one day to the next, but you cannot always count on that. Trend traders should generally wait until after 10:00 Eastern

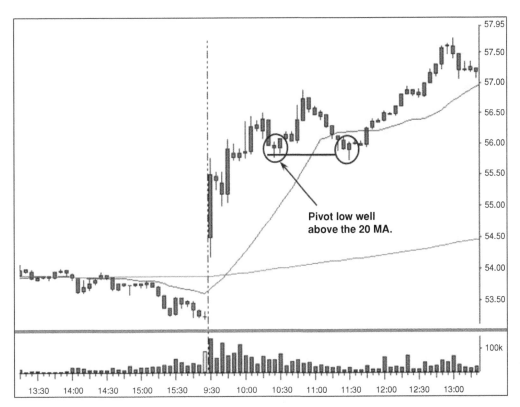

FIGURE 10.24 A Very Strong Stock That Failed on Its First Pivot
Chart courtesy of Mastertrader.com.

time every day. Figure 10.25 is example of a trend that continued nicely from one day to the next, although you can see how sloppy it became during the opening half-hour of the new day.

Finally, I want to discuss trend analysis versus the actual entry of a trade. When we reviewed the formation of pivots, we discussed how a major pivot is more secure than a minor pivot and more likely to indicate a reversal on the small time frame. However, do not forget that it is where pivots form in relation to each other that forms the trend in the bigger time frame, and is the basis for actual trades. For example, every downtrend will normally form major pivots whenever it makes a lower low. However, these major pivots are not to be played long because the bigger time frame is in a downtrend. It is when we are in an uptrend that we care about the new lows that are forming, as we want to make sure they are higher lows.

While the trend is best solidified once a major pivot forms, we will likely be entering the trade well before the major pivot forms. As you recall from prior chapters, our Pristine Buy Setup (PBS) would occur as soon as you cross the high of the prior bar. This technically would be entering the trade before a minor pivot even forms. If you let the bar close before entering, then you will have entered upon the completion of a minor pivot.

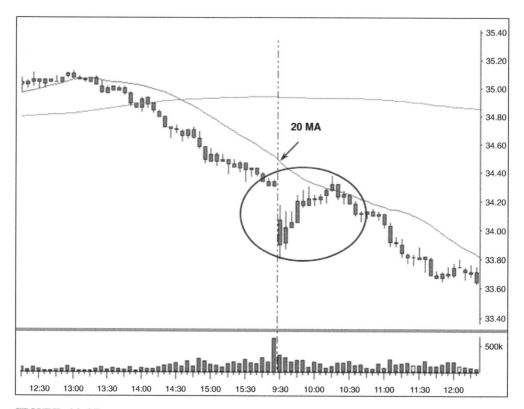

FIGURE 10.25 Use Caution with Trends Continuing from One Day to the Next
Chart courtesy of Mastertrader.com.

The reason we are so aggressive with the entry to a trade is because we are playing in the direction of a trend and assuming that when the current bar trades above the high of the prior bar inside of a buy setup, it will close forming a minor pivot, and the following bars will complete a major pivot. If you wait for a major pivot to form before entering, you will have very late entries on all your trades.

IN SUMMARY

Playing with the trend is perhaps the most important rule in trading. It is the oldest adage, but still the truest. Remember, there are different trends occurring in different time frames. We always want to be playing in the direction of the trend of the time frame we are playing, and it is certainly best to have the time frame above us in agreement. For example, a 15-minute downtrend can form inside of a pullback in an hourly uptrend. The better trade however, will be waiting for the 15-minute uptrend that occurs inside of the rally of the hourly chart uptrend.

Next, in determining the trend we are in, we want to look first to price, which means looking to see how the pivots form in relation to each other. Higher highs and higher lows form uptrends, lower highs and lower lows form downtrends, and relatively equal highs in equal lows form sideways trends. At any moment in time, the price pattern will be in one of these three trends. The next question we want to answer, in order to make an acceptable trade, is when do we have a high-quality trend? This means a trend that has a very tight pattern with consistent formation of pivots, as opposed to a wide and whippy pattern. We also want to see the formation of pivots forming a nice orderly trend with respect to a 20-period moving average or a trend line. We also want to pay attention to how the price pattern is responding to support and resistance areas, and to the formation of wide range bars.

When you properly understand trends, you will be able to find the highest-odds trades. Through proper trend analysis, you will understand when trends are weakening, and see the trades that are becoming lower odds. This will also help you identify when trends actually transition and become the beginning of the new trend. Once you understand trends, the next step is to make sure you understand the interaction of trends in different time frames. We discuss multiple time frames in a later chapter.

Next, in Chapter 11, we go on to a new and popular topic: How to play those morning gaps.

Shoot the Gap

What Is a Gap?

Gaps are a category unto themselves. They are unique because whatever caused the gap often follows into the trading day and can create high-volume, large trading swings, and a stock that often ignores what the market is doing. This combination of events can often make for excellent trading opportunities. Before we get into the possible opportunities, we have to define just what a gap is, discuss the many fallacies about gaps, and then look at gaps both on a daily chart, and on and intraday basis.

The word gap refers to the space that is left behind on the daily chart. It is the empty space between one day's close and the next day's open. Although this is where the word gap got its meaning, stocks can also gap into the prior day's trading range, leaving congestion behind rather than a gap. These are not as obvious to see on a daily chart. Gaps can be either up or down. They can happen to all stocks, as well as markets. You can see the different looks that these two types of gaps have in Figures 11.1 and 11.2.

A gap is what we have on the chart when a stock (or market or index) opens at a significantly higher or lower price than it closed the prior day. When we are discussing gaps, we are generally talking about gaps that occur on the daily chart. The gap occurs due to the fact that the market is closed for a period of time which allows for news and other events to increase the supply or demand for a stock between the time that it closes and the time that it opens the following day. Naturally, intraday charts will also reflect this gap during the first bar of the trading day. However, gaps do not occur on intraday charts during the middle of the day. If you ever see something like this, it is only because the stock is trading so thin that it literally did not trade for a period of time in between the formation of bars. This event has nothing to do with the topic of this chapter. That is just an indication of a stock that is trading so thin traders should move onto another stock.

A gap is measured from the prior day's 4:00 P.M closing price to the opening price of the following day at 9:30 A.M. In other words, it is a change in price from the regular

FIGURE 11.1 This Gap Leaves a Void of Prices on the Daily Chart
Chart courtesy of Mastertrader.com.

market close of the major exchanges to the opening of these exchanges. The post- and pre-market activity do not affect the gap for our considerations. Stocks can and do trade before and after regular market hours through ECNs (electronic communication networks), but this is not currently considered regular market hours. For example, let's say a stock, XYZ, closes the regular market session at 4:00 P.M. at $23.50. News comes out about the stock, which drives the price down in afterhours trading as low as $22.25. The next morning in premarket activity, the stock begins trading even lower down to $21.50. However, during the rest of the premarket activity the stock continues to trade higher and ends up opening the regular market session at 9:30 A.M. at $23.90. The bottom line is that we would say the stock has gapped up 40 cents.

Another issue to deal with is what actually qualifies as a gap. There are thousands of stocks trading every day and technically almost every one of them gaps if we're going to count one penny as a gap. By implication, for our purposes, we are only interested in stocks that gap a significant amount. Unfortunately, the discussion about what is a significant amount is not a simple one.

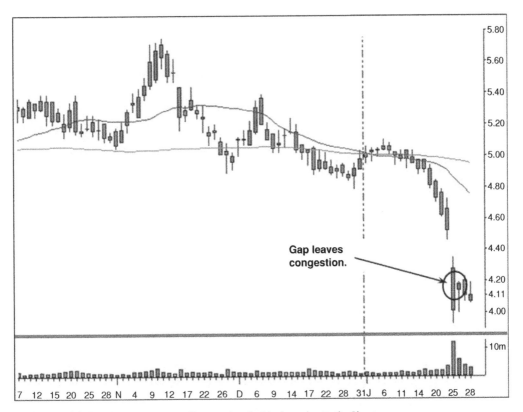

FIGURE 11.2 This Gap Leaves Congestion behind on the Daily Chart
Chart courtesy of Mastertrader.com.

One idea of how to define significant is to simply pick a number, above which everything would be called a significant gap. In other words, anything gapping more than 20 cents is significant. The problem with this, as you might realize, is that if a three-dollar stock gaps 20 cents, it may be significant. If a three hundred dollar stock gaps 20 cents, it will not be noticeable. A better idea would be to use a percentage. Say, anything gapping more than 2 percent would be considered significant. This is a much better idea than using a fixed dollar amount, however it is still may not be accurate. A 2 percent gap may be almost meaningless on a very volatile stock that frequently gaps. A 2 percent gap on a very nonvolatile stock may be a record-breaking amount.

Using a percentage is an acceptable way to sort the morning list of stocks for significant gaps. At least this will limit the very long list of stocks that are gapping any amount to a smaller number of stocks that are gapping at least by a certain percentage. However, in determining what is really significant for the list we want to keep with us throughout the day, or to look at swing trades, we need to use a different approach. We need to look at each individual daily chart and determine what a significant gap is on that particular chart. We need to look at prior gaps that have occurred on the chart, and we need to see

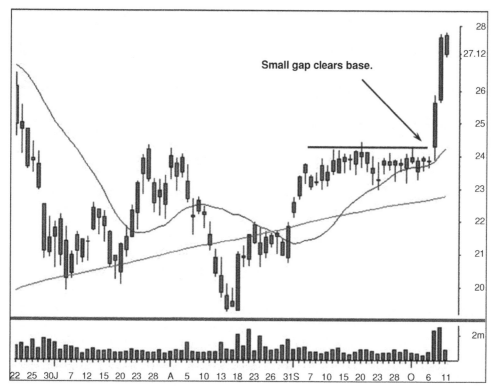

FIGURE 11.3 A Small but Significant Gap
Chart courtesy of Mastertrader.com.

where this particular gap will open, and what it will look like. We want to find those gaps that will open in an area significantly different from where it closed. Figure 11.3 shows a fairly small gap that was still significant. (Later in this chapter, we will develop a better understanding of what significant means on the daily chart.)

WHAT CAUSES A GAP?

A gap is caused because of a change in the supply-demand relationship in the stock that happened while the market was closed. The change in the supply-demand relationship is usually news driven. News has come out about the stock since the market closed and this news is being looked upon either bullishly or bearishly for the next day. The news may be statements that the company is releasing regarding new products, changes in management, an analyst upgrade or downgrade, an earnings report being released or commented on, message board posts, miscellaneous rumors, key people in the company buying and selling their own stock, or anything else that traders have perceived to be good or bad news. It is also possible that there is no news evident and there is simply demand for the stock. The stock may also be gapping because the entire market is gapping. The entire market may be gapping up due to a wide variety of various economic reports, news on the economy, political news, or major world events. The entire market, or any sector, may gap just like an individual stock may gap. When the entire market is gapping up, most stocks will also be gapping up, some perhaps more than others.

Whatever the exact reason, gaps are the result of some kind of event happening while the market is closed and the result is that either buying or selling pressure at open the next day will make the stock open at a different price from where it closed. This can be important because the sudden move by the stock, the sudden change in demand or supply, is often the beginning of the bigger move. There are swing-trading strategies that capitalize on entering the gap, and intraday tactics to capitalize on one or two day moves that frequently occur.

For example, let's say a stock closed at $13 and after the close, news was released on the stock, and it was perceived to be good news by traders. As the stock is getting ready to open the following morning, we may not see any sellers at all until somewhere over $14. In other words, due to the good news, nobody is willing to sell their stock for less than $14. We may also see that buyers are willing to pay $13.75 for the stock even though it has not traded yet. Somebody has to be the first trade, and the first trade will be the result of the first person that is willing to either buy the lowest offer, or sell to the highest bid.

One more comment on the cause of gaps. While it is often news that causes the gap, I do not care whether the cause of the gap is news or not. If it is news, I also do not care what the nature of the news is that is causing the gap. Trying to interpret the news can cause confusion. The news is out, and the gap is already happening. The question is not whether the good news will make the stock gap up—it has—the question is, "Now that the stock has gapped up, will it trade even higher, or will it trade lower, or is it at equilibrium?" What information do you have to say a stock is not at equilibrium? This is why we play the charts. No matter how good the news seems, it may already be totally built into the price before the news was even released. This is why a stock can post a great earnings report and trade lower for weeks after the announcement.

FALLACIES ABOUT GAPS

There are many untrue beliefs about gaps in the market. The first thing that we must understand is that in most cases, news or some event has happened that is causing a change in the supply-demand relationship. However, by the time the stock opens at 9:30 A.M. millions of buyers and sellers have digested the information, have made their decisions, and zeroed in on a new price for the stock. It must be initially assumed that all of this thinking and reasoning has established a new equilibrium and a new price for the stock. There is no reason to suspect that this new price is wrong.

The first thing that many traders do is try to determine the quality of the news and just how good or bad it is. This is a huge mistake. Even if you can be sure that you have access to all of the news and information, you do not have any idea what will be perceived by big money. We also do not know if the gap has already fully accounted for the news, has discounted the news, or has overcompensated for the news. Good news does not mean the stock will continue higher. Good news may mean that the good news has been expected and the stock price had already adjusted for the news, and a gap up today will actually set the high for months to come. So the first rule we have to remember is that we do not look at the quality of the news, and whether the news is perceived to be good or bad, it has no bearing on where the stock will go after the gap has occurred.

Similar to this reasoning is a belief that all gap ups are bullish and all gap downs are bearish. This is simply not true. There are many things we will discuss in a few moments to determine where a gap may go, but whether or not a gap up continues higher or trades lower is really a result of whether the gap was actually a novice or professional gap. Either one can happen, each affecting stocks differently.

Another untrue notion is that gaps have to be filled. In a sense, if you extend the time period to forever, I suppose most gaps do get filled. But they may not be filled for days, weeks, months, or years. Over a long period of time the market will usually have big swings and, often, gaps eventually get filled. But it is not a trading philosophy to trade for the fact that gaps will fill. Many professional gaps will not be filled on the day of the gap, and will continue higher for months or years.

Another falsehood is the belief that really large gaps will fade. The term "fade" is used to talk about going the opposite direction of the gap. In other words, if a stock gaps up a large amount, playing it short when it gapped would be fading the gap. Again, the size of the gap may be one factor we look at, but very large gaps do not automatically mean we begin trading against the gap. Prices often continue in the direction of the gap despite the fact that the gap was very large.

And finally we have to discuss that infamous word, extended, as it applies to gaps. I have mentioned several times throughout this book, that the word extended is a very subjective term and should be reserved only for making visual descriptions of a chart and not used to base trading decisions. It is often the case that extended moves simply become more extended. The false notion of extended is even more important when discussing gaps. Let's say a $20 stock gaps to $22. That is a 10 percent increase in the price of the stock, and many may call that extended just due to the percentage. If you believe in fundamental analysis, the P/E ratio just went up 10 percent, as well as other accounting numbers that fundamental traders may look at to determine whether or not a stock is a good purchase. However, we know that in fact the only thing that makes a stock move up is a surplus of buyers, that is, strong demand for the stock. If you want to use the word extended in a technical sense, it has to mean that we are running out of buyers and the stock is extended to the upside. The ironic part is that when the stock gaps from $20 to $22, there have been exactly zero buyers that have purchased the stock in order to make the stock gap that far. This price void in the chart is created without any actual buys or sells. It is only the presence of the potential buyer that makes a stock open where it does.

It is therefore very difficult to call a stock extended when it has gapped two dollars, when not one single bull has bought the stock yet.

GAPS AND THE DAILY CHART

When we look at gaps on the daily chart there are several relevant points we want to look at to determine if a stock is more likely to go higher or lower after the gap. The most basic of these premises is the determination of whether or not this gap is going to be a novice or a professional type of gap. If the stock is gapping up, a professional gap would imply that this gap up is beginning a new direction upward. In other words, the prior trend for the stock was either down or sideways for an extended period of time on the daily chart. Professional gaps are likely to continue in the direction of the gap, sometimes without ever filling the gap, and sometimes after filling the gap. See Figure 11.4.

If a stock is gapping up, a novice gap would imply that the gap is going to end the current direction. In other words, the prior direction of the stock had been up for so long that this gap up is going to be a profit-taking opportunity for all the current bulls that

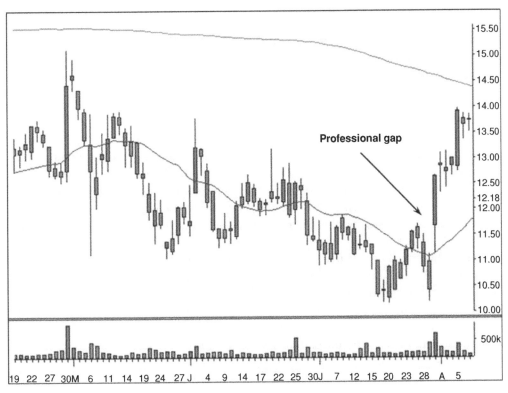

FIGURE 11.4 A Professional Gap Reverses the Trend
Chart courtesy of Mastertrader.com.

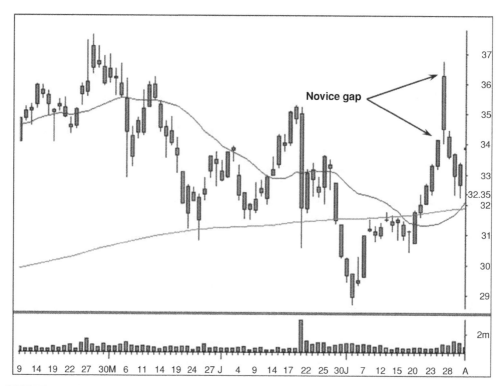

FIGURE 11.5 A Novice Gap Reverses the Trend
Chart courtesy of Mastertrader.com.

are long the stock. A novice gap up may set the high for many days or weeks to come. Figure 11.5 is an example of a novice gap up that reversed the trend, at least on the intraday pattern. Whether or not the daily chart changes trends is not yet determined but, at the very least, prices just had a severe five-day pullback from the novice gap.

As always, both of these statements are equally true of novice and professional gaps when a stock is gapping down. A professional gap down would imply that the prior trend was either up or sideways and this gap down will begin a new move. A novice gap down means that the stock has been declining for so long that the gap down will put an end to the decline and bring in new buyers to take the stock higher in the future.

We make the professional–novice determination by looking at several things. The first is to determine where this gap is going to land in terms of support and resistance. If a stock is gapping up, gapping into a resistance area will imply that the stock may head lower after the gap up. Gapping over a resistance area may imply the stock will move higher, if the gap is not too far beyond the resistance area. Figure 11.6 is an example of a stock that has gapped up and cleared a nearby resistance area.

Likewise, if a stock is gapping down we want to see where it lands in terms of the nearby support area. A stock gapping to or above support is more likely to rally after the gap, and a stock that is gapping down beneath the support area is more likely to

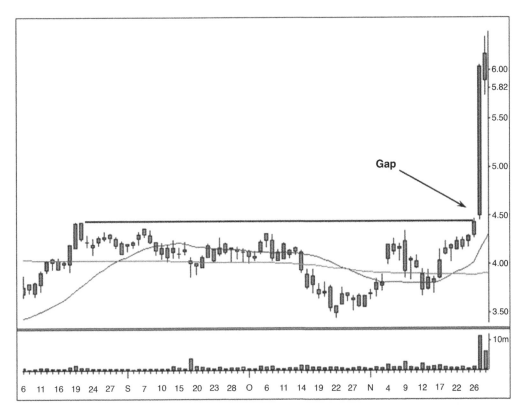

FIGURE 11.6 A Stock Clears Resistance on the Gap
Chart courtesy of Mastertrader.com.

continue to decline. Figure 11.7 is an example of a stock that gapped down but landed on the support area.

Much of the information in Chapter 3 on support and resistance applies in gap analysis as well. Support and resistance areas can gain strength or weakness depending upon how far the stock has to run in order to encounter these areas. In other words, in gap terms, a stock that gaps up a large amount is more likely to react bearishly to a resistance area. A stock that gaps down a large amount is more likely to react bullishly to a support area. After a long run, stocks are tired. Meaning, the long run causes traders to be less willing to take positions since prices have already moved so much and they will have a more difficult time eating through their respective supply and demand areas.

Be careful here however. As I just discussed, in the true sense of the word, stocks are never extended just because of a large gap. What is just as important, or even more important than the size of the gap, is the pattern preceding the gap. Looking at it this way, a stock that has been up for several days in a row and then gaps a large amount into a resistance area would be the best candidate to stall on the morning of the gap up and begin to decline. Likewise, a stock that has been down for several days in a row and

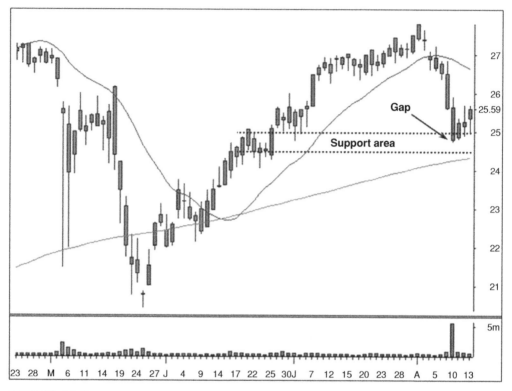

FIGURE 11.7 Stock Gaps Down into a Support Area
Chart courtesy of Mastertrader.com.

then gaps down a large amount to a support area is the most likely candidate to rally sometime during the morning of the gap. See Figure 11.8.

This analysis that we are doing of a stock that is gapping on a daily chart has three purposes. First, if our gap analysis determines a short-term bullish or bearish bias, we may look to trade the stock on an intraday basis by finding a complementary entry. We will discuss this concept in the next section. Second, if our gap analysis determines a long-term bullish or bearish bias on the daily chart, this pattern could be an excellent pattern for a swing trade on the daily chart. The patterns we have discussed above are likely candidates for stocks that could be held for two to five days to play out the bullish or bearish bias of the gap that occurs.

For example, a stock that gaps a significant amount after a very bullish run on the daily chart could be an excellent short sale and be held as a short swing trade if the stock closes red. The third purpose can be to use an exceptionally potent gap as a permanent reversal point on the daily chart. If you study daily charts you will find that the long-term inflection points are set the vast majority of the time by either a climactic reversal, or a gap that reverses the pattern. These powerful gap reversals often set lows that hold for months at a time. These types of patterns can have very safe entries as the high or low

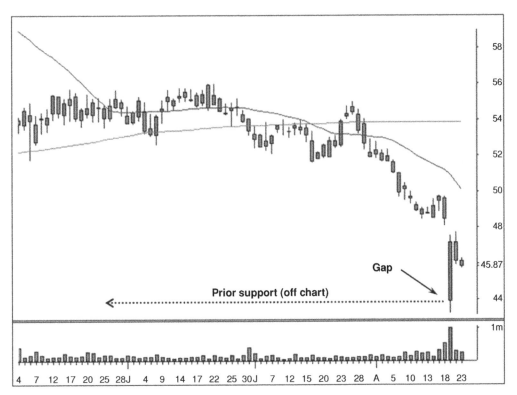

FIGURE 11.8 A Steep Decline Plus a Large Gap to Support Means a Bullish Move
Chart courtesy of Mastertrader.com.

that is left behind and the daily chart is often a very secure area. Traders can also use this new reversal point to begin trading the upcoming new pullbacks in the new trend.

In Figure 11.9 the daily chart set a permanent reversal because of a very bullish gap. The stock had been falling for a long time, and was near climactic in nature at the time it gapped up a significant amount, clearing nearby resistance areas and setting a new bullish course for the future. It is a great practice and a great learning experience to go through daily charts of many stocks and to note all the significant turning points on the daily chart and see what types of patterns cause these turning points.

In review, a bullish gap may happen in a couple of different ways. It may come in the form of a professional gap up that changes the prior trend of the stock from down or sideways, to up. It does this by gapping significantly to clear resistance. It may also come in the form of a novice gap down, that ends the move down by gapping down a large amount after the stock has fallen a long time, especially if it fell hard the prior day. When the pattern is extreme, such as gapping totally over a large red bar, the low left behind may be suitable for core trading.

Remember, the same concepts apply to bearish gaps. The gap may be bearish because the gap comes in the form of a professional gap down that changes the prior trend

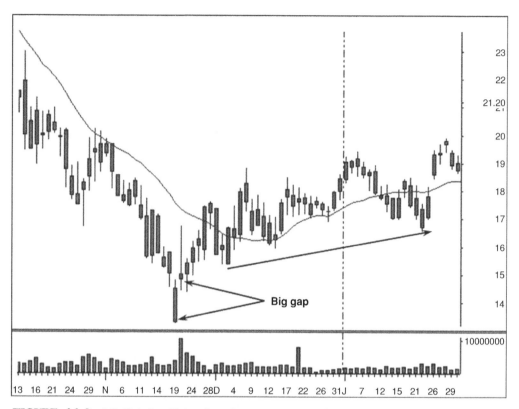

FIGURE 11.9 A Bullish Gap Makes for a Permanent Reversal on the Daily Chart
Chart courtesy of Mastertrader.com.

of the stock from up or sideways, to down. It does this by gapping significantly to clear support. It may also come in the form of a novice gap up, that ends the move up by gapping up a large amount after the stock has rallied a long time, especially if it rallied hard the prior day. When the pattern is extreme, such as gapping totally over a large green bar, the high left behind may be suitable for core trading. Figure 11.10 shows a professional bearish gap.

Also, a bullish or bearish gap may cause a nice move up or down the first day that intraday traders want to capture. It is not uncommon for a large move to occur during the first 30 minutes of trading, which makes gap plays a focus for many traders.

THE INTRADAY PLAY

Different gaps can have different reactions after they open. Stocks may sometimes have a very bullish gap up, but they gap so far that prior holders of the stock continue to sell and take profits, preventing the stock from moving higher the first day. These stocks may have very bullish moves in the days to come, but just go sideways or fall the first

FIGURE 11.10 A Professional Bearish Gap
Chart courtesy of Mastertrader.com.

day. Figure 11.10 is an example of a stock that had a bullish gap on the daily chart, but didn't look so bullish the first day.

Some stocks have a gap that surprises traders and catches many traders on the wrong side of the trade. These gaps can often have a very sharp move on the first day, or even on the opening minutes that it trades. The concept as an intraday trader is to find these potential movers, and find a way to enter them with a reasonable risk to reward.

The most likely candidates to have big moves the first day are stocks that have the following criteria. If it is a bullish gap, it will clear nearby resistance, but not by an excessive amount. It will reverse the recent short-term pattern, causing a surprise to traders who are currently short the stock. This creates a sense of urgency at the open, which will often lead to one of three types of patterns when the stock opens. First, the stock may open on the low of the day and start moving up immediately, sometimes fairly quickly. Second, the stock may trade down a little for a few minutes, and then trade above the high of the day and keep going. Third, the stock may have an orderly pullback over the first 30 to 60 minutes, and find support early, well before filling the gap. Let's take a look at how to play each of these on an intraday basis, but first a word of warning.

Trading anything during the first minutes of the day is very risky. Stocks can move quickly and they are often thinner just after the open, making them harder to enter and exit. They may also have bigger spreads (the difference between the bid and offer), making them more costly to enter. Traders can get trapped if they do not get out in a quick move, and that may generate a larger than anticipated loss.

That being said, let's start with the safest intraday entry, and the only one that all but the most aggressive traders may look at, the morning pullback. A stock that gaps above some resistance areas may pullback and test those areas. Remember, this area will become a minor support area. Visit the chapter on support and resistance if you forgot this concept. Whether the stock trades through a resistance area, or gaps through the resistance area, when it pulls back to test that area it will be a strong support area of some kind. If the pullback meets all the requirements of a Pristine Buy Setup (PBS), and reacts to the new minor support area, this is often an excellent entry to a gap play. Figure 11.11 shows a stock that gapped up bullishly and did a PBS on a support area.

There are two choices for timing on this that work the best. A morning pullback that finds support around 10:00 Eastern Standard Time (EST) can be played on a quality five-minute PBS. As long as the pullback remains clean, it can also be played on the 15-minute chart around 10:30. These are the best and most likely times. Another

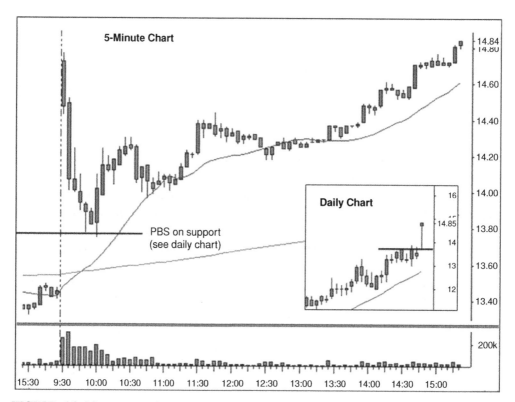

FIGURE 11.11 A PBS on Support after a Bullish Gap
Chart courtesy of Mastertrader.com.

possibility that works very well is the 15-minute PBS that occurs over lunch. Many times the gap is bullish, but the gap is too much and the stock needs half the day to overcome the profit takers. Buying a 15-minute pullback over lunch is acceptable and does not violate the concept of not playing during lunch, because these are the types of plays that should be done—healthy pullbacks off the 15-minute chart. Lunch may still be sloppy, so you may want to give the initial entry more room to start.

While the morning pullback is the safest entry to these aggressive plays, trying to play the stock right out of the open is by far the most aggressive. To do this, you literally have to play the stock long as it starts moving up, and put your stop a little below the low of the day. This will lead to more frequent stops, as the stop is tight, and these plays are usually not orderly in nature. You may ask why anyone would play them. The reason is simple. With the greater risk, comes the greater reward. If you have the right entry, you will capture the entire move, all with a fairly tight stop. Keep in mind, if you play the stock aggressively this way and it stops out, do not be afraid to play it again using one of the other two entries, if it sets up properly. Some traders may even take the attitude of using two entries on every play like this, accounting for the fact the first one may not work. Figure 11.12 shows a not uncommon chart: a bullish gap that opened on the low and never pulled back. Notice the lack of any bottoming tail.

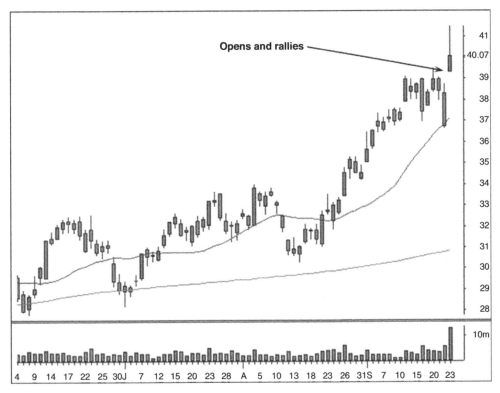

FIGURE 11.12 A Bullish Gap Opens on the Low of the Day
Chart courtesy of Mastertrader.com.

The third way to play these is similar to the first, but a little less aggressive. It is to let the stock trade down initially, and then play it long over the five-minute high. This is less aggressive than the first way for a couple of important reasons. First, playing a stock after five minutes of trading is often much less aggressive. Wide spreads are often reduced, and the stock will usually be somewhat easier to enter and exit. Also, because we are letting the stock trade down initially, then trade above a five-minute high, the stock is proving in some small way that it is going to be bullish, as it fought off the initial selling. There is a much better chance that the low it leaves behind will hold as support. This is consistent with what I taught you earlier, because the entry will have a one-minute pivot beneath the trade, rather than just the low of a bar. See Figure 11.13.

Naturally, the downside is obvious. This style of entry may lead to no entry. If the stock just opens on the low and takes off, there will be no initial move down, and the initial move up during five minutes may be so big that there is no entry, unless you used the most aggressive style. As with any trading there is always a trade-off, but with more risk comes more reward.

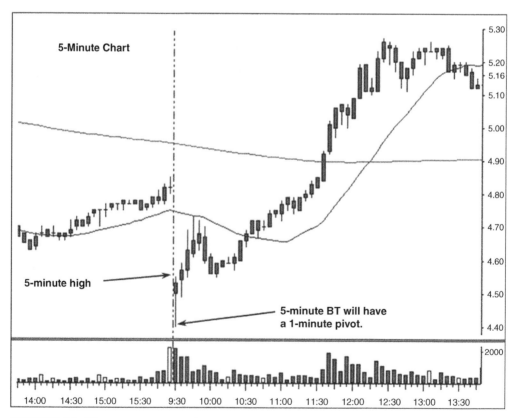

FIGURE 11.13 A Five-Minute High Is a More Secure Entry
Chart courtesy of Mastertrader.com.

As you become more familiar with gaps and develop a style that complements the plays you find, remember this about the entry you pick. There is a relationship between the quality of the gap, and the aggressiveness of the entry. The really high quality gaps are the only ones in which you should attempt an aggressive entry. The gaps that are not as clear, or are more extended, give them time to sort themselves out and wait for the quality pullback on the 5- or 15-minute chart. You will find that many gaps end up being best left alone, and this option will let you do just that.

IN SUMMARY

Gaps offer a unique opportunity in the market. Some traders may opt to trade gaps early and aggressively as their main form of day trading. Many index futures traders will trade the morning gap each day for a potential gap fill, which happens much more often with this trading instrument. Some traders may use gaps to signal swing and core entries. Some traders may take note of gaps, and play the resulting trend that occurs after the gap. Some traders may ignore gaps all together. At the very least, be aware of them and understand gaps are often special opportunities on the day.

Next up is a very important chapter I have referenced many times. In fact, it is almost impossible to discuss as much as we have without mentioning this topic. We now take all that we have learned, and put it together through the eyes of different time frames. This is known as "multiple time frame analysis."

CHAPTER 12

Frame-by-Frame

The Concept of Multiple Time Frames

When talking about trends, or support and resistance levels, you may have been asking yourself, "What time frame are we talking about," as well as, "How do the various time frames interact with each other and how can I use this interaction to my advantage when trading?" Up to this point, the time frames has not mattered. Everything we have discussed previously applies to any and all time frames and always will. If you have a two-minute uptrend, and you have a two-minute Pristine Buy Setup, it is a legitimate play. If you have resistance on a two-minute chart, it is valid resistance. Now, what we want to explore is whether that two-minute chart will have better odds if the 15-minute chart is an uptrend. Do we need to look at the daily chart? How about the weekly chart?

WHICH TIME FRAMES?

A common misconception some people believe is that all time frames need to be pointing in the same direction. While theoretically there is a moment in time when this will happen, it is simply not necessary. What we really want to see is that the time frame we are playing has enough room to continue its trend for a significant period of time. Beyond that, it is much more important that the quality of the trend we are concerned about is a high-quality trend. This is much more important than trying to find a moment when every time frame in the universe is pointing in the same direction.

For example, if you are playing a two-minute uptrend, your duration to hold the trade is likely going to be anywhere between a few minutes to a few hours. Even a few hours is going to be on the far end of reasonable. If we only need the stock to go up for a few hours, is it necessary that the weekly chart be an uptrend? Are you really concerned whether or not the stock will continue for several weeks when we are going to be exiting

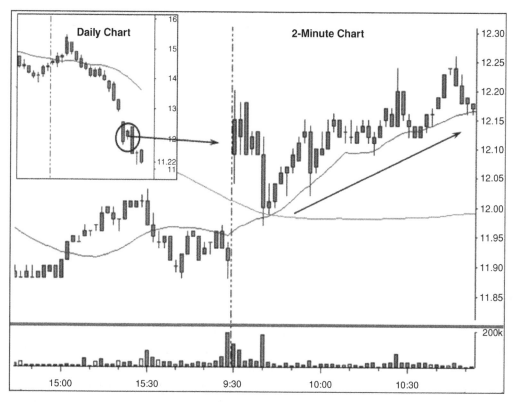

FIGURE 12.1 A Two-Minute Rally Inside of the Daily Downtrend
Chart courtesy of Mastertrader.com.

the stock in a couple of hours? If you are playing a two-minute chart for that matter, is it really even relevant that the daily chart is in an uptrend? A downtrending daily chart may rally for three or four days and still be in the downtrend. If the stock is up for three days, is there enough room to hold the stock long for two hours? Absolutely! See Figure 12.1.

Whenever you are about to play a strategy, you are looking at it in a certain time frame. What we are actually concerned about is that a dominant time frame above that time frame is in the same trend as the time frame in which we are going to play our current strategy. For simplicity, we can call the bigger time frame the "macro" time frame, and the one we are looking to play the "micro" time frame and we want to see an alignment between them. See Figure 12.2.

Next, we ask what time frames can be macro to which micro time frames? In other words, if we are playing the two-minute chart, what is the macro time frame we want to see in alignment? The time frames that we usually reference when trading at Pristine are: one-minute, two-minute, five-minute, 15-minute, 60-minute, daily, and weekly. For longer-term trading, traders may reference the monthly charts, and sometimes traders will use a 180-minute or a 30-minute chart to supplement the hourly chart. These are all fine, but I will stick to the original list we use at Pristine for this discussion.

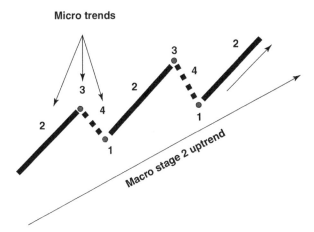

FIGURE 12.2 The Micro Time Frame Aligns with the Macros During All of the Macro 2s Chart courtesy of Mastertrader.com.

As a rule of thumb, for intraday trading we want the time frame two frames above our current time frame to be the major time frame. For example, when trading a one- or a two-minute chart, we want to see the 15-minute chart in alignment. When trading a five-minute chart, we like to see the hourly chart in alignment. When trading the 15-minute chart, we would like to see the daily in alignment. See Figure 12.3.

For larger time frame, as a rule of thumb, one time frame above is sufficient. For example, when trading the hourly chart we want to see the daily chart in alignment, and when trading the daily chart we want to see the weekly chart in alignment.

THE FIRST GOAL OF USING MULTIPLE TIME FRAMES

One of the most powerful yet basic concepts to trading the Pristine Method is to find a powerful macro trend and then to have the patience to wait for the micro trend to align with the macro trend. For example, if you want to play a two-minute Pristine Buy Setup as a long position, your first job would be to find a stock that had a very nice quality 15-minute uptrend in place. Note, that during the 15-minute uptrend, there are times when the stock is rallying to make new highs, and then times when the stock is pulling back to set higher lows. Using the concept of a macro to micro stage match, you would want to focus on playing the two-minute uptrend right after the 15-minute chart pullback ends, when the new move up in the 15-minute uptrend begins. See Figure 12.4.

Not following this rule can actually lead to some of the biggest trading debacles you could ever encounter. For example, during some of the great declines in recent years, many traders have been fixated in trying to go long on any rally that occurs on the daily chart. All of these rallies, however, were occurring inside of the weekly downtrend.

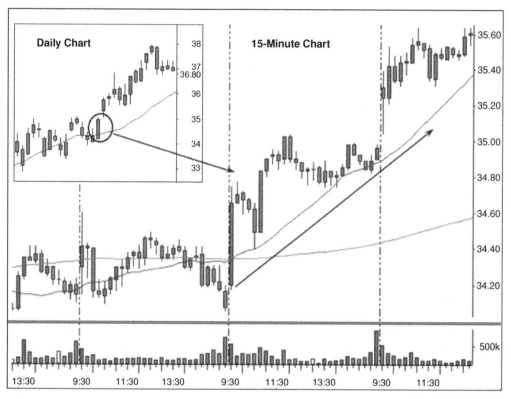

FIGURE 12.3 A 15-Minute Uptrend Inside of the Daily Uptrend
Chart courtesy of Mastertrader.com.

This means the daily rallies were short-lived, and new lows were soon to come. Any trader who understood this stage-to-stage match would never have been buying additional long positions off the daily chart during the crashes in 2001 or 2007. Perhaps you are guilty of going long when the weekly chart looked like the one in Figure 12.5?

We sometimes talk about this stage-to-stage match as trading in the sweet spot of the bigger time frame. For example, in Figure 12.4, you would be trading the 2-minute chart long in the sweet spot of the 15-minute chart. What about the reverse of this concept? In other words, if you are trading as described in Figure 12.4, and you are long the two-minute chart on all pullbacks inside the 15-minute uptrend, does there come a time where there is a sour spot, so to speak, on the 15-minute chart? Yes there is. This is referred to as a conflict in time frames.

Dealing with Conflicts in Time Frames

There are many examples of conflicts in time frames. Our first job as traders is to identify when these possible conflicts could arise. Our second job then is to determine whether

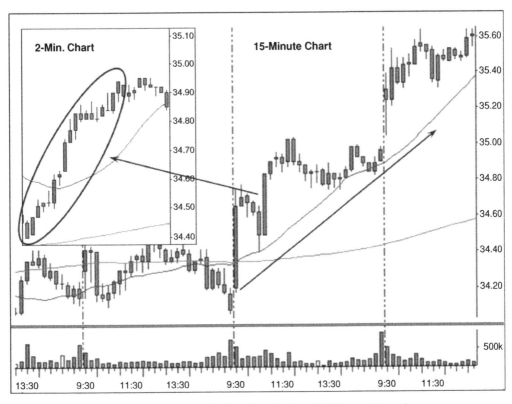

FIGURE 12.4 A Two-Minute Uptrend Aligned and with a 15-Minute Uptrend
Chart courtesy of Mastertrader.com.

these conflicts are sufficient to warrant us exiting a trade or turning down a new trade. Next, we look at some examples of where conflict would exist.

The simplest and easiest concept to understand is that when playing a micro uptrend inside of a macro uptrend, there will come a time when the macro uptrend meets some kind of resistance. There are several types of resistance that may be encountered, and each one may yield different results. Figure 12.6 depicts a basic example of this concept. Here a trader could be properly playing long during the rally that has occurred, but now you can see we are encountering a significant prior high in the stock's macro uptrend.

When this happens, there are two technical considerations when deciding whether to exit a trade or to reject a new trade in this area. First of all, any time you are currently long and deciding what to do when this happens, if you cannot come up with a better answer, simply sell half of the position and keep half. Also if undecided, it is always better to pass a new trade under the theory that missed money is better than lost money. All that being said, when reaching a prior high, if we have been on a very extended run which has lasted more than two to three pivots on the macro time frame, it is better to treat this resistance area as significant and to pass any new trade or to exit current positions.

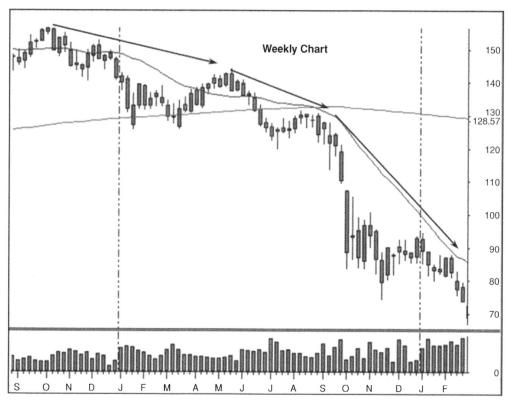

FIGURE 12.5 When the Weekly Chart Is in the Downtrend, It Is No Time to Be Buying Daily Rallies
Chart courtesy of Mastertrader.com.

This is because a very extended run is more likely to be affected by prior resistance areas. It isn't an absolute that it will, it's just common sense.

If however, you are simply encountering the prior high from the very last pivot on the macro time frame, it is safe to continue to play long because a basic definition of an uptrend is to make higher highs, which means that the prior high should be dealt with and overcome.

Another type of resistance that may be encountered by the macro time frame is when it runs into a downtrending area on a bigger time frame. This may start to sound a little confusing, but the concept is very simple. For example, say we are playing the two-minute chart long or even the 15-minute chart long because they are in uptrends. If the daily chart or hourly chart are actually in downtrends when the rallies on the 2- and 15-minute charts take us into the area that could produce a sell setup in the downtrend of the hourly or daily chart, it is time to stand aside or to sell current long positions. This should begin to sound somewhat familiar because at the beginning of this chapter we discussed how many time frames we need to look above the one we are currently using. While we may decide to play a two-minute uptrend inside of the daily downtrend that

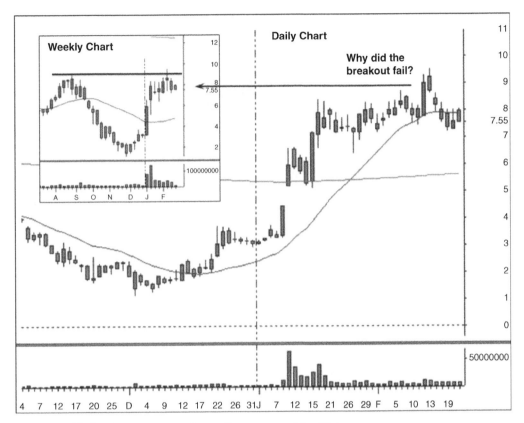

FIGURE 12.6 The Macro Time Frame Encounters a Prior High
Chart courtesy of Mastertrader.com.

does not mean that you should ignore the exact resistance area of the daily downtrend when you encounter it. This should seem like a good deal of common sense. Figure 12.7 shows a very playable uptrend that is now encountering an area that should be respected in the downtrend.

As a footnote to this discussion, given a choice between continuing to play long at the prior high and continuing to play long when meeting a significant downtrend area, it is always better to favor the long that is meeting the prior high. Before reading on, can you think of the reason why? (Again, it is quite simple and you should have the knowledge now to understand this.) When you are encountering a prior high, the examples we looked at had the price pattern still in an uptrend. Meeting resistance in an uptrend is not the same as meeting resistance in a downtrend. Resistance in a downtrend should always be respected because that keeps you following the major trends. This ultimately is what trading is all about.

The last item to consider when the macro time frame is meeting resistance is not really a new type of resistance but rather the quality of that resistance. If you go back

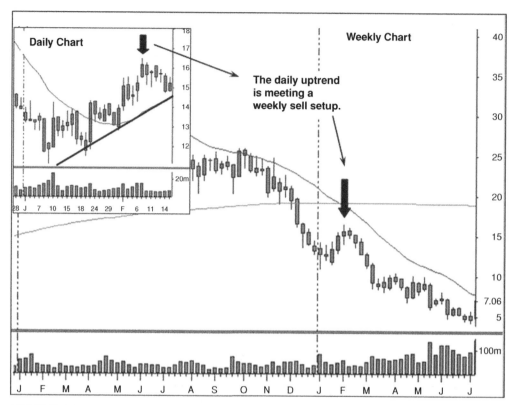

FIGURE 12.7 A Strong Micro Uptrend Meets a Larger Time Frame Downtrend
Chart courtesy of Mastertrader.com.

to Chapter 3 on support and resistance, simply note the different types of resistance and remember that the stronger forms of resistance are the ones that we want to avoid. For example, picture a price pattern simply returning to the prior pivot high on the macro time frame, and that prior area was a very difficult square top filled with failed breakouts. That strong type or resistance area was discussed before and it is the type of resistance that may prevent us from making a new high. Likewise for this discussion, if the quality of that resistance is strong, it could warrant selling long positions or passing on the next long trade even though it is only the prior high in an uptrend. See Figure 12.8.

A POWERFUL CONCEPT EMERGES

This leads perfectly into a very advanced discussion about a concept that, once understood, extends well beyond the current use of multiple time frames. We just discussed what the expectation is when a smaller time frame uptrend meets a larger time frame downtrend and that there are higher odds of failure for the smaller time frame uptrend

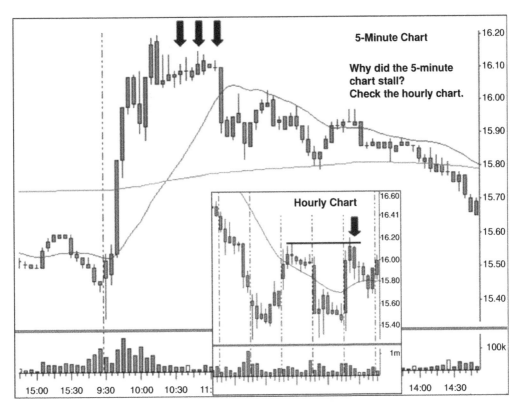

FIGURE 12.8 Strong Resistance in the Macro Time Frame
Chart courtesy of Mastertrader.com.

when it encounters a larger time frame downtrend. Since the larger time frame is the one we should be paying respect to, when you have a price pattern that shows that it is likely to roll over in an area near the downtrend, one way to get confirmation of that downtrend continuing is when the smaller time frame uptrend fails. This is really just the reverse, or the positive way, of reiterating what we have just discussed. We were looking at why not to play the smaller time frame in the situation, because it might fail. However, the failure of that small time frame actually leads to a larger time frame resuming its original trend. Herein lies the magic.

This concept really gives us three incredible rules for trading. First, as we just discussed, do not continue to play the smaller time frame uptrend when it encounters a larger time frame downtrend because the odds of failure become greater. Second, we can get the best indication of that larger downtrend continuing once we have a failure of the uptrend on the smaller time frame. Third, and perhaps the best and most advanced topic, is that we can actually use the failure of the smaller time frame as our entry criteria for the larger time frame downtrend.

Naturally, if the bigger time frame is in a proper downtrend, the sell setup that occurs in the downtrend is the proper entry. However, when you have a more questionable

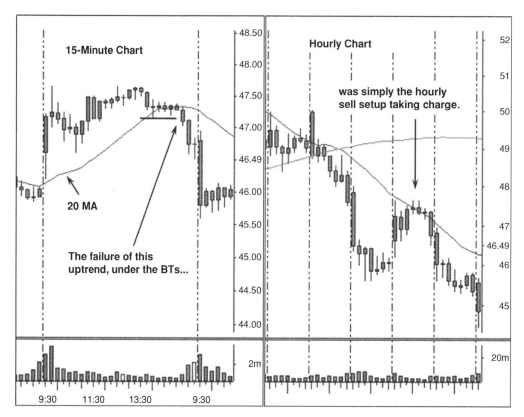

FIGURE 12.9 The Failure of the Smaller Time Frame Uptrend Resumes Larger Downtrend
Chart courtesy of Mastertrader.com.

downtrend, or you are not as sure of the exact point at which the downtrend may continue, using the failure of the smaller time frame uptrend is often a great way to get confirmation of the proper area to short. Figure 12.9 shows an example of a small time frame failing which sets the larger time frame in motion.

WARNING SIGNS IN THE MICRO TREND

We just finished discussing how a breakdown in the shorter-term time frame should always be treated seriously when it is occurring in some kind of danger area in the larger-term time frame. However, what about weakness on the smaller time frame in general? Can this be interpreted as an early warning sign of weakness in the larger time frame?

As a rule, the answer is "No." This should be fairly obvious at this point. Remember in the course of any macro uptrend, there will be micro downtrends. In other words, there will be weakness all the time in smaller time frames even when the larger time frame is still in a very secure and reliable uptrend. So generally, we cannot assume that the tail will wag the dog, and that any weakness in the small time frame is automatically going to spell trouble for the big time frame.

However, there are several exceptions. I want to present two instances of them, where the shorter-term time frame can exhibit a powerful enough pattern that it should be respected. Respecting it, at the very least, means to be extra cautious if playing the longer time frame uptrend. It could also mean that it is advisable to avoid playing the uptrend altogether. In extreme cases, aggressive traders may even look at some of these signs as a valid reason to short.

The first instance occurs on a type of pattern under the general heading of a "failure pattern." There are several ways to use failure patterns, and the first one is used here in the discussion about multiple time frame analysis. It is a fairly simple concept. It occurs when you are playing a time frame long and in the middle of the uptrend a perfect bullish move occurs to the upside, and immediately after the breakout or buy setup rallies, the bears take over and make the pattern fail immediately. The most important point here is distinguishing a perfectly valid bullish move that should not move higher and fails, as opposed to a pattern that was not ready to move up yet.

In other words, if the pattern was too extended or was attacking a prior area of resistance, it may be perfectly acceptable for the first breakout attempt to fail but that does not mean that the bullishness is over. What we are looking for here is that near perfect setup that begins to move up as we expected it should, and then fails miserably. It is also important to note that immediately after the failure, it does not rebound more than halfway back to the height of the breakout. Sometimes a bullish stock will have a sharp decline and snap back almost immediately. This is known as a "shakeout." It is much different than the failure to breakout that we have been discussing. The name for this type of concept is often abbreviated BBF, and stands for Breakout Bar Failure. See Figure 12.10 for an example of a BBF.

As with all technical analysis, I believe it is good that you understand the reasons why price action occurs on a chart. Simply memorizing a set of rules will give you a set of rules. Knowing the reasons that the rules are formed will help you develop new rules of your own and better trading concepts. The reason that a Breakout Bar Failure can be used to indicate trouble, not only for the current time frame, but also for the larger time frame is because of the extreme bearishness that is taking place. When a stock is strong, the bulls will always maintain control. If the pattern is sloppy or if it becomes extended, some bearishness may set in but prices should always snap back. When a perfectly bullish play is unable to hold the attention of the bulls, this type of action is likely to continue into the future, which will make it extend to the larger time frame. Again, it is critical to make sure that you see a real failure and not just a sloppy price pattern.

The second instance where the smaller time frame may give us an indication of trouble in the larger time frame is a pattern that is known as the "M pattern." The M pattern is a type of pattern that interrupts a bullish move and can spell trouble not only for the current time frame but also for the larger time frame. The comparable concept when ending a downtrend is known as the "W pattern."

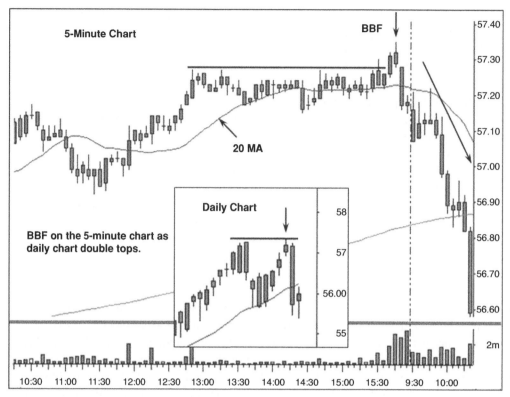

FIGURE 12.10 A Breakout Bar Failure Spells Trouble for All Time Frames
Chart courtesy of Mastertrader.com.

There are two movements that should happen to form an M pattern. First, prices usually extend or accelerate slightly into the final high. This is not always required, but usually present. Second, we have what amounts to a change of trend on the current time frame. In other words, the next rally attempt back into that extended high retests the prior high but fails to make a new high. The pullback from there breaks the pivot that began the last rally, which in fact breaks the uptrend and puts a stock in a presumptive downtrend. Figure 12.11 shows an example of a stock with an M pattern.

Now is an especially good time to remind you of a rule to always keep in mind. Our job is always to analyze all the information to try and draw the best conclusion that we can, based on the price action in front of us. I recently discussed examples indicating when a very bearish shorter-term pattern may indicate a change of the longer-term pattern. It will not always be the case that this will follow through to the downside, and again you need to look at all the information at hand. At the very least, this should raise enough of a question for you to stand aside if you are unsure about what is going on. You need much more evidence to actually take one of these patterns and play it as a short.

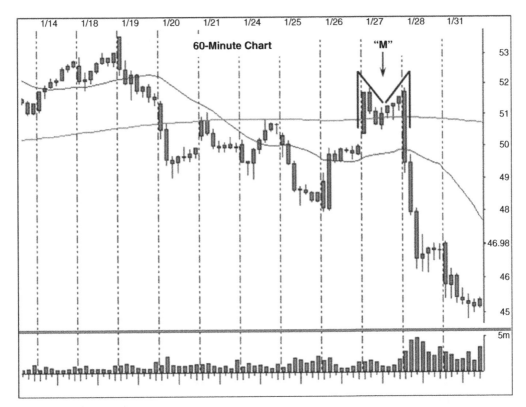

FIGURE 12.11 The M Pattern Ends an Uptrend
Chart courtesy of Mastertrader.com.

Another thing to note is that, over the course of this book, I have focused on discussing one constant direction in price action to keep things simple. In this chapter, I have always discussed a bullish micro time frame inside of either a bullish or bearish macro time frame. But remember that all of these concepts apply in reverse equally as well. In other words, a micro downtrend running into a prior low on the macro time frame may signal the end of the downtrend. Like with everything in technical analysis, you can go through this entire book and swap all of the bullish words for bearish words and the concepts will hold true.

HIDDEN PATTERNS

One final area of multiple time frame analysis I want to cover is what we call "zooming down" at Pristine. It refers to moving one time frame lower in order to get a clearer picture of what is actually happening.

One of most common uses for this is when a pullback in a bullish uptrend does a proper retracement to a minor support area and looks like an excellent opportunity

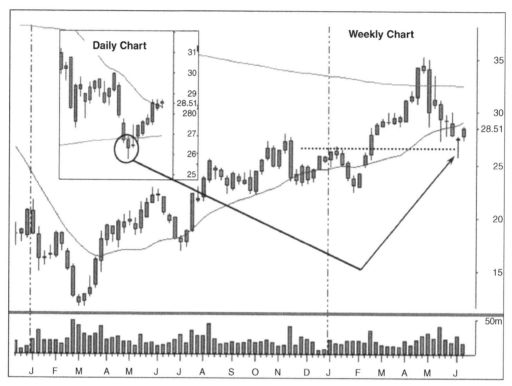

FIGURE 12.12 The Daily Chart Entry Is Used to Enter a Sloppy Pullback on the Weekly Chart Chart courtesy of Mastertrader.com.

for a PBS, but does not form the PBS properly. It only has two bars or does not form the requisite pattern we want to see, but still appears to be very bullish. As long as the retracement is correct and we are in a proper support area, we can drop down one time frame in order to pick up enough bars to form the proper buy setup. Figure 12.12 depicts an example of a bullish time frame that pulled back but never formed the proper set up. The smaller time frame actually formed a nice Pristine Buy Setup to take the stock higher.

Another instance when we can use a hidden pattern is when the current time frame we are playing produces very wide bars, which makes the entry or exit very difficult. Wide bars can produce very wide stops and if the play is otherwise set up properly, it may make sense to zoom down one time frame to find a better entry. In this case, the word better means more precise, not necessarily higher odds. When we zoom down a time frame we are engaging in one of the oldest trade-offs in trading. We are giving up some reliability, for a higher reward-to-risk trade. This is always a trade-off that you will find in trading.

Figure 12.13 shows a nice PBS but the problem is that the last bar is so wide that waiting for the entry over that wide bar will give us a very wide stop. This will produce a trade with the lower reward-to-risk. However, note that this pattern will also be a much

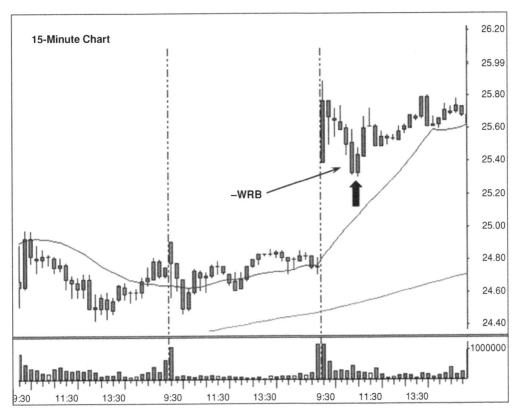

FIGURE 12.13 A PBS Forms with a Wide Range Bar on the 15-Minute Chart
Chart courtesy of Mastertrader.com.

more reliable trade because it will be very difficult for the pattern to stop out underneath the bullish bars that must form in order to negate the high of the big red bar. When the odds become this skewed toward safety over reward-to-risk, we may want to zoom down to a smaller time frame and trade the PBS that occurs in the smaller time frame.

Figure 12.14 is the same pattern shown on a smaller time frame that gives us an entry with a reasonable reward-to-risk ratio. Of course, the trade-off is that by entering the trade earlier on the smaller time frame, it has a greater chance of stopping out because it has not yet negated the big red bar.

Another time that we can find a hidden pattern is when a congested area forms on a smaller time frame that is not clearly visible on the time frame we are playing. Sometimes the current time frame shows a pullback that has some minor disruptions to it, but when zooming down to the smaller time frame we see a serious failure has occurred, or at least a very congested pattern has formed that may reduce the odds of the current long play we are contemplating. See Figure 12.15, where we have a pullback that looks a little sloppy but may still be acceptable.

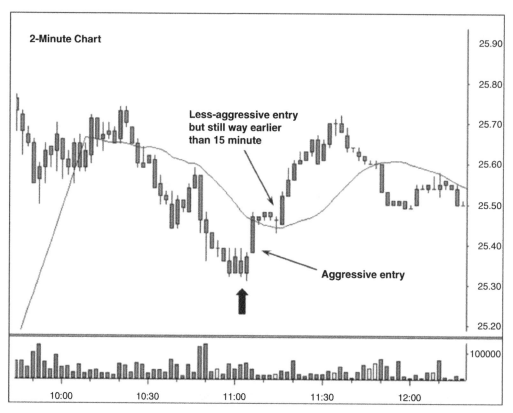

FIGURE 12.14 The Two-Minute Chart of 12.13 Provides a Better Reward to Risk
Chart courtesy of Mastertrader.com.

Then Figure 12.16 shows that the disruption in the pattern is actually more severe than it looks on the original time frame. By zooming in on a time frame, we see a more congested pattern and a failure that occurred that gives this trade lower odds of moving up on the next rally.

IN SUMMARY

Once you understand the basic concepts that account for price movements, using multiple time frame analysis is one of the best ways to increase your odds on every trade. Using multiple time frame analysis enables us to do several important things. It always keeps us in check with following the trend. Following the trend is one of the most basic, but still most important, concepts in technical analysis. We often lose sight of the bigger trend when looking at the smaller time frames. Multiple time frame analysis keeps us looking at the forest and not the trees when picking our plays.

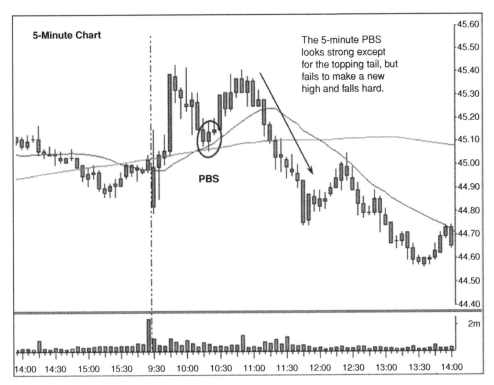

FIGURE 12.15 The Pullback Looks a Little Sloppy
Chart courtesy of Mastertrader.com.

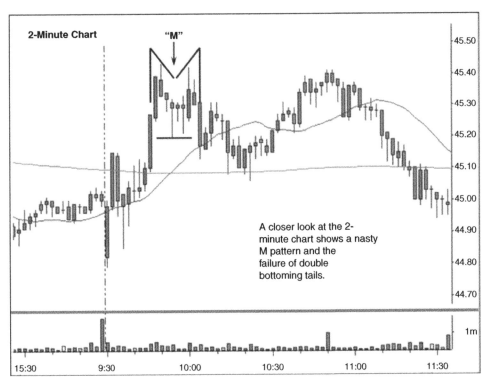

FIGURE 12.16 The Smaller Time Frame Shows More Congestion
Chart courtesy of Mastertrader.com.

Multiple time frame analysis also gives us the ability to have a better look at the current price pattern by zooming down and seeing what is happening underneath the surface. By adding the concept of multiple time frame analysis to what you have already learned about price patterns, you begin to reach the upper levels of trading mastery.

Things should really be pulling together for you as we finish this chapter. We talk about some very important topics in the remaining chapters and the next one, Chapter 13, is one of my favorites: Making failure work for you.

CHAPTER 13

Making Failure Work for You

Recognizing When Patterns Fail

You might wonder, "What is the purpose of having a chapter that discusses failure?" Obviously, if you are this far into the book you realize that not all patterns work, no matter how accurate the method. It is always a matter of probability and trying to get the odds in our favor as much as possible on every trade. Therefore, some good patterns will fail, and that is precisely why we put a protective stop loss in place. If we can always maximize the potential gains from our winning trades, and limit all of our losing trades to the intended amount as designated by the original stop loss, we will be good traders as long as we can pick reasonable plays. So, since the stop loss is our failsafe, why even have a discussion about failure? There are several reasons, which we will discuss in this chapter.

First, from a psychological point of view, it is good to determine, before we even place a trade, at what point we will have considered the pattern a failure. Determining this helps us accept our stop loss and to exit the trade when there is no hope of recovering. Traders who always hang on to the hope for recovery always turn into losing traders. Defining the points at which decisions should be made before getting into the trade is always the proper thing to do. See Figure 13.1.

Second, under a similar theory, when a particular play stops out, it does not necessarily mean that the strategy being implemented has failed. For instance, we may be expecting a certain price area to hold and, as prices begin to move up the first time, the move fails and the play stops out, based on the tight stop that was used when the play triggered. However, it is quite possible that the second time the stock tries to rally it will be successful. You will also find this to be a common occurrence if you zoom down time frames to find an entry. For example, if you are looking to buy a 60-minute Pristine Buy Setup and you are zooming down to the 5-minute chart to find an appropriate entry, the 5-minute chart may stop you out, yet the 60-minute Pristine Buy Setup turns out to be successful. Does this mean your whole strategy failed, or simply the first attempt at en-

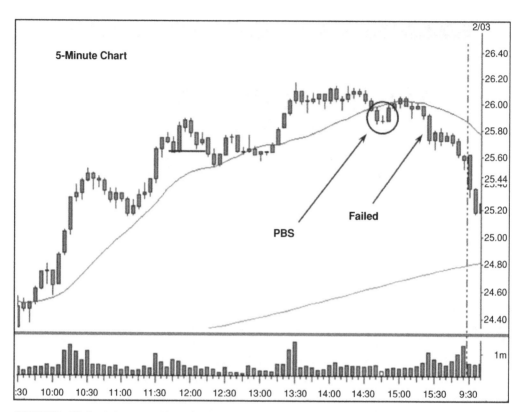

FIGURE 13.1 A Pattern Fails and Moves Quickly in the "Wrong" Direction
Chart courtesy of Mastertrader.com.

tering failed? Understanding these differences is important so we can know whether it is acceptable to replay a trade that stopped out initially.

Third, sometimes excellent patterns do fail and this situation often tells us that things may be changing. The trend is our friend because it is so reliable, but trends do change. One of the best signs of the trend changing is the actual failure of that trend to continue from a pattern that it typically would have come from. It sounds obvious, but noticing failures at the appropriate times can help you find new plays in a new direction. Remember, too, in Chapter 12 on multiple time frames (when discussing M and W patterns, and breakout bar failures), we pointed out that failure on a smaller time frame can sometimes give us a clue as to the beginning of failure on a larger time frame. Whether or not we were a victim of the failure, we still want to be able to participate in profiting on what the failure is telling us. The move from an objective failure often sets up a measured move, something I will discuss in detail later in this chapter.

Lastly, many failures are not really failures to a Pristine-Trained Trader (PTT). Many traders not trained in the methods of Pristine misuse subjective indicators. When Pristine traders see prices responding temporarily to the self-fulfilling prophecy that is brought about by a subjective indicator, and yet there is no corresponding price action to justify the move, we can often predict the failure of the pattern other traders are looking at and, when we play a failure like this, we are participating in profits in two different ways:

1. First, by virtue of the fact that we felt a failure would happen, we are actually playing the stock in the correct direction.
2. Second, because many people ended up failing on this play, we will be profiting by taking the stock in the direction it will go as traders' stops trigger.

We will be participating in profits from trader stops being hit rather than being stopped ourselves. These subjective failures also can set up a measured move.

DID THE PLAY STOP, OR DID THE PATTERN FAIL?

By definition, anytime a pattern fails, the trade should have stopped out. However, every time a trade stops out, does it mean that the pattern failed? Perhaps it is a matter of semantics, but the answer is, "No." In theory, some kind of failure has happened. That particular entry failed, but that is not enough information to say that the pattern failed and that we should play the stock in a different direction. Also, do not think that any time a stock does not go up, it must go down. That is also poor logic. We want to find the best possible patterns moving in either direction.

Sometimes when a stock has trouble going higher, it will simply go sideways. There is a big difference between saying that a pattern failed and we should leave it alone, and saying that a pattern failed so let us take it in the new direction. One of the things to look at is if the failure has a tradable void or, in other words, the relevant support areas are violated and there are no more price support areas to the immediate left.

In Figure 13.2 you will see that a play was made in a strong support area and that the pattern simply failed to hold that support level. The time frame we played actually failed and the pullback was already at a level from which we would not have been interested in playing the stock long. This is the type of failure in which we have no interest in playing long, and would consider shorting the failure of the stock to go higher. Notice in Figure 13.2 that the lack of support is the same as saying that there was a tradable void beneath the area from which the stock attempted to rally.

In Figure 13.3 we see a different story. The stock tried to rally at the top of a support area, and a smaller time frame triggered a buy setup. When that entry attempt failed, the stock fell. There was a void, but it was a small one. The stock held on to the support area from the bigger time frame. Also, if the strategy was based on the bigger time frame, it did not fail. Only the early entry on the smaller time frame failed.

Also, we were still above the last area of support on the bigger time frame or, in other words, there was not a tradable void underneath this immediate area.

FIGURE 13.2   The Time Frame We Are Playing Fails and There Is No Support to Be Found
Chart courtesy of Mastertrader.com.

WHEN GOOD PATTERNS FAIL

We always have to accept that anything can happen in the market at any time. As traders, we are always looking to develop odds that are in our favor. But even if we have huge odds in our favor, there are still times when those odds will not play out. Therefore, the first quality of a good trader is to understand and accept that anything can happen and when the trade is not going as planned (even when the play is truly good), to take the appropriate response. It is only common sense to understand that while the trend is our friend, no trend will last forever. If trends do eventually change, it implies that the current trend at some time will fail. If we are involved in playing the stock at the time the trend fails, we need to exit our position accordingly and reevaluate the situation. You can see a play in Figure 13.4 that appeared to be in an excellent trend, but the play did not work, and the result of the failure was a change in direction of the trend.

In this situation, if you chose to be stubborn and not accept what was actually happening, you would have suffered a great deal of pain when the stock changed direction as a result of the failure. The only time to exit this situation, the only appropriate time,

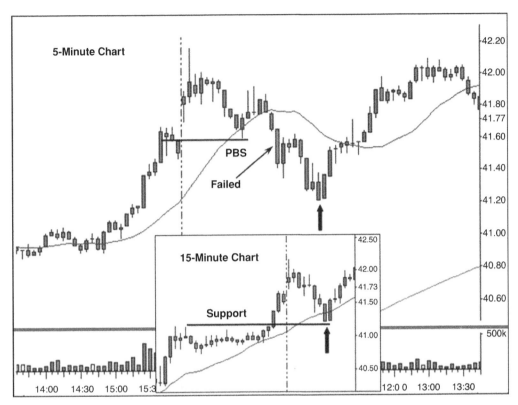

FIGURE 13.3   This Failure Is Not a True Failure on a Bigger Time Frame
Chart courtesy of Mastertrader.com.

was when the original play failed. The first and most important rule of what to do when a good play does fail is to accept the failure and to exit with the understanding that this is just one of those plays that did not work. Whether or not a new play should be made in a different direction is a function of the setup that actually occurs. When a trade fails, it is not a good idea to just assume a new trend has started. Often times, prices simply go sideways in a confused manner looking to create new support or resistance levels.

The decision to make a new play in a new direction would be based on whether you have a new strategy occurring. In other words, perhaps the bigger time frame ran into resistance or perhaps the current move was becoming climactically extended. These events could generate strategies that would allow you to go against the prior trend as soon as it breaks. Without any events like this, it is generally better to wait until you have a new strategy: Let the new trend develop in the new direction and begin playing the new trend. Remember that your first goal is always to find clean patterns. Many trends form very difficult and sloppy patterns when they are in the process of changing.

There are actually several reasons why good patterns may fail. A very common reason is playing the stock at the wrong time of the day. Strong rallies that continue in one direction right into the middle of lunch will often fail to continue that trend through to

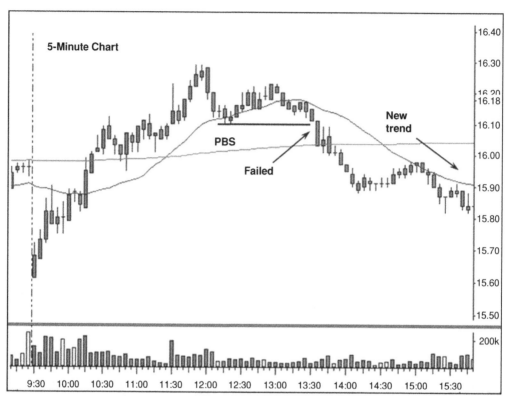

FIGURE 13.4   This Failure Actually Changes the Direction of the Trend
Chart courtesy of Mastertrader.com.

the end of lunch (see Figure 13.5). In addition, sharp moves into reversal times often change direction and may break the trend they were following going into the reversal time.

Another common reason for good patterns to fail comes from playing an overly extended pattern. Two prior chapters discussed how big volume or wide range bars toward the end of a run can often signal the end of the current move as these types of moves become exhaustion moves and can use up the last of the buyers or sellers. The first pullbacks after these moves often fail. Figure 13.6 shows an example of a very extended move that was not able to rally again because of the exhaustion of buyers. You should be able to recognize these patterns and anticipate these failures (if we even choose to call them failures at all.)

Also, remember our discussion about support and resistance in Chapter 3. When stocks form very difficult prior pivot areas, prices often have a difficult time moving beyond those pivots and can cause the pattern to fail. In an uptrend, if the stock has a difficult time and forms a round or square top, the next pullback may fail to make a new high on the next rally. Figure 13.7 shows a stock that was not able to continue its current trend because the prior reference point was a congested area.

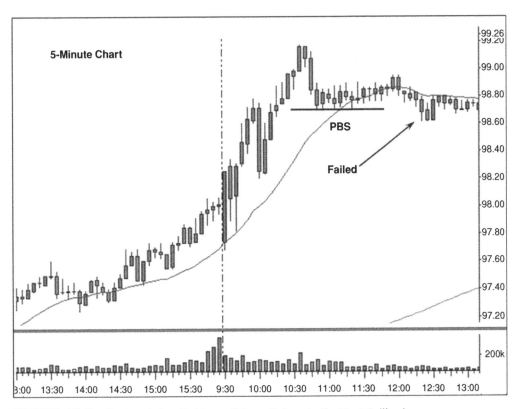

FIGURE 13.5 The Lunchtime Doldrums Bring a Failure to the Next Pullback
Chart courtesy of Mastertrader.com.

When we do have a clear strategy to begin playing the new trend, we will often find that the first move in the new direction is a measured move from the move that lead into the failure. Let us look at a play that might have been done based on the failure of the smaller time frame as the failure was anticipated due to the larger time frame running into resistance. In Figure 13.8, you see a trend breaking on one time frame, only because the larger time frame is no longer in a clear trend. This causes the smaller time frame to fail, and it is not uncommon to see a move after the failure that is equal to the distance of the movement of the failure. This is what we call a measured move. Measured moves can happen both when the failure was very unpredictable, and when the failure was very predictable.

Naturally, there is a bit of semantics involved here because if any of these conditions exist, it should be somewhat expected that the pattern would fail and therefore is not a good pattern. The only true shocking failures are the ones that come from perfect patterns that simply fail for reasons we never understand. Anytime there are issues that could affect the continuation of the trend, it becomes more likely and more expected that the pattern will fail. At some point, the pattern may become so poor that the failure becomes obvious. At this point, some of these patterns are expected to fail because only

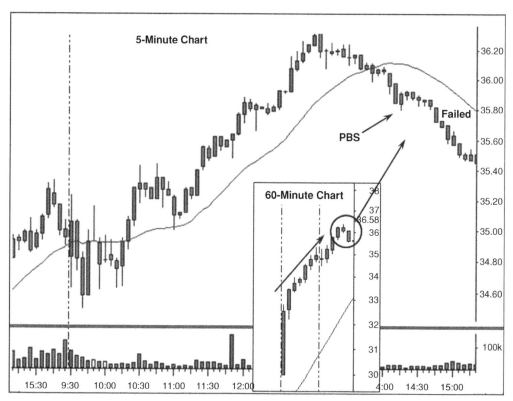

FIGURE 13.6 Exhaustion Move Often Means That the Next Rally May Fail
Chart courtesy of Mastertrader.com.

novice traders will be looking at them, and good traders will be looking to take advantage of their failures when they happen.

CAPITALIZING ON PREDICTABLE FAILURES

On any day when the market is flat, the market is a zero-sum game (actually a negative-sum game when you include commissions and slippage), which means that the sum of all the winners equals the sum of all the losers. Sometimes the loser of the trade is a good trader who was on the right side of a high-odds trade but the odds did not play out. More often, though, the loser is someone who is not experienced in the market and is paying his or her dues on a daily basis. These traders often rely on a fly-by-the-seat-of-the-pants method rather than any real strategy. They rely on things that seem to make sense intuitively, but they are rarely correct. The market is famous for taking money from the inexperienced. Most losing trades and most losing traders rely on information that is not properly used, like subjective indicators. These types of failures can actually be used by the experienced trader to make money from the minute the pattern fails.

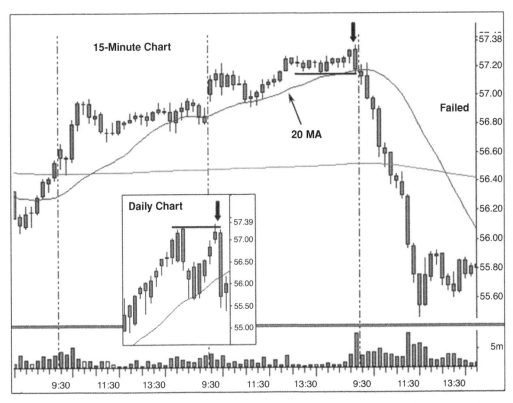

FIGURE 13.7 The Prior Congestion Forms a Difficult Area Making It Hard for Prices to Move Higher
Chart courtesy of Mastertrader.com.

This first example comes from playing weak support levels in a downtrend. Many traders have a perpetual bullish bias whether they are aware of it or not. They are always looking to buy stocks that fall, even when they are likely to continue to fall. Figure 13.9 depicts an example of a stock that tried to bounce when it hit its prior pivot low in a downtrend. An experienced Pristine trader knows that this prior pivot low is expected to fail because prices are in a downtrend. The self-fulfilling prophecy of the prior pivot often makes for a small bounce, and as traders enter into this on the long side, they are destined to fail. As the stop gives way, experienced traders can short and take advantage of the stops being triggered by the incorrect bulls, as well as play the correct side of the downtrend.

A second great example involves those subjective indicators we have discussed previously. Subjective indicators often give traders the excuse to take trades when there is no real price support available. Many traders look at the subjective indicators as being the Holy Grail so that they do not have to truly learn or understand price action. There are many examples of this, but one of the most common is the simple concept of using a moving average as support. The 200-period moving average is perhaps most

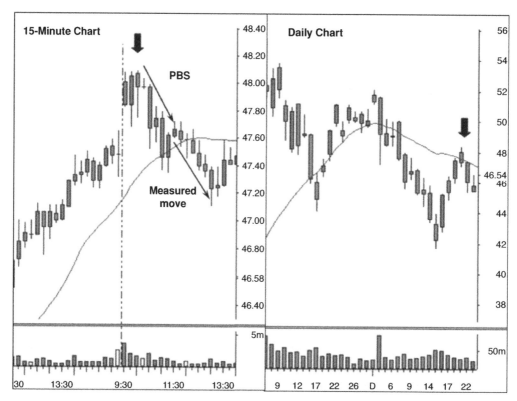

FIGURE 13.8 The Small Time Frame Fails, Causing a Measured Move to the Downside
Chart courtesy of Mastertrader.com.

well known and the best self-fulfilling prophecy that there is when it comes to support. It is so strong as a self-fulfilling prophecy that it will often make a stock bounce for no other reason but the fact it is there. However, the bounce will be temporary if there is no true price support to the left. In that case, the moving average will provide only temporary relief from the decline. Inexperienced traders go long as the stock bounces on the 200-period moving average. Experienced traders short the failure of this bounce (see Figure 13.10).

Again, there may be some semantics at play here. We have now come full circle to the point where, to a Pristine trader, these are not really failures because we play them to fail and we move in the new direction. These are the most playable events because we are actually playing on the correct side of the odds.

EXPECTED (OR UNEXPECTED) FAILURE

Obviously there are some in-between situations where price movements are not terribly clear as to whether they are failing at the moment or not. It also may not be clear whether

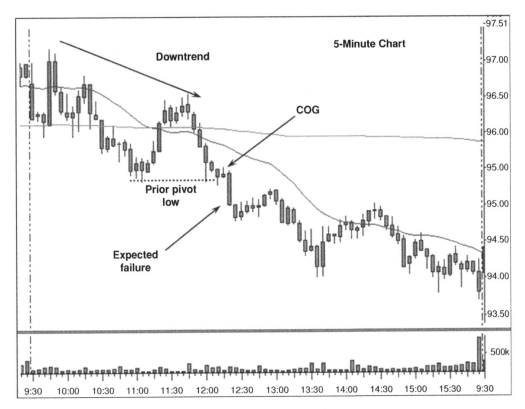

FIGURE 13.9 The Prior Pivot Low Does Not Offer Any Real Support
Chart courtesy of Mastertrader.com.

we should expect the pattern to fail or not. So how do we handle these in-between situations? There are two ways:

1. There is an old adage that is an excellent rule to trade by: "Missed money is better than lost money." It aligns with one of the key concepts for trading that you should have heard several times in this book: "If there is not a clear tradable pattern, pass the trade." While this book is going to great lengths to show you various price patterns, it is best to remember that actual trades should be taken on the clearest and best-formed patterns. If you are not sure what is happening, stand aside. With all of the stock symbols and markets, and all of the various time frames, there is always an excellent trade out there somewhere.

2. To better analyze how a particular failure is shaping up, use bar-by-bar analysis techniques. If the pattern begins to fail, but it is not clear to what extent the failure will develop, evaluate every bar that forms and continue to recalculate the odds as a price pattern develops. Using bar-by-bar analysis keeps you in the moment and constantly assessing the odds of what may happen. This, again, helps your selection in determining when it is appropriate to exit a bad trade, exit what was a good trade, stand aside, or play a new trade in a new direction.

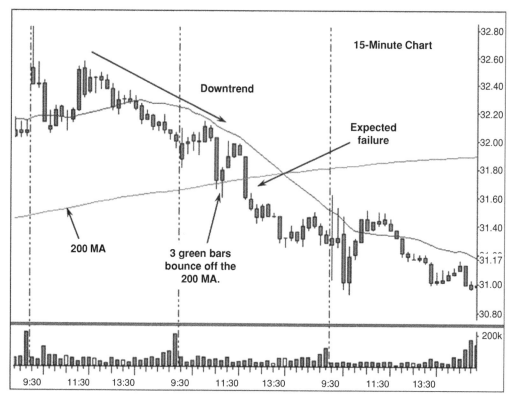

FIGURE 13.10   The 200-Period Moving Average Provides Only a Temporary Bounce
Chart courtesy of Mastertrader.com.

IN SUMMARY

Remember, anything can happen in the market at any time. Without question, many things happen repeatedly and set up high-odds events, which give traders a huge edge in the market. The key is to recognize and follow these events and only act when they are present. Remember that most failed patterns are really the failed expectations of traders. The initial pattern was created by a belief that something would occur (no matter whether that initial belief was legitimate or not) and now something different has happened, and it is causing traders to react a certain way. We study failure patterns first and foremost because they are an excellent psychological tool to reinforce the exit of a trade that is no longer performing to our expectations. Having these moments defined ahead of time and understanding when our expectations have failed will help us react at the right time and in the right way.

All trends come to an end at some point, no matter how reliable the trend was, and we use failure patterns as focal areas to note the change of a trend or a pattern that is occurring. The failure of the trend to act as we expected is the first indication the trend is changing. Knowing to stay away from that trend, or being ready to play in the new direction, can be helpful to traders and these instances are brought about by understanding how the failures of good patterns occur.

What some traders consider failures may be very expected outcomes to other, more experienced traders. By noticing false moves that are brought about by an incomplete understanding of technical analysis, or by the use of subjective indicators, we can actually create new opportunities for ourselves by playing prices in the correct direction after other traders feel a failure has occurred. By mastering the concept of failures, you round out your trading persona and take your trading to a new level.

After all we have covered about finding the best plays, it is now time to talk about what to do with a play once you are in it. I am talking about how to manage plays, which is perhaps one of the most important topics to making money, and it is the focus of Chapter 14.

CHAPTER 14

Manage the Trade and the Money

The Missing Link

A s you grow as a trader, you become more accustomed to technical analysis and how price action works in a predictable manner. You gain confidence in reading charts and see plays move in the direction that you desire them to move. Understanding all of the workings of price action takes some education and experience but it is all at a level that can be learned by anybody. Naturally, the quality of your teacher and the quality of the education makes all the difference as to how well you learn to read charts.

After gaining the proper chart reading experience, the next hurdle in good trading is management; how to translate a price movement on a chart into having the money end up in your bank account. The first big topic in trade management is how to manage the money and there are a few different levels to this which we will go over in this chapter. If you lose large amounts of money on your losing trades, and only make small amounts of money on your winning trades, it will be difficult to be a successful trader. Next comes the ability to manage the trade. Here we also have several possible levels through which traders develop. The overall goal is to capture large price movements when they occur, yet not give up significant gains when your plays have already had their maximum move. There is admittedly some art to this as there is to all of trading. However, there are very manageable rules to guide you through it.

MANAGING THE MONEY—SHARE SIZE

When someone comes to the market without any education and takes their first sets of trades, they probably have no real money management concept whatsoever. They may have some vague notion that based on the size of their account they should be taking 100 or 1,000 or 2,000 or 5,000 shares, but there may be very little rhyme or reason to the rules they follow. At some point they probably develop the notion that their share size should vary not only with the size of their account, but also with the price of the stock they are playing. A five-dollar stock may only have a 20-cent move on a good day, whereas a $150 stock may move several dollars without any problem. Buying equal shares of both these stocks would yield greatly different results. But while this is a step in the right direction, it is not nearly close enough.

Before delving into some of the money management concepts you will use as a trader, ask yourself this simple question: "If you develop as a trader to the point that you have significantly more winning trades than losing trades, and all of your winning trades have a significantly higher percentage of gain on the chart when compared to the losing trades, does this mean you will be a profitable trader?" It may astound you, but the answer is, "No." This is because of the trader placing larger bets on the trades that end up being losers.

In trading, placing a larger bet translates to the number of shares that you carry on each particular trade. If you have a high percentage of winning trades, and all those winning trades move a significant amount, it will not translate to many dollars in the bank account if you have a very small share size on those winning trades. The same problem exists if you start with a significant share size but sell most of it very early, capturing only a small part of a move with most of the shares. Then, if you feel exceptionally confident about one of the trades and it turns out to be a loser, you may have a very large share size which turns into a large dollar loss that wipes out all of your winning trades. Many traders reading this may have experienced this exact phenomenon: You feel like a winning trader because you get a significant number of trades right, but one or two losing trades wipe out all of the winning trades and you are back to negative.

The way to avoid this is to make sure that every similar trade will lose approximately the same amount of money. This ensures that all trades are equal, which has many advantages. First, when all trades are equal, you manage them all in a similar way and do not favor one over the other. When one trade carries a higher risk amount, traders tend to manage it differently and sell earlier. Second, we are going to discuss other issues regarding the management of an account for the day, and those issues will become very difficult to accomplish if every trade loses a different amount of money. Third, and perhaps most importantly, if you are following a trading plan and take only the highest quality trades, it becomes very difficult to argue that one trade is far superior to another. Proper risk amount should be taken on the best trades, and the lesser-quality trade should not be taken at all. This is called share sizing.

Share sizing so that all similar trades have a similar risk is just a simple matter of math. When we enter a trade, there are three numbers that always need to be present: the exact price upon which we will enter this trade, the exact price upon which we will exit the trade as a failure, and the approximate areas that we will exit the trade for profit. Based on these, we always know the exact distance between the price at which we will enter and the price at which we will exit. Let us say for example that we are going to enter a long trade and we are willing to risk $300 on the trade. If we are willing to enter the trade

Your preset risk amount in dollars

The size of the stop in dollars

Example:
Risk amount = 300.00
Entry = 20.50
Stop = 20.20

$$\frac{300.00}{(20.50 - 20.20)} = 1000$$

FIGURE 14.1 How to Mathematically Calculate Your Share Size
Chart courtesy of Mastertrader.com.

over $22.50, and exit the trade for a loss underneath $20.20, that is a 30-cent move that the stock will travel in the event of a stop out (it technically will be 32 cents by the time you enter and exit even without any slippage but, for simplicity, we will use 30 cents). Figure 14.1 shows you the formulas that you can use to make these calculations.

You can see in Figure 14.1 that you could purchase 1,000 shares and you would contain your loss to $300 in the event of a stop out, assuming there was not any slippage and not counting commissions. By using this simple math formula, you ensure that all similar trades will have a similar loss amount if stopped out. And notice that I said the loss would be $300 "not counting slippage and commissions." The word slippage means that the stock moves as you try to enter because there are not enough shares available at the price you want. For example, if you go to buy 1,000 shares at $22.50, and there are only 300 for sale at $22.50, you will only get filled on the 300 shares. You will then have to pay more for the rest, or keep bidding at $22.50 and take the chance of not getting filled as prices move away from you. If you enter a market order to exit because it was at your stop loss, you would be filled on the 300 shares at $22.50, and the rest where there were offers. That means you may pay $22.51, $22.52, or much higher to get filled. That additional amount you pay is called "'slippage."

There are two different ways that you can account for slippage and commissions when figuring share size. The simplest one is to use a risk amount for the calculation that is slightly lower than your true risk amount. For example, if in the above example the amount you are willing to risk per trade is $350, using a $300 number for calculations will keep your total loss under $350, including an average amount of slippage and commissions. The other way to do this is to figure in an additional amount based on the slippage you are likely to encounter on each particular stock. In other words, in the above example, if this were a very volatile stock and you calculated it would take an average of four cents to enter and four cents to exit, you would perhaps use $.40 as a total stop amount which would allow for slippage to get in, slippage to get out, and a couple cents for commissions. With this in mind, can different plays have different risk amounts? As you might guess, it is acceptable to use different risk amounts on different types of trades. Next, we will look at the reasons why you would change risk amounts.

First, different time frames may justify different risk amounts. Obviously, a core trader entering one or two trades every month or every three months is likely to risk more on each of those trades than a scalper taking three to four trades every hour. It is not uncommon for traders to have different risk amounts set up for each of the major time frames from core, to swing, to day trades, to scalps.

Another reason that you may choose to legitimately increase the risk on one trade is the frequency with which it occurs. Perhaps you have a very reliable strategy as a day trade and you only find the occurrence of this once every week or two. If you have a track record that shows this is an accurate trade and you would like to do it more often, but simply do not have the opportunity because it does not appear frequently enough, it would be acceptable to risk more on that trade when it does occur. A real-life example of this comes up for traders who like to trade gaps in the morning. There are some gap plays that are fairly reliable but do not occur very often. Figure 14.2 is simply an example

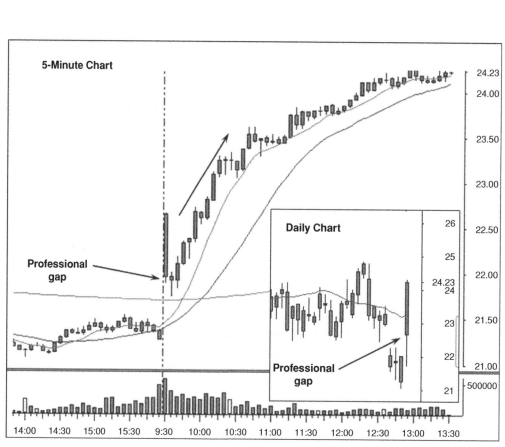

FIGURE 14.2 A Rare Gap Play Causes a Large and Reliable Move
Chart courtesy of Mastertrader.com.

of a powerful but rare trade and if you are able to trade the strategy accurately, it justifies a higher risk amount per trade.

There is one last category that would allow you to increase the risk on a single trade. This would apply only to well-established traders who have tracked their trades by strategy and have proven that a very well-defined strategy has an exceptional frequency of success. This is very different from traders who simply decide to risk more on a trade in the heat of the moment because they feel that it is a great trade. Many trades feel great in the heat of the moment, but can stop out as quickly as any other trade. It is only a proven track record that can justify increasing the risk amounts on a particular, well-defined trade.

All of the above exceptions have something in common: They are all well-defined exceptions and are all decided ahead of time in the form of a written trading plan. The decision to risk more money on one trade is never made while the market is open. Yes, you do have to decide if this trade is a swing trade and justifies more risk, or if this trade is your favorite gap play, but those decisions are fairly objective to make. Traders should never decide in the middle of the day to risk more money on a trade if it was not clearly spelled out ahead of time.

HOW MUCH TO RISK

Now that you know how to calculate share size to a fixed loss amount, how do you determine what that amount is? There is no definite answer to this because every trader's situation varies. One of the considerations will be whether or not your trading account is one of the basic accounts to your financial future, or whether the account would be considered high-risk capital to you. In other words, if you have saved your whole life and have the money in one account, and this is the money we are talking about, you must be very conservative with it. If you already have accounts which are taking care of your future and this account would not affect you financially if it were lost, you can be more aggressive with the account. In any event, it should never be the case that you risk more than 1 percent of your trading capital on any single trade. By risk I am referring to the amount of money you would lose on a trade that stops out. One percent is very much on the high side and should only be considered for longer-term positions. More realistically, traders should not be exceeding .50 percent or even .25 percent for day trading unless a well-established record has been proven. Remember these are just rules of thumb and you must take your total financial situation into account, which may include talking to other professionals if you use them.

Far more important than determining your risk amount is determining how to work up to that risk amount. The next couple of paragraphs are perhaps some of the most important in this book because they offer advice that can save you from disaster. The risk amount just discussed should not be used until you have proven that you can trade successfully. All traders should start by paper trading until they can prove that the strategies they have chosen to play and the way they have decided to play them will make money on a consistent basis. Many trading platforms will let you go into paper trading mode, where you can simulate live trades on your trading platform. This is a great system to use and you should take this practice time very seriously. You should not advance to risking even one dollar on a trade until you have proven:

- You know how to use your trading platform.
- You know your trading plan is effective.
- You can effectively follow your trading plan.
- Your trading plan produces successful results.

Until all of these criteria are in place and rock solid, do not trade real money.

Some view paper trading as a waste of time, and it is if you take trades that you know you would not have taken with real money or, most importantly, trades that are not in your plan. Once you have defined a trading strategy and have proven that it has good odds, paper trading it doesn't make sense. Realize that while trade setups (patterns) are similar by definition, each trade has different market forces at the time that can influence the outcome. This being the case, it's not possible to know everything that may influence a trade and it's not necessary. The major point of paper trading is to see if you will follow the trading plan that you have written out. Using paper trading in this way makes it a valuable part of the learning process that should not be disregarded.

Once you have proven success at paper trading, begin with a very small risk amount: about $10 or less. You will find a big difference in your ability to trade when there is even one dollar on the line. That is because this becomes your official record and you start getting concerned about hitting targets and taking stops. Naturally, at these low levels, you will not be making money even if you trade successfully because the commissions will be greater than any profits you could possibly make. That is okay at this level; you have to consider commissions as simply being one of the expenses of learning to trade. It is a very small expense when you consider the other alternatives. I have seen way too many traders begin trading on day one with full risk amounts and get very frustrated as the money did not roll in. That frustration leads to trading higher risk amounts to try to make the money back and soon they are out of an account.

From here you follow the same policy: Do not advance above that $10 amount until you prove that you can make money on a gross basis. Making money on a gross basis means that you are making money not including the expense of commissions or other account fees. As you trade higher and higher share size, those fees will become meaningless. Once you can make money on your trades on a consistent basis not counting commissions, then you may increase the risk amount. Increase it slowly and only increase it based upon what you have defined to be successful trading at that level. You may want to set up a gross dollar target at each level that must be achieved over the course of the week or something similar, but keep it objective and do not advance unless your goal is met. You then continue to do this until you work your way up to the risk amount we discussed in the prior section of this chapter.

You should also establish a standard for demotion. In other words, if you fail to make your goal for two weeks in a row, or if you actually lose money one week, you should demote yourself back down to the prior risk amount. This will make sure you do not advance too quickly and then become stuck at a losing level for a long time. You will find it more difficult to trade the higher your risk amount becomes, because the psychological factors start to play a more important role as the amount of money risked becomes more meaningful to you.

MANAGING THE MONEY—THROUGHOUT THE DAY

Once we have set up money management rules that contain our loss on any single trade, we now need to manage the whole day. To fill out the rest of the money management rules it is a good idea to set up parameters to be used throughout the day if you are a day trader. As for swing trading, issues of managing on a day-to-day basis would not apply. Swing traders need to manage the account as a whole and I will discuss those issues shortly.

The first thing we want to set up is maximum loss amounts for the day. Most struggling traders can trace back much of their problem to having several really bad days (meaning, the type of day that wipes out many good days of trading and does much to destroy a trader's morale as well as their account). Traders must accept that there will be days when things just do not go right and the best option is to shut down before the damage gets worse. This allows you to come back to trade another day. This is done very simply by setting a monetary limit at which you will stop trading. This is exactly how professionals are taught. They are shutoff automatically by the system when they hit their daily loss limit.

Some traders may feel this is a bad idea because they will argue that there have been times where they were down a significant amount of money and fought their way back. This may be true, but it is not relevant. The issue here is not even whether or not it makes sense to shut down or not based on how well you handled disastrous days in the past. This actually is a form of insurance. Some days or some trades can become so disastrous that they can do irreparable damage to the account. These days have to be avoided at all costs even if it means sacrificing the ability to come back on some other days.

The policy here is fairly simple: Just set a dollar amount for the day at which you will shut down. The only rule is that this dollar amount must relate to the dollar amount you will lose on a single trade in a way that makes sense. Depending on the frequency with which you trade, this amount may vary. For example, if you are a fairly active day trader or scalp trader, it would make very little sense to risk $300 per trade and have a $500 cut off for the day. It would mean that you could only lose one trade before you would have to shut down. As an active trader, it is likely that you would want to have at least three or four attempts that failed before you had to quit for the day. If you are a less active trader who perhaps takes two to three day trades per day at the most, then perhaps

Share Sizing with:	$100,000 Account
Maximum Risk per Day:	1% of capital = $1000
Maximum Loss per trade:	$250.00
Maximum Losses per Day:	4
Stop	Maximum Share Size
$0.10	2500
$0.20	1250
$0.30	833
$0.40	625
$0.50	500
$0.60	416
$0.70	357
$0.80	312
$0.90	277
$1.00	250

FIGURE 14.3 A Sample Money Management Table
Chart courtesy of Mastertrader.com.

one or maybe two trades would be all you would be willing to lose before you quit for the day. Figure 14.3 shows you an example of the table that you might have set up in your trading plan to outline some of these things.

CONSIDERATIONS WHEN SWING TRADING

Regarding swing trading, the rules need to be slightly different because of the additional risk that applies to holding stocks overnight.

There is nothing wrong with swing trading and core trading, as long as the risk is managed properly. Long ago traders would routinely hold stocks for weeks and months at a time without even considering earnings reports or anything else. While this long-term buy and hold policy is no longer an acceptable method for an investor or trader to use, many have gone to the other extreme and feel that anything overnight is too risky. All risk can be managed by proper share sizing. However, you do need to understand that when you hold positions overnight, the stocks can gap either up or down, and if that move is against your position, there is nothing you can do but take the loss. See Figure 14.4.

Note there is a misconception out there that if traders have protective stop orders in place that they will not suffer the effect of the gap. This is very untrue. Protective stop orders simply mean that you will exit the trade as soon as the market opens, which will be at the new price, and if this price is not favorable, you will bear the full loss. It is never possible to go backwards and sell or exit a position at the prior day's price. Due

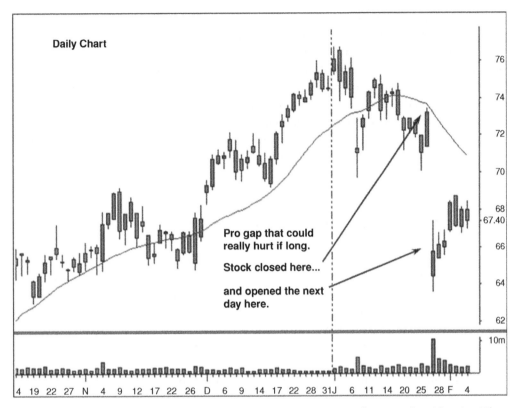

FIGURE 14.4 The Possibility of Large Overnight Gaps Must Be Taken into Consideration When Share Sizing Swing Trades
Chart courtesy of Mastertrader.com.

to the issue that unexpected gaps can occur, we have to install additional rules when swing trading.

The section about share sizing to an equal risk amount per similar trade still applies with swing trading. However, the number of shares you calculate may have to be reduced based on other calculations. In other words, that number you arrive at will be the maximum that you would ever have as a swing trade. Picture a situation where you have found a very tight stop on a very volatile stock. While that $.15 stop may justify you holding 2,000 shares for the day because you know you can exit for a $300 loss, you need to consider the effects of a possible gap down the next morning. If the stock were to open $1.50 against you, it would cause a loss of 10 times the amount of money you contemplated losing. When swing trading, you must temper the share size with other considerations.

First, you need to understand the potential volatility of the stock. Some stocks should not even be held overnight, such as pharmaceuticals and highflying biotech stocks. The stock shown in Figure 14.4 is an example of such a stock. These types of gaps are not rare and they often can have huge gaps based on drug approvals and FDA comments. Second, there are a variety of other stocks that frequently have larger gaps. Look at Figure 14.4 and calculate what you would expect a disastrous gap to be, and figure the effect that would have on your account. In a disaster, you do not want to lose more than 10 percent of your account. Another good rule is to limit the total capital you are using to purchase any stock to a fixed percentage of your account. Regardless of how good a trade is or what other parameters are in place, you do not want to have 50 percent of your account value tied up in any one play. Following these additional rules for swing trading will help you avoid the disasters that can happen from unexpected overnight gaps.

BASIC TRADE MANAGEMENT CONCEPTS

There are a variety of ways in which trades can be managed. The method you choose will depend largely on the time frame you are playing, the intended duration you expect to hold the trade, and the expected target you are looking for. Also at play will be your own personal ability to hold positions. Some traders have a hard time holding any position for more than a few minutes while some traders do not understand why you would ever sell anything. Before deciding on how to manage a trade, decide first what the expectations are for the trade, as well as your tendencies.

But first, realize trade management is perhaps one of the most critical times where psychological issues come into play. A trader does not need a great deal of technical knowledge to manage a trade properly. While there are more advanced techniques for managing trades, the basic techniques would do fine for the average trader if they would follow them. The real issue is actually following the methods once you are in a play. There is a huge tendency for traders to want to exit positions very early, to want to lock gains to breakeven, or to lock in very small gains. This comes from the desire to avoid being a loser. While these methods may satisfy the need to not be a loser, they do not promote getting maximum profits out of a trade. You need to be aware of how these issues may influence you in your trading so you can avoid being guilty of not following your trade management policy.

While mastering the psychology of managing trades is not simple, there is a trick that can help everyone to some extent: to manage the trade, *not* manage the money. Traders often react when they see profits beginning to show in their trade because they do not want to let those profits get away. However, it is better to simply watch the chart and to make the appropriate management decisions at the appropriate time. Therefore, actually hiding your trading platforms position screen which shows your net profit can help you manage the trade better. The problem of making bad decisions because you are watching the money instead of the chart is called "dollar counting" and it is a bad habit to get into. If you want to make a handsome profit on trades you are going to have to let the money pile up. If you react with poor management every time your play gets in the green, you will never make a good profit.

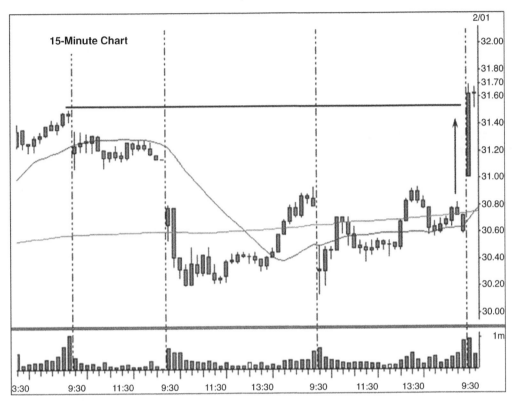

FIGURE 14.5 If All Trades Hit Their Targets There Would Be No Need for Management
Chart courtesy of Mastertrader.com.

At Pristine, the goal in trade management is simple: Have a target in mind and always try to reach that target. In one sense, then, it is possible to argue that there is no need for management at all. Since the inception of the play, there is an entry point, a stop loss to limit the downside, and the target is reasonable enough to be achieved. There is not necessarily any need to manage the play. As shown in Figure 14.5, if you choose plays and hit their targets, the only thing management can do is decrease your profits.

The reason management is an issue for many traders is because of the difficulty in setting targets. While there can be great precision in setting entries and stop losses, the target is always a general area, and often a guess to even the most experienced traders. You have probably seen many instances where you thought you picked a very generous target, yet the stock went leaps and bounds beyond the area you chose. Conversely, you have also probably set rather conservative targets and found the stock did not make it halfway there. You have probably also experienced the effect of seeing a stock come within pennies of your target, and then pull back to give back a significant part of the gain. This is where management comes into play for many traders. It is the attempt to lock in some of the gains if the total target is never achieved. Naturally, your first goal should always be to manage in a way to get to the target. When it becomes clear that the target is not going to be achieved, you will want to go to Plan B and lock in as much profit as you can. Usually, Pristine's definition for a stock no longer being able to hit its target is that it fails to follow the trend that was expected to continue all the way to the target.

MANAGING THE TRADE—STAYING WITH THE TREND

When managing a trade from beginning to end there are a few things to remember and you can use any combination of these for yourself, but remember to always keep your main goal in mind.

You want to achieve the target whenever it is going to be hit. The first concept of management, despite what most traders think, is to do nothing. Remember, you have a protective stop loss in place from the minute the trade is entered—you are protected, so there is no need to take any action. At least in theory you have spent a long, hard time finding the best play you could possibly find. It does not make much sense to say that 45 seconds after you enter the trade it is no longer a valid trade unless something drastic really happens. Your stop loss is there to protect you in case the trade does not work. What you want to manage is the protection of profits upon a significant successful move toward your target. Therefore, the first step is to do nothing until prices have advanced a significant amount away from our entry point. You will need to define that amount for yourself, but some suggestions would include waiting until you are 50 percent of the way to your first target, or until you have at least two solid bars advancing toward your target on the time frame that you are playing. Once you achieve that threshold (see Figure 14.6), then you can begin to institute a management policy that would have you raising the stop at some point.

The most secure way to manage a trade is to raise the stop whenever a pivot forms on the time frame you are playing. The reason that this is a very sound method of trail stopping is because a trend (say, an uptrend for this example) is formed by a series of higher pivot highs and higher lows. Therefore, whenever a pivot forms, if you trade below it, you are breaking the uptrend. If you are breaking the uptrend, it perhaps makes sense to exit the trade because your trade has significantly lower odds of reaching your target once the trend breaks. Refer to Chapter 10 on pivots: If you are going to raise your stop, it is best to do so once a significant pivot has formed. Do not raise them due only to minor pivots, because these will frequently be violated without the trend actually breaking (as shown in Figure 14.7.)

While this is a good starting point, it may not fully accomplish the goal that you want. Look what happens next to the price action in Figure 14.8. You have the ability to raise the stop, but only by a small amount.

Prices then run almost all the way to the target without forming another pivot. This means that a play would have come pennies from the target and could possibly go all

FIGURE 14.6 There Is Nothing to Manage until the Trade Begins to Make a Move in the Desired Direction
Chart courtesy of Mastertrader.com.

the way back to negative. If that thought is unbearable to you, a secondary form of management would need to take place. In other words, once a trade gets even closer to a target, say 75 to 90 percent, it may cause you to institute another level of management. You could begin managing with pivots on a smaller time frame, or switch to a bar-by-bar trail stop in order to tighten the reign on the profits you currently have. Keep in mind, though, this must be spelled out ahead of time in your trading plan. If not, you will find yourself always finding a need to trail tighter and be taking your profits when they are only fractionally on the way to their targets.

MANAGING THE TRADE—ZOOMING DOWN

Finally, let us look at a couple of examples regarding how to handle the situation just described. Remember that targets are general areas and they are used to set up the initial trade. As the trade progresses, you have to look at the type of advances and pullbacks a

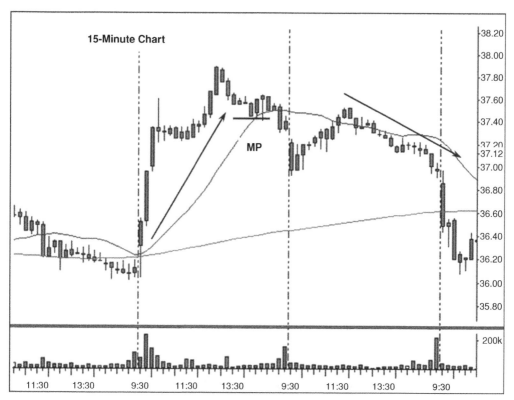

FIGURE 14.7 Once a Significant Pivot Breaks, the Odds of Hitting a Target Have Decreased
Chart courtesy of Mastertrader.com.

stock is making, and how it is performing compared to the general market. In addition, you need to look at the timing to make sure the stock is not peaking at a key reversal time. When taking all this into consideration there may be times when you are very close to a target and need to manage in a way that locks in profits better than following pivots on the original time frame.

Figure 14.8 is an example of a stock that had a strong advance but did not yet hit its intended target. The trailing stop based on pivots is very far behind. Say that in your trading plan we developed a threshold that once we are 90 percent of the way to a target, you have the right to use a tighter method of trail stopping. If you allow yourself to go down to a bar-by-bar trail stop method, you would be able to use a low of each consecutive bar once you cross the threshold of 90 percent. When using a bar-by-bar method, you have the option of either exiting the trade as the low of the prior bar is breached, or waiting to exit until the current bar closes below the prior bar. This is a very simple way of tightening the trail stop, but it has the disadvantage of using prior bars as focal points. As reference to earlier discussions in this book, remember that while every bar is the first focal point of support or resistance, many bars have virtually no real support in them.

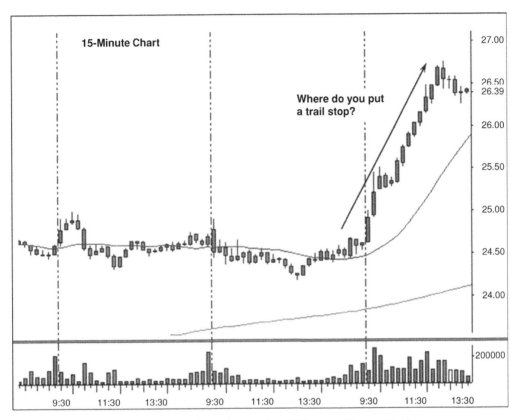

FIGURE 14.8 Strong Advances Often Make It More Difficult to Manage Trades
Chart courtesy of Mastertrader.com.

The other option is to zoom down one or two time frames and use the pivots that form on the smaller time frame. Figure 14.9 shows the zoomed down time frame from the rapid advance seen in Figure 14.8.

By using this method, once a stock crosses that 90 percent level, you would have the right to come down to the smaller time frame and raise your stop to the pivots that form, just as discussed earlier in this chapter.

IN SUMMARY

The psychology of trade and money management will be a very important part of your trading career. Be sure to refer back to this chapter several times as you progress as a trader. While there is much to be learned about technical analysis—and most information is devoted to that—all of technical analysis can be learned. The problem with trade and

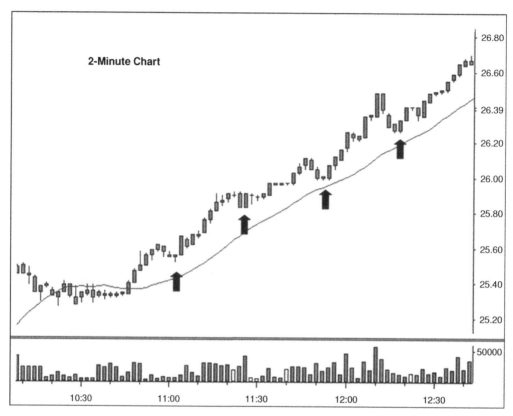

FIGURE 14.9 The Smaller Time Frame Shows a Clear Pivots Chart
Chart courtesy of Mastertrader.com.

money management is that many traders learn the technique, but they never actually take the correct action at the appropriate time.

Remember not to fall into the habit of dollar counting. Manage the chart and have preset money management rules. Do not react based on the money you are making or losing at the moment. Always keep in mind that anything can happen in a trade and that is why you have predetermined areas in which you will exit. Remember to let trades develop and not overmanage at the beginning of the trade. Make sure all of your money management rules and all your trade management rules are written into your plan and are followed consistently. Check them every day to make sure they are being followed. Your goal is to remove emotion from the decision-making process while trading.

If you find yourself having a difficult time with the above strategies, here are a few questions to keep in mind:

- Are you trading with scared money? Scared money never makes money. If you need to make money on any particular day in order to live, you will never be a successful trader.

- Are you suffering from a tremendous lack of confidence? Without having a successful track record, it is difficult to manage trades properly when you are never sure of the outcome.
- If you are having trouble, can you reduce your share size? Most bad decisions come from having too much money at risk. Cut back to a share size where you no longer care about your open position and you will find that you manage much better.

As a final topic, let's take a look in Chapter 15 at how to tie together some of these topics, and see how some professionals handle the trading day.

Getting Through a Typical Trading Day

Strategies to Incorporate into Your Daily Routine

This chapter walks you through the typical daily routine of the day trader. All of this knowledge is really only valuable if you are organized properly. Many traders tend to get overwhelmed by information or experience overload and become so scattered that they cannot make effective decisions. It is good to keep in mind that while you want to initially look at a broad spectrum of ideas to assist you in being a good day trader, you will eventually want to be very focused when it comes to placing actual trades.

BEGINNING YOUR DAY

The first thing you will do is come to the market armed with watch lists that will help you find the types of plays you like to trade. One of the more important watch lists you can bring with you is a watch list created by reviewing the daily charts. As a swing trader, it is imperative to look at the daily charts. However, the daily charts have even greater value for the intraday trader. If you want to find strong trending stocks on an intraday basis, there is no better ground to search than stocks that are already trending nicely on the daily chart. When looking at daily charts, you should be looking for the technical setups that really stand out. Finding nice, clean, quality uptrends and downtrends are at the top of the list. Finding those wide range bars that are igniting new moves are also great ideas to bring to the table every morning. As you get more experience, you also learn to recognize failed patterns on the daily chart and consolidations that can be playable as well. When using these stocks as a watch list intraday, the next step is to find the setups that complement the move on the daily chart.

Another watch list to bring with you every morning is one that you cannot form until shortly before the market opens: the list of stocks that are gapping that morning. Stocks that gap often have unique patterns and large moves and are a great place for the day trader to look (for a refresher on this subject, see Chapter 11 on trading gaps).

The next thing you want to do to prepare for the morning is to develop a market bias by applying the Pristine Method on the market itself. By looking at the current trend on different time frames and where support and resistance areas are, try to find the areas where you would be looking for the market to rally or for the market to decline. Another way to look at this is, throughout the day, or throughout various parts of the day, you want to know if you should favor buying pullbacks or shorting rallies. Your market bias is your guide for doing this.

When looking at support resistance levels to help determine your market bias, do not ignore the premarket activity. Many times significant reversals form before the U.S. market opens and these areas can be significant support and resistance areas. In order to see these you either need to be able to chart the E-mini futures contracts on the NASDAQ and/or the S&P 500 or, if you only care to see a couple of hours prior to the open, you may also track the premarket charts of the QQQ and the SPY. Figure 15.1 is an example of how to look at premarket activity using the futures.

Next you want to take a look at the longer-term market. Take the time to review the chapter on market internals. Before the market opens, turn to your setup of charts that

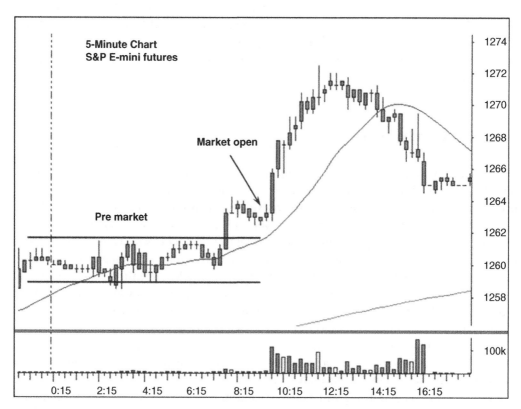

FIGURE 15.1   The S&P E-mini Future Contracts Showing Premarket Support
Chart courtesy of Mastertrader.com.

show the longer-term market internals to see if they are confirming the current market trend or if you should be cautious of a reversal. When the market internals are screaming something different than the market has been telling you the last couple of days, it is often a great indication to sit and watch for the morning to see what develops. Do not feel compelled to trade right at the open, especially when the internals are signaling a warning. Ten o'clock or 10:30 will typically be when the highest odds of a turn will occur. Good traders want to be most aggressive when the market is in a clear trend and the market internals are confirming it.

When reviewing the daily charts, you may have already looked at the patterns of various sectors. Finding daily charts of exceptional stocks that are in the strongest trending sectors are always a good place to look for ideas. In addition to that, you want to see how the overall sectors are complementing one another. In strong trending markets, the concept of sector rotation is alive and well and you will notice that even though some sectors have selloffs, the money immediately flows to another major sector. If you are not aware of this, you may form an incorrect bias in the market. For example, it is quite possible that the semiconductor stocks could be in a serious intraday downtrend over the last several days. However, if the money is going into financials and those stocks are accelerating strong, that is overall very bullish for the market. The reverse of that is when a sector sells off, and the money leaves the market. This is evident because no other sectors are having a corresponding rally to match the decline in the weak sector.

Do not make light of the step of forming a market bias. You will recall from earlier discussions in this book that the market is the tide that lifts all boats. While it is nice to find trades that perform on their own and ignore the market, they are not always easy to find. When you do find them, they are often not evident until later in the morning. Staying with the flow of the market will increase your profitability greatly.

PLANNING YOUR TRADE, TRADING YOUR PLAN

At this point, you should be prepared to open the market. The next question is perhaps one you will ask the most frequently every day: What are you going to trade? However, this decision should not be made at this time; it should have been made a long time ago in the form of a trading plan. The importance of a trading plan has been mentioned continuously throughout this book and it is here that you really need to understand the importance of planning everything you do ahead of time. All trades have a way of looking excellent when you are watching them during the day. It is important that you plan out exactly what type of trade you are going to take and what the requirements are for you to enter. This must be objectively written out in a way so that after the trade you can review it to see if you successfully accomplished what the trading plan said to do.

Your plan needs to dictate exactly what times of the day you are allowed to trade. It needs to indicate the exact setup as well as all of the necessary criteria for entry. It needs to discuss whether or not the market bias must be involved, and how that bias is going to be formed. It must outline how the trade will be managed and how targets will be taken. It is your guide throughout the day and the purpose of that is to limit the decision-making process during market hours. Naturally, you need to look at charts and decide which patterns are going to meet the criteria of your plan during the trading. However, this is not the time to create new strategies or new plans. You can always note any ideas you have and then look to incorporate them in your plan the next day. If you change your plan during the trading day, you do not have a plan at all.

Notice that up to this point you have been looking at many things before taking that first trade. You have looked at many stocks in order to form various watch lists of interest and examined the market, both premarket and from prior days. What is important now is that you take all that information and synthesize it down to the best of the best ideas to be looking at for the first 30 minutes of the day. You may have started by looking at hundreds of stocks, and then reduced that down to dozens of watch list items, but now is the time to find the best one or two possible plays to be watching for the first 30 minutes of the day. It is not a time to be hopping around looking for what else could be done. Focus on the stocks that you feel are the best trades for the morning, and wait for the appropriate entries. Have the patience to have the entry come to you, and do not chase the stock.

As part of that plan you should incorporate some kind of quality trade checklist. This would be a last-minute summary of the things that you need in order to validate your strategy and to enter a trade. Figure 15.2 is an example of a quality-trade checklist.

Throughout the trading day, it is very important to note reversal times and the major phases of the trading day. If you were to look at the volatility throughout the trading day, and if you were to assign a "one" to the volatility during lunch, afternoon volatility would be a "three," and the morning volatility would be a "five." Naturally, every day can be a

Setups (in your plan):	Entry Criteria:
PBS & PSS	✓Trend on multiple time frames
Gap list from A.M.	✓Tight vs. whippy
Volume spike	✓On support/resistance
PBO & PBD	✓Relative strength
WRBs at S-D	✓MAs
Tails—BT & TT	✓Good reward to risk – Void
Failed patterns	✓No pending news reports
CBS/CSS	✓Adequate volume
Engulfing bars	✓Timed with market internals

FIGURE 15.2 Checklist to Determine a Quality Trade
Chart courtesy of Mastertrader.com.

little different, but this is what to expect on average. The morning is often so volatile that traders who get stuck on the wrong side of a trade may have a difficult time getting out. The early morning is often full of quick reversals and patterns that many traders feel are unplayable. You may have read that traders should avoid the opening 30 or 60 minutes of the day. This is nonsense; experienced traders know how to trade the first hour of the day. However, it must be handled differently than other parts of the day. Likewise, at lunch many traders get frustrated because the market often goes nowhere. Breakouts and breakdowns fail and prior trends often stall or are reversed. The last third of the day can be a good time to take trades as long as you find the proper setups. (As a refresher on this point, you can review the chapter on reversal times earlier in this book).

AFTER THE CLOSE

The time you spend after the market closes can perhaps be some of the most important time that you devote to your trading, especially as a new trader. If you were to look at how most new traders spend their time, you would probably find that 90 percent of their time is spent sitting in front of the screen during market hours trying to find trades. They perhaps spend 5 to 10 percent of their time preparing for the market and 0 to 5 percent of their time after the market. Especially for a new trader, these numbers should be much closer to equal across the board. The market is open six and a half hours, so it is not suggested that you put in a 19-hour day. However, you should not be trading the entire time the market is open. You should have your select hours that you focus on trading and use the rest of the time for other things. Spending at least a third of your total time in after market analysis is perhaps one of the most important steps you can take when starting out.

The first thing you want to do as the market comes to a close is to review and consolidate your watch lists. You may often be able to begin doing this 30 minutes before the market closes, as the last 30 minutes do not offer many trading opportunities. You want to take and review all of the stocks that you had on your list before the market opened and see which of these are still valid for the following day. Throughout the day it is likely that you accumulated many more watch list ideas while scanning as you were looking for plays. You should also take a look at these and decide which ones should carry over to the next day. Get rid of all the others and have one consolidated list of ideas for the next day as part of your end-of-the-day routine. Naturally, the following day you will be adding more ideas from the daily watch list and the gap list as you did this day.

Next, you will want to take a review of your current day's market bias, see how it played out, and begin to form a bias for the next day. Note what happened to the current trends on various time frames, and how support and resistance areas were handled. It is a good idea here to print intraday charts of the market and to mark off support and resistance areas for the next day.

This next step is perhaps the most important. You need to review each of the trades you executed during the trading day. It is recommended that you print charts of each of your trades and compare what your trading plan says to what you actually did. The first and most important question you will need to ask is if the chart that was printed is actually the reflection of a strategy that you have in your trading plan. You will find that the majority of mistakes you make, and the majority of your losses early in your trading career, will be attributed to taking the plays that are not in your trading plan. You will need to review to see if the strategy was a valid one, if you used the proper entry criteria, how you managed the trade, and how you actually exited the trade.

While it is okay to print the charts during the trading day, it is very important that you do not do this review until well after market hours. Anytime you look at a trade immediately after taking it, it is likely that you will justify the trade. You need to wait until your head clears after market hours and make a very objective review of what you actually did. If you are a very active scalper, to the extent that this becomes too much of a burden to do, simply print every third or fourth chart on a random basis to review your trading tendencies. Do not skip this step just because you are a more active trader. It is also a good idea to print these charts out and to manually mark on the face of the chart with a pen or pencil. Figure 15.3 is an example of a chart that has been marked up.

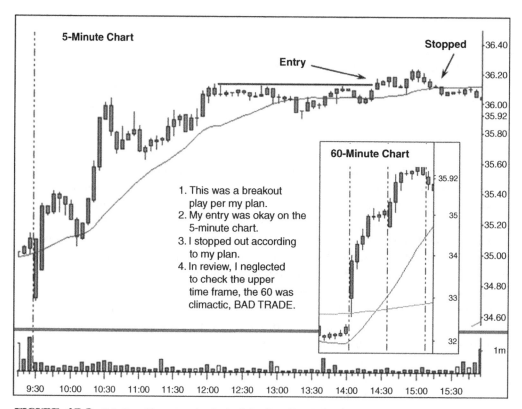

FIGURE 15.3 Printing Charts at the End of the Day Can Help Eliminate Mistakes
Chart courtesy of Mastertrader.com.

Printing these charts helps you to see and then eliminate the most common mistakes. As you identify problems, write the nature of the mistake on the front of the chart. Save the charts that have problems and make note of the most repetitive problems. Make it your goal to eliminate these mistakes as you uncover them; doing this will make you improve as a trader.

Finally, here are a few key things to keep in mind regarding this process. First, this process cannot be initiated if you do not have a written well-defined trading plan. There is nothing to compare your actions to if you do not have a plan. Second, the most common mistake you will initially uncover is that you are taking trades that are simply not a part of your plan. If you cannot quickly and immediately identify the chart you printed, you need to stop and either take a look at your trading plan, or develop the discipline to follow your current plan. Third, if you see that most of your mistakes are in management or in not reaching targets, consider the possibility that you are trading too many shares for your level. Most management mistakes come from the fear of trading with too much money at stake. Cut back in the share size until you are able to handle the position properly.

MAXIMIZING THE WINNERS, AND HANDLING THE LOSERS PROPERLY

If you follow the aforementioned procedures and make it your goal to eliminate mistakes on a consistent basis, you will always be maximizing your potential as a trader. If you start by paper trading and slowly increase your risk amounts until your desired limits are reached, it will be difficult to damage your account. If you are still having trouble, the likely culprit is simply the lack of technical knowledge. Getting more education or gaining more experience will help in this area.

Once you are successful, problems may still set in. Be sure you continue to do the aftermarket trade analysis, and also make sure that you follow your proper share sizing policies as outlined in your trading plan. Good traders may still run into occasional bad streaks, and it is important that you handle them properly. The first, best, and most effective step is to simply take a day or two off. Clearing your mind and getting a fresh start is often all that is needed. Take that time to do a second review of your trades to see if you find any consistent problems. Study your records to see if one of your strategies that used to be successful is no longer delivering the same results. The market changes, strategies change, and trading plans need to be updated. You may be blindly following a prior strategy that is no longer effective. Determine if your problem is trading strategies that are not effective, or not following your current strategies. After a day or two off, come back to the market and start trading again with a very small share size. Get back in the flow of being a winning trader and handling the trades properly. Go through a process of rebuilding your share size as you did when you originally started. You can step up the pace a little without needing to take months to build your share size again, but use some objective criteria to move up share size as you continue to be successful.

Continue to remind yourself that your job is to ascertain the best odds at any time. No matter how proficient you become there will still be losing trades. No matter how high the odds are in your favor, there will still be times where your trades will not work. Always remember your job is to maximize the winning trades, and to handle losing trades properly.

I've mentioned many times in this book that there is only one truth, and now perhaps you have a better understanding of that concept. The upcoming final chapter is a must-read and a summation of this important concept.

CHAPTER 16

There Is Only One Truth in the Markets

Price action is the only truth in the markets. It is that simple and it seems too obvious to be true. Most traders spend a good deal of their career looking for other answers that do not exist. The constant pursuit of the Holy Grail has been a quest of traders since the beginning of trading, of any kind, centuries ago. Yet, by definition, any other method will always be secondary to price.

PRICE IS KING

Here is a simple analogy: You are going to travel to Spain on a business trip and, not knowing the native language, a friend suggests that you study Italian because it is somewhat similar to Spanish. Another friend suggests you study French because it is the native language of the bordering country. Another friend suggests you study Latin because it is the base language of Spanish. But while all of these may help a little, the obvious question becomes, why not simply study Spanish?

While this may seem like a ridiculous analogy, it is exactly what most traders do every day. The quest for finding technical indicators or special formulas to predict price action all use price in the computation, so why not just focus on the actual price action to understand its direction? Learning the language of price action is the only answer to understanding the markets.

If you have ever been to a trading expo or a money show, you may have noticed that there are frequently large crowds around the company that is selling the newest fangled indicator or magic formula that is going to be the next predictor of price. This is because of that continuous drive for people to find that Holy Grail. The desire for quick profits, the desire for it to be easy . . . these things fuel the fire for people to continue to look for something that is easy to use and requires little thought, work, or training.

As you can imagine, few things in life work like that. Remember the market is a zero-sum game. That means by mathematical definition it is impossible for any indicator to deliver profits to everyone at the same time. For every winner there is a loser and the only way to win at the market is to outsmart another group of people. This is something that will never change and it is one of the reasons that technical indicators cannot work for the masses. There is a charting platform available that comes loaded with over 200 technical indicators and they claim that their website has an additional 800 available to be downloaded. If there are over 1000 technical indicators available, which one is the right one? Which one is the magic bullet? Obviously none of these is worth anything or there would only be one indicator that people use. Again, simply put: Price is king.

CEOs of companies lie. Chief financial officers create books and ledgers that cannot be trusted or are downright fraudulent. News commentators say whatever they are told to say or give day-old explanations for what happened the prior day. It does not matter what anyone says about a company; what matters is whether big money is buying the stock. When big money buys a stock, the price action shows up on the chart and it supersedes all other information that is available. When a CEO says the outlook of his company is fantastic and he will be buying the stock as fast as he can, but the price is falling every day, which can you believe? Analysts upgrade stock so that their company can sell their profitable shares to the newly buying public. This happens all the time. On which side of the equation do you want to be?

Anything that is truly worth achieving comes with a price. Reading price action is both a skill to be learned and an art to be acquired, but it is not an impossible task. It requires some diligence and some patience but it is achievable by anyone. There are different levels at which you will acquire skill. Things will work for a while because you have achieved a certain level, but then you get confused again as things become more complex. There is a simple explanation. There are many participants in the market at any moment. You may be right about the movement of the stock, but it simply is not going to happen this afternoon. Perhaps it happens tomorrow morning or the day after tomorrow. You have to learn to recognize the signs on all time frames to have things make sense.

If you go back to the learning Spanish analogy, you can draw upon it further. Let us say in preparation for your trip to Spain you study a set of CDs that teach you Spanish. Over the course of a week, you learn many key phrases and are able to make your way through your trip to Spain. You may have felt quite confident navigating your way through restaurants and purchasing items in stores. However, would this training have taken you through a complex business meeting in Madrid? The answer is "No." The same is true for technical analysis: You may learn a certain level of expertise, only to get confused as new price patterns emerge. This is normal and eventually the whole puzzle will fit together for you the more you learn and trade. Much of it comes from the understanding that at any moment in time there are a variety of money sources possibly moving the market or a single stock at any moment.

Once you understand price action, it is amazing how it makes sense 100 percent of the time. Naturally, this 100 percent comment is always looking in hindsight. Once you understand technical analysis, understanding why something happened always makes total sense. The true skill comes in seeing the price patterns emerge in real time and understanding which pattern is the dominant one. Good traders can do this the vast majority of time with great confidence. For traders taking shortcuts, these patterns will never make themselves visible.

Abbreviations

BT	Bottoming Tail
TT	Topping Tail
BOF	Breakout Failure
BDF	Breakdown Failure
BBF	Breakout Bar Failure
CAH	Close at High
CAL	Close at Low
CBS	Climactic Buy Setup
CSS	Climactic Sell Setup
+COG	Bullish Changing of the Guard
–COG	Bearish Changing of the Guard
DT	Double Top
EOD	End of Day
HH	Higher High
HL	Higher Low
LH	Lower High
LL	Lower Low
MR	Major Resistance
mR	Minor Resistance
MS	Major Support
mS	Minor Support
–mP	Level 1 Pivot (minor)
mP	Level 2 Pivot (minor)
MP	Level 3 Pivot (major)
MP+	Level 4 Pivot (major)
+MP	Bullish Major Pivot

−MP	Bearish Major Pivot
NH	New High
NL	New Low
NB	Narrow Body
NRB	Narrow Range Bar
NFT	No Follow Through
PBS	Pristine Buy Setup
PSS	Pristine Sell Setup
+WRB	Bullish Wide Range Bar
−WRB	Bearish Wide Range Bar
YC	Yesterday's Close
YH	Yesterday's High
YL	Yesterday's Low

Trade Types

T he following is a list of the most common trade types, complete with a brief description of each style of trade. These trade types should not be confused with the many specific, proprietary trading strategies and tactics taught in Pristine's trading seminars.

Scalp trade: A style of trading that is designed to capitalize on small moves, using price setups that present exceptionally low-risk opportunities. The typical objective for a scalp trade can be a few cents or more. Scalping demands a familiarity with Level II (see Glossary, "Commonly Used Technical Terms") as well as the use of a direct access system such as Mastertrader (www.mastertrader.com) for instant order execution. The best scalping opportunities are found in liquid stocks (trading 500,000 or more shares a day) with quality market maker representation. Pristine's scalp setups are typically found using charts in smaller intraday time frames such as 1, 2, 5, and 15 minutes.

Day trade: Conventionally speaking, a day trade is a position initiated and closed out in the same trading session. In Pristine's real-time trading rooms, a day trade is an opportunity with the potential to become an overnight (O/N) and/or develop into a swing trade but, because it occurs early in the day, it is typically treated more aggressively in terms of locking in partial or complete profits. Day trades also typically employ tighter stops than the average swing trade does. We have found that the best day trades usually have room to run, with resistance (or support) being far enough away to warrant holding through a brief pullback or period of consolidation if necessary. Day trades are typically found using intraday charts with medium length time frames, such as 15-minute or hourly charts.

Overnight trade: An overnight trade is typically a position entered late in the day in a stock which is closing at or near its high (or low, for shorts), with the potential to gap up (or down), or see follow-through the next morning. As mentioned earlier, an overnight can also start as a day trade that closes strong (or weak) enough to warrant holding past the close and into the following day. Overnights are frequently closed out in the early going of the following morning (if not right at or before the open) with some traders opting to sell only half, with the remaining half held for a longer period and a potentially larger price gain.

Swing trade: A swing trade is one that is entered with the idea of profiting from the natural ebb and flow of a stock's daily movements. Swing trades are usually initiated in an area of significant support (or resistance, for shorts), and seek to capture between $1 to $4 in profits (on an average $30 stock), depending on the situation. Typically held for a period of two to five (or more) days, swing trades take advantage of a very profitable market niche overlooked by most active investors. Too brief for large institutional concerns to take advantage of and, at the same time, too lengthy for floor traders (who typically don't hold positions overnight) to be comfortable with, this time frame offers the perfect opportunity for independent traders who possess the expertise necessary to profitably exploit it. Swing trades are found primarily using daily (and weekly) charts, with occasional reference to a 60-minute chart as well.

Glossary

accumulation   Term usually applied to the transfer of stocks into the institutional sector, or buying pressure resulting in increased stock values.

advance-decline line   Each day's number of declining issues is subtracted from the number of advancing issues. The net difference is added to a running sum if the difference is positive or subtracted from the running sum if the difference is negative.

American Depositary Receipts (ADRs)   Receipts held by an American bank that represent shares in a foreign company.

arbitrage   Technique of buying and selling securities to take advantage of small differences in price.

auction market   Trading securities on a stock exchange where buyers compete with other buyers and sellers compete with other sellers for the best stock price. Trading in individual stocks is managed and kept orderly by a specialist.

bear   A person who thinks that a market, an industry, or prices in general, will decline.

bear market   Generally a period of time when security prices decline 15 percent or more.

Big Board   Another name for the New York Stock Exchange.

block trade   Buying or selling 10,000 shares of stock or $200,000 or more worth of bonds.

blue chip stocks   Stocks of companies known for their long-established record of earning profits and paying dividends.

Bollinger bands   Fixed lines calculated to be above and below a security's average price. As volatility increases, the bands widen.

bottom fishing   Trying to buy stocks whose prices appear to have bottomed out or fallen to low levels.

breakaway/runaway gap   When a tradable stock exits in a range by trading at price levels that leave a price area where no trading occurs on a bar chart. These gaps appear at the completion of important chart formations.

broker-dealer   A securities firm that sells mutual funds or other securities to the public. The broker-dealer is responsible for oversight of their affiliated brokers.

bull market   A period of time when security prices increase.

call option   Agreement that gives an investor the right, but not the obligation, to buy a stock, bond, commodity, or other instrument at a specified price within a specific time period.

candlestick charts   Price activity is aggregated and displayed for specific periods of time and coded in the form of candlesticks. The convention of candlesticks visually posts the open, high, low, and close price of the period.

cash market   The trading of securities according to their current or spot price, as opposed to trading in a security for future delivery.

channel   In charting, a price channel contains prices throughout a trend. There are three basic ways to draw channels: parallel rounded, and channels that connect lows or highs.

Chicago Board of Trade (CBOT)   A commodity trading market.

Chicago Board Options Exchange (CBOE)   An exchange set up by the Chicago Board of Trade to trade stock options.

circuit breakers   Measuring used by some major stock and commodities exchanges to restrict trading temporarily when markets rise or fall too far and/or too fast.

closing price   The last trading price of a stock when the market closes.

composite trading   Total amount of trading across all markets in a share that is listed on the New York Stock Exchange or American Stock Exchange. This includes transactions on those exchanges, the five regional exchanges, and on the NASDAQ Stock Market.

congestion area or pattern   Series of trading days in which there is no visible progress in price.

consolidation   A pause that allows market participants to reevaluate the market and sets the stage for the next price move.

Consumer Price Index (CPI)   A gauge of inflation that measures changes in the prices of consumer goods. The index is based on a list of specific goods and services purchased in urban areas, and is released monthly by the Labor Department.

correction   A reverse movement in the price of an individual stock, bond, commodity, index, or the stock market as a whole.

curbs in   An indication that trading curbs have been installed on the New York Stock Exchange.

cyclical stocks   Shares that tend to rise during an upturn in the economy and fall during a downturn.

crossed market   A situation in which one broker's bid exceeds the lowest offer of another or vise versa. NASD rules prohibit a broker from intentionally entering such bids or offers.

cup and handle   Accumulation pattern observed on bar charts that generally lasts from 7 to 65 weeks. The cup is in the shape of a BUY and the handle is usually more than one or two weeks in duration. The handle is a downward drift with low trading volume from the right side.

daily chart   This is a chart where the periods are set to equal one-day periods. The value that is charted is typically the closing price for each day.

day order An investor's order to buy or sell stock that will be canceled by the end of the day if not filled.

day trading Day trading is a mentality that traders follow to take advantage of the liquidity and execution available through real-time trading systems like Mastertrader. Traders enter the day flat (with no inventory or predispositions), trade on intraday moves, and exit the day with no open positions.

dead cat bounce Market rebound that sees prices recover and come back up a small amount after a big move down.

defensive securities Stocks with investment returns that do not tend to decline as much as the market in general in times when stock prices are falling. Those include companies with earnings that tend to grow despite the business cycle, such as food and drug firms, or companies that pay relatively high dividends, such as utilities.

delayed opening The postponement of trading of an issue on a exchange beyond the normal opening because of market conditions that have been judged by exchange officials to warrant such a delay (that is, an influx or imbalance of buy or sell orders and/or pending corporate news).

dip A slight decline in securities prices followed by a rise.

discount rate The interest rate charged by the Federal Reserve on loans to banks and other financial institutions. This rate influences the rates these financial institutions can charge their customers.

double bottom/top Price action of a security or market average where it has declined (advanced) two times to the same approximate level, indicating the existence of a support (resistance) level and a possibility that the downward (upward) trend has ended.

Dow Jones Average There are four Dow Jones Averages that track price changes in various sectors. The Dow Jones Industrial Average tracks the price changes of the stocks of 30 industrial companies. The Dow Jones Transportation Average monitors the price changes of the stocks of 20 airlines, railroads, and trucking companies. The Dow Jones Utility Average measures the performance of the stocks of 15 gas, electric, and power companies. The Dow Jones 65 Composite Average monitors the stocks of all 65 companies that make up the other three averages.

Dow Jones Industrial Average (DJIA) Often referred to as the Dow, it is the best known and most widely-reported indicator of the stock market's performance. The Dow tracks the price changes of 30 significant industrial stocks traded on the New York Stock Exchange. Their combined market value makes up a large percent of the market value of all stocks listed on the New York Stock Exchange.

earnings Income after a company's taxes and all other expenses have been paid. Also called profit or net income.

earnings per share Calculated by dividing the number of outstanding shares into earnings.

economic indicators Key statistics used to analyze business conditions and to make forecasts.

Elliot Wave theory   Originally published by Nelson Elliot in 1939, it is a pattern recognition technique based on the thesis that stock markets follow a pattern or rhythm of five waves up and three waves down to form a complete cycle of eight waves. The down waves are referred to as correction waves.

emerging markets   Financial markets in nations that are developing market-based economies and have become popular with U.S. investors.

exchange   A centralized place for trading securities and commodities, usually involving an auction process.

fade   Selling a rising price or buying a falling price.

fair value   A mathematical relationship between the S&P 500, cash, and the futures index.

Federal Funds Rate   The interest rate banks charge on overnight loans to banks that need more cash to meet bank reserve requirements. The Federal Reserve sets the interest rate.

Federal Open Market Committee (FOMC)   The policy-making arm of the Federal Reserve Board. It sets monetary policy to meet the Fed's objectives of regulating the money supply and credit. The FOMC's chief tool is the purchase and sale of government securities, which increase or decrease the money supply, respectively. It also sets key interest rates, such as the discount rate.

Federal Reserve   The central bank of the United States that sets monetary policy. The Federal Reserve oversees money supply, interest rates, and credit with the goal of keeping the U.S. economy and currency stable. Governed by a seven-member board, the system includes 12 regional federal banks, 25 branches, and all national and state banks that are part of the system.

Fibonacci numbers   Fibonacci numbers are a sequence of numbers in which each successive number is the sum of the two previous numbers: 1, 2, 3, 5, 8, 13, 21, 34, 55, 89, 144, 610, and so on. There are four popular Fibonacci studies: arcs, fans, retracements, and time zones. The interpretation of these studies involves anticipating changes in trends as prices near the lines created by the Fibonacci studies.

flag   A sharp price spike followed with a sideways consolidation with a bias counter to the rally. Prices usually break out of this consolidation pattern with an objective equal to the mast preceding the flag.

float   The number of outstanding shares in a corporation available for trading by the public.

fundamental analysis   Analysis technique that looks at a company's financial condition, management, and place in its industry to predict a company's stock price movement.

hedging   Buying or selling a product or a security to offset a possible loss from price changes on a future corresponding purchase or sale.

index fund   A mutual fund that seeks to produce the same return that investors would get if they owned all the stocks in a particular stock index, often the Standard and Poor's 500-stock index.

index arbitrage   Buying or selling baskets of stocks while at the same time executing offsetting trades in stock-index futures. For example, if stocks are temporarily cheaper than futures, an arbitrager will buy stocks and sell futures to capture a profit on the difference or spread between the two prices.

indexing   Buying and holding a mix of stocks that match the performance of a broad stock market barometer such as the Standard & Poor's 500 stock index.

Initial Public Offering (IPO)   The first time a company issues stock to the public.

insider   A person, such as an executive or director, who has information about a company before the information is available to the public.

inside trading   In one respect, it refers to the legal trading of a security by corporate officers based on information available to the public. In another respect, it refers to the illegal trading of securities by any investor based on information not available to the public.

intermarket trading   An electronic communications network linking the intermarket trading systems (ITS) floors of the seven registered exchanges to foster competition among them in stocks listed on either the NYSE or AMEX and one or more of the regional exchanges.

lagging economic indicators   A composite of seven economic measurements that tend to trail developments in the economy as a whole. Those indicators are duration of unemployment, ratio of inventories to sales, index of labor costs per unit of output, average prime rate, outstanding commercial and industrial loans, ratio of outstanding consumer installment credit to personal income, and Consumer Price Index for services.

leading economic indicators   A composite of 11 economic measurements developed to help forecast likely changes in the economy as a whole. The components are average work, unemployment claims, orders for consumer goods, slower deliveries, plant and equipment orders, building permits, durable order backlog, material prices, stock prices, M2 money supply, and consumer expectations.

Long-Term Equity Anticipation Securities (LEAPS)   Options that won't expire for up to three years.

Level I   Sometimes called "quick quote," Level I is trade and quote data that only shows current bid, ask, last trade value and volume, and some daily summary information. You do not see who is buying and selling, nor do you know the number of shares for sale at all price levels.

listed stock   The stock of a company that is traded on a securities exchange.

long bond   Slang for a 30-year bond issued by the U.S. Treasury. It is considered a key indicator, or benchmark, of trends in long-term interest rates.

margin call   A demand upon a customer to deposit money or securities with a broker. Margin calls are made in accordance with Regulation T, which governs the amount of credit that may be advanced by brokers to customers for the purchase of securities.

market capitalization   The total market value of a company or stock, which equals the number of shares times the current market price of the shares.

market minder   A customizable table that allows you to isolate and display key information fields on a list of stocks or indexes.

market sentiment   A measurement of the bullish or bearish attitude of the crowd.

market timing   Shifting money in and out of investment markets in an effort to take advantage of rising and fading prices.

momentum   Momentum is the most basic concept in oscillator analysis. Momentum is the rate of change at which the market is rising or fading.

NASDAQ   An electronic stock market run by the National Association of Securities Dealers. Brokers get price quotes through a computer network and trade via telephone or computer network.

NASDAQ Composite Index   An index that covers the price movements of all stocks traded on the NASDAQ Stock Market.

NASDAQ National Market   A subdivision of the NASDAQ Stock Market that contains the largest and most actively traded stocks on NASDAQ. Companies must meet more stringent standards to be included in this section than they do to be included in the other major subdivision, the NASDAQ small-cap market.

National Association of Securities Dealers (NASD)   A membership organization for securities-brokerage firms and underwriters in the United States that promise to abide by association rules. It sets guidelines for ethics and standardized industry practices, and has a disciplinary structure for looking into allegations of violations. The NASD also operates the NASDAQ Stock Market.

New York Stock Exchange   Founded in 1792, it is the roughly 23,000 companies whose shares are listed there, totaling about $5 trillion.

NYSE Composite Index   An index that covers the price movements of all stocks listed on the New York Stock Exchange.

odd lot   Order to buy or sell less than 100 shares of stock.

offer   Same as the ask price. See "ask" under the following section Commonly Used Technical Terms.

open order   A buy or sell order that has not yet been executed or canceled.

options   An agreement allowing an investor to buy or sell stock during a specific time for a specific price. Options are traded on several exchanges, including the Chicago Board of Exchange, the American Stock Exchange, the Philadelphia Stock Exchange, the Pacific Stock Exchange, and the New York Stock Exchange.

Over-the-Counter (OTC)   Market where transactions are conducted over the telephone and computer network of dealers rather than on the floor of an exchange.

penny stocks   While many legitimate companies have share prices that low, the term "penny stocks" includes stocks that are priced at $5 and below and usually refers to speculative companies with little or no real business that are heavily promoted by hard-selling brokerage firms.

pink sheets   The printed quotations of the bid and ask prices of over-the-counter stocks, published by National Quotation Bureaus, Inc.

point   A change of $1 on the market price of a stock is equal to one point.

portfolio   A collection of securities held by an investor

private placement   The sale of stocks or other investments directly to an investor. The securities in a private placement don't have to be registered with the Securities and Exchange Commission.

Producer Price Index (PPI)   A group of statistics compiled by the Labor Department that are used as a gauge of inflation at the wholesale level. The index for finished goods, which tracks commodities that will not undergo further processing and are ready for sale to the ultimate user. It is the most prominently reported of the statistics.

profit taking   Exiting securities after a recent, often rapid, price movement in your favor.

program trading   Stock trades involving the purchase or sale of a basket including 15 or more stocks with a total market value of one million dollars or more. Most program trades are executed on the New York Stock Exchange, using computerized trading systems. Index arbitrage is the most prominently reported type of program trading.

put option   An agreement that gives an investor the right but not the obligation to sell a stock, bond, commodity, or other instrument of a specified price within a specific time period.

put/call volume ratio   The volume of trading in puts (options to sell) divided by the total calls (options to buy) for a security or an index.

quote   A bid to buy a security or an offer to sell a security in a given market at a given time.

reversal gap   Chart formation where the low of the day is above the previous day's range and the close is above the day's open.

reversal stop   An order to reverse position when a specific price is hit.

round lot   A unit of trading or a multiple thereof, generally consisting of 100 shares of stock.

Russell 2000   A small-capitalization stock index. It consists of the 2000 smallest securities in the Russell 3000 ($RUT.X).

secondary market   Market for issues that were previously offered or sold.

secondary offering   The sale to the public of a usually large block of stock that is owned by an existing shareholder.

sector funds   Mutual funds that invest in a single-industry sector such as biotechnology, gold, or regional banks. Sector funds tend to generate erratic performance, and they often dominate both the top and bottom of the annual mutual fund performance charts.

Securities and Exchange Commission (SEC)   The federal agency that enforces securities laws and sets standards for disclosure about publicly traded securities, including mutual funds. It was created in 1934 and consists of five commissioners appointed by the president and confirmed by the Senate to staggered terms.

secular   Long-term as opposed to seasonal or cyclical.

security   A financial instrument that indicates the holder owns a share or shares of a company (stock) or has loaned money to a company or government organization (bond).

share   An investment that represents part ownership of a company or a mutual fund. See also **stock**.

short covering   Trades that reverse, or close out, short-sale positions. In the stock market, for instance, shares are purchased to replace the shares previously borrowed.

Short interest   Total number of shares of a given stock that have been sold short and not yet repurchased.

small cap stocks   Shares of relatively small publicly traded corporations, typically with a total market value, or capitalization of less than $600 million.

stock   An investment that represents part ownership of a company. There are two different types of stock: common and preferred. Common stocks provide voting rights but no guarantee of dividend payments. Preferred stocks provide no voting rights but have a set, guaranteed dividend payment. See also **share**.

stock index futures   A contract to buy or sell the cash value of a stock index by a specified date.

stock option   An agreement allowing an investor to buy or sell shares of stock within a stipulated time and for a certain price.

stock split   A change in a company's number of shares outstanding that doesn't change a company's total market value, or each shareholder's percentage stake in the company. Additional shares are issued to existing shareholders, at a rate expressed as a ratio. A 2-for-1 stock split, for instance, doubles the number of shares outstanding. Investors will own two shares after the split for each share they owned before the split. Stock splits are typically viewed by investors as bullish.

stop limit order   A stop order that becomes a limit order after the specified price has been reached.

technical analysis   Research of a security or market sector that uses trading data, such as volume and price trends, to make predictions on stock movements.

third-market trading   Over-the-counter trading in stocks that are listed on an exchange.

ticker   Display of the final sell price that can be set to display market maker positioning and/or trade details and are color-coded in order to easily recognize market direction.

ticker symbol   Letters that identify a security for trading purposes. A security's ticker symbol also may be used in news and price-quotation services to identify the security.

time and sales   Time and sales ticker displays information about specific trades as they go off. The selling institution is responsible for posting the trade (within 90 seconds) and traders use this to see where the market sentiment is at a certain time.

timed out   After you place an order, the order will only be "live" for a specified amount of time. Then your order has timed out, which means that it has run out of time and it will be automatically canceled by the proper exchange. Time constraints vary for each type of order.

trade date   The actual date on which your shares are purchased or sold. The transaction price is determined by the closing net asset value on that date. This date also determines the eligibility for dividends.

traders   People who negotiate prices and execute buy and sell orders, either on behalf of an investor or for their own account.

trading curbs   One of several circuit breakers adopted by the NYSE and approved by the Securities and Exchange Commission in response to the October 1987 stock market crash.

triple witching   Slang for the quarterly expiration of stock index futures, stock index options, and options on individual stocks. Also known now as Quad witching, since futures options are included. Trading associated with the expirations inflates stock market volume and can cause volatility in prices. It occurs on the third Friday of March, June, September, and December.

unlisted stock   A security not listed on a stock exchange and generally traded in the OTC market.

up to bid   This happens when a market maker moves his or her current bid to the highest bid. This is a bullish sign because the market maker will now pay a higher price to buy a stock than any other market maker at that time.

volatility   The characteristic of a security or market to fall or rise sharply in price in a short-term period.

VIX   The CBOE's volatility index.

volume   Number of shares traded in a company or an entire market during a given period.

wedge   Technical pattern where two converging lines connect a group of price peaks and troughs.

whipsaw   Losing money on both sides of a price swing.

GLOSSARY OF COMMONLY USED TECHNICAL TERMS

The following are commonly used technical terms. Please read and become very familiar with them, as this will maximize your learning growth to trading mastery.

ask   Low ask (offer) is the lowest price that someone is willing to accept for a security.

bid   High bid is the highest price that someone is willing to pay for a security. "Hit the bid" means to sell a stock on the current bid price.

breakout point   When the market price moves out of the trend channel.

Doji   A candlestick in which the open and close of the stock price are the same, or substantially the same.

downtick   A sale of a listed security that occurs at a lower price than the previous transaction.

Electronic Communication Network (ECN)   Electronic Communication Network consists of networks that work as order-matching systems and allow traders to advertise a price better than the current bid or offer. By using ECNs, traders can bypass the market makers and can make markets by playing or splitting the spread.

futures   An agreement to purchase or sell a given quantity of a commodity, security, or currency at a specified date in the future. Also called a futures contract. We use the governing S&P 500 futures contract (changes each quarter) as the key leading indicator of the equity market. See also "arbitrage" under Commonly Used Market Terms, preceding.

inside day   Day in which the price range is within the previous day's price range.

inside market/price   The highest bid and the lowest ask (offer) at any given time for an Issue.

intraday   Price and volume information that occurs during a single trading day as opposed to daily information, which summarizes trades on a day-by-day basis.

Level II   Level II data is a real-time display of market maker or ECN bids and offers. Studying this data allows a trader insight into the intentions of the market makers and the propensity that the stock has to move multiple levels.

limit order   An order to buy or sell a stock when it reaches a certain price.

market internals   Market internals are used to gauge market strength or weakness. These may include the futures contracts, the TICK, TRIN, bond futures and the strength or weakness of particular sectors, among other things.

market maker   In a stock market, a trader responsible for maintaining an orderly market in an individual stock by standing ready to buy or sell shares. On a stock exchange, a market maker is known as a specialist.

market order   Order to buy or sell at the best available price.

mid-day doldrums   Slang for the period between 11:15 A.M. to 2:15 P.M. EST. This is the time when breakouts often fail. This is typically a slow time, when many Wall Street market makers are off at lunch and doing other things besides trading. Pristine suggests that only experienced traders trade during this period. Pristine uses the mid-day doldrums to search for stocks that have favorable setups for possible afternoon scalping plays or swing trade opportunities.

momentum trading   A style of trading where a trader attempts to identify short bursts of buying or selling pressure in order to quickly enter and exit stocks.

moving average   Moving averages are one way to view historic price levels. A moving average takes into account some number of price periods (a new period is added and the oldest is dropped from the calculation) to show average price over time. It is possible to weight more recent prices by linearly or exponentially recent prices smoothing the average lines. The longer the averaging period, the more lag you will see between the average and the most recent prices.

offer out   Price at which a market maker sells his or her stock and the general public buys. When you "offer out," you are in essence taking the role of a market maker by offering to sell your stock on the offer, typically on an ECN.

refreshes   Essentially the same as "he stays." Used when a market maker has filled someone at the bid or offer and the market maker remains, continuing to buy or sell stock at the quoted price.

reversal times   Over the many years of trading and study of the markets, Pristine has noted and profitably used various reversal periods. These are the times during which the direction of the market often changes course.

sell off   A period of intensified selling in a market that pushes prices sharply lower.

short covering   Trades that reverse, or close out, short-sale positions. In the stock market, for instance, shares are purchased to replace the shares previously borrowed.

short selling A trading strategy that anticipates a drop in a share's price. Stock or another financial instrument is borrowed from a broker and then sold, creating a short position. That position is reversed, or covered, when the stock is repurchased to repay the loan. The short seller profits by repurchasing the stock at a lower price than sold for in creating the short positions.

specialist A stock exchange member who is designated to maintain a fair and orderly market in a specific stock. They are required to buy and sell for their own account to counteract temporary imbalances in supply and demand.

spread The difference between the bid and asked prices.

Standard & Poor's 500 Stock Index A benchmark index of 500 large stocks, maintained by Standard & Poor's.

stop (protective stop) The price at which a trader will close out an existing position to cut losses in the event the trade does not move in the intended direction. A trailing, or progressive stop, is a technique that trails the price of a stock up with a stop right behind it.

ticks Upward or downward price movements in a security or index. A downtick is the sale of a security at a price below the preceding sale. An uptick is a sale executed at a price higher than the preceding sale.

tick spread The difference between the high and low of the NYSE tick indicator of each trading day. For intraday trading, Pristine views the tick of under 1,000 as oversold and over 1,000 as overbought, and looks for intraday reversals (bounces) when such levels correspond with other extreme levels in the S&P futures and TRIN.

TRIN The short-term trading index (or "ARMS Index") measures the breadth of the market while taking volume into account. The index measures the concentration of the volume in advancing and declining stocks. TRIN is a ratio of the advance/decline ratio to the up volume/down volume ratio. TRIN readings above 1.0 indicate oversold conditions or more relative volume in declining issues, while values below 1.0 indicate overbought conditions, or more relative volume in advancing issues.

uptick A sale of a listed security that occurs at a higher price than the previous transaction.

About the Companion Website

T o enhance your reading of this book, please be sure to visit the companion website at www.wiley.com/go/capra (password: trade123). Following is a brief overview of the contents you will find there:

- Full color, detailed views of all of the charts and pictures in this book.
- A video by Greg Capra, President and CEO of Pristine.com, explaining how the Pristine Method handled recent market swings.
- Several detailed chart analyses done by Greg.
- Specially-written software for Mastertrader charting platforms that show bullish and bearish patterns graphically.
- Links to several sites at Pristine.com with free information about trading and investing in the market.

Index

Printed and bound by CPI Group (UK) Ltd, Croydon, CR0 4YY

16/04/2025

14658460-0004